-all artwork in this book was c

MW00462735

Mari!

Keep on adventuring!

and keep being A

John-Michael

Life In The Festivals

A journey into the perpetual hope machine

By

John-Michael Thomas

Table of Contents

This book is dedicated to...

Penny Suphunthuchat
David Isaac
Cameron St Denis
Christopher McArthur
Cassandra Alicia
Naira Hart
Dougie Campbell
Ashley Booth
Evan Meyer
Jerry Brandt
Megan Gersh
Andrei Kipres
Cin Kats
Paul Kats
Ryan Averbukh
Stacey Storey
Zach Puchtel
Kitty Mach
Erin Eskila
Josh Orem

These are the people, who are creating the festivals, that are shaping our city, to change the world.

Some Remarks

This book was written between April of 2014 and September of 2014. I went into this experience not knowing how I would come out. I do not claim to be an expert; I am an outsider who decided to peer in. This is what I saw.

"Here ends another day, during which I have had eyes, ears, hands and the great world around me. Tomorrow begins another day. Why am I allowed two?"

- GK Chesterton

Prologue

This story has to have a happy ending. I keep telling myself this as I stare at the throng of people, sitting Indian style, elbows on knees, palms pointing towards the sky. I see in their faces lies. They nod and agree, but I can tell they are wishing it were true, wishing so strongly that they really believe it. And maybe that's the trick to all of this. To really analyze the human condition, you must understand that most of us are losers.

The thing is, these people may actually be right; if nothing matters, then why not believe in something? Why not make happiness the end all be all of everything you do? Why not be selfish? Why not escape? Why not play and love? Why not live forever in the now, never looking forward or back?

These people, they may be right. They probably are right. But I just keep thinking, this story has to have a happy ending, and they don't seem that happy.

The preacher talks through one of those microphones that attaches to his ear. It's very 'corporate retreat' for a group of hippies. He refers to the guests as "Human Beings of the Planet Earth." There is something about this that annoys me, yet everyone in the audience finds it profound.

He speaks in a great temple. Many in the audience helped construct this giant wooden monolith: it's part of the culture to build the community you reside in. It is raw and impressive, even if the smell is of porta potties, puke and sex. Almost no one here has bathed in three days.

"This is what human beings of the planet earth do not to understand."

He has a slight accent, probably Indian. Americans were always suckers for accents. Maybe it's our daddy complex of knowing we are the rowdy kids who ran away from mother England. But a crowd like this is a sucker for all things foreign, dark skin, Eastern spirituality. How could you not find everything that comes out of this man's mouth profound..? It's funny how we choose our tribes, even when we think we have chosen none.

I call them hippies, but that is not fair. It's a strange mix, from the ultra poor who live for the next festival, or warehouse party, to the mega rich who have been worn down by the life of the tech world and want to experience something ethereal.

We need to name them, they deserve that, they are something special. Whether you hate or love them, something is going on, an allegory for what all first world people are going through, maybe what all "Human beings of the planet earth" are going through in this strange modern age, where you can see everything this planet has to offer from the comfort of your computer, while ignoring everything your neighborhood has to offer while you look down at your smart phone.

They have no label. I hear them call themselves

"Burners," some say "Tribal", many just say "Spiritual." Yet the most common word I hear is "transformational," transformational festivals, transformational groups, transformational music and experiences. Maybe it's time we let a counterculture name itself, maybe they are just Transformationals.

A woman asks the preacher a question about animals, it's a loaded question; "How can we, the human beings of the planet earth, learn to respect animals?" It's obvious she wants her life decisions to be validated. But the preacher doesn't fall for the trap. Any leader knows giving the answer one expects bring you down to the level of your peers.

"What human beings of the planet Earth do not understand is that animals are actually smarter than we are," It was a great answer, no one saw it coming, "A dog is never concerned with anything more than being a dog, they have no grand ambitions, they live completely and totally in the now, just living the life of a dog."

I can't help but think of the sadness I see on my puppy's face every time I leave the house. Dogs are the most co-dependent creatures in the history of this planet. They are the exact opposite of the individuals I see on display at this festival. They don't live in the now, they live for their masters. That's why we love them so much. No human of this planet Earth will ever love us as much as our dog will, nor should they.

I look back to the audience; I see the enlightenment on their faces. Sure half of them are stoned… Who am I kidding half of them are on acid and 90% of them are high on some sort of concoction. It makes me wonder why the enlightened rely upon drugs so much? Do drugs really cause us to live in the now? Are drugs really being "spiritual?"

"The key is to change yourself, you must be love, but you can't force this change upon others, you must glow, make others want what you have."

It's amazing, because I agree with so much he has to say, yet everything about this place, this speaker, this whole spectacle, reeks of wanting to find truth, where there is none. Why did I hate everything this man was saying while agreeing with everything he said? I am a result oriented person, but it was the means that were driving me insane. Was I the hypocrite?

"You must change your perspective, your perspective is your reality, quit your ambitious life, you must focus on being, not having, not doing."

Maybe it's because if everyone lived this way, we would still be in the Stone Age. Without ambition there would be no rocket ships to the moon, no cures for diseases, no LED lights… Actually, I am wrong about that. Without ambition, there would be no high finance, no venture capitalist, no war, no politicians. Rocket ships are pure, rocket ships come from nerds doing what they love to do, tinker and create… Could this preacher be right? He doesn't seem right.

I have been using the word "preacher," but no one would call him that. Honestly I don't know what he is called, probably a spiritual advisor, or life coach. They use terms with broad definitions, these Transformationals are afraid of specifics. "preacher" equates to "religion." advisor? Well, everyone needs an advisor.

I come from the world where if something can be everything, then it is nothing. But that's me, I am out of place here, I have no experience with drugs or festivals, I have no experience with these art installations. I know nothing about the world I am in.

"Think with your heart, not with your mind," he says. Something I hear again and again. Another statement that says nothing, therefore means everything. Everything means nothing, and nothing means everything. I don't know the truth, but I guess this is life in the festivals.

Part I

The First Festival

"I am going to tell you how to achieve your dream," he said, "I'm not saying you will actually succeed. I am just offering to send you on the path that will make anything you desire possible. Following that path to its end, is up to you."

Sometimes everything you know turns out to be a lie. It's hard to tell when you are on the verge of something great. My heart says everything is about to change, but my mind says that I am again wasting my time. I know change happens at the margins, but margins are boring, I want an adventure.

Chapter One:

The First Trip

Cocaine's not even really a drug. I know this may come as a surprise to you, but to think of cocaine as a drug is like saying you just like the taste of coffee. Cocaine is about regulating your life. Regulating your sleep, your mood, your experience.

I had a friend who became a meth addict, the last thing he told me as I dropped him off at rehab was, "The problem with meth, is that by the time you found out anything was wrong with it, you were living in an alley."

It had no downside. You are more productive, you feel better, needed less sleep, and everyone seems to like you more. You then decided you were lied to all these years by everyone who claimed to know better, and it would become a daily routine, not any different from your morning shower and cup of joe. Two years later you would find yourself with no teeth, blots on your skin and your house was the dumpster that sat behind the apartment complex of your local meth dealer.

It's kinda like this mime I saw performing in front of city hall. He was standing still, his hand clasped around some imaginary object. I walked into the courthouse and paid a ticket. When I returned, the mime was still there, but now his hand was up to his mouth, and he was taking a bite out of the imaginary apple he had been holding the whole time. He was moving so slowly you could never tell that he was in motion. Life is like that. You know what else is like that? Cocaine.

...Ahh Cocaine, unlike meth, you never lose your teeth, your skin doesn't rot, maybe you get a few more nosebleeds, but that is it. No, what cocaine does is make you lose everything of value you have ever created as a human being. Your house, your company, your family. They are all sucked up into your nose, and you are aware of it, you are acutely aware of slowly becoming a beast of a man. All so that you can continue to have fun every night, be the life of the party, fuck young girls and have the confidence to take over the world.

People are often confused by cocaine. They don't understand the appeal. A man takes a bump and doesn't feel any different. Then he sees a cute girl at a bar and walks up to her. No mind games, no wondering what to say, no worry of rejection, no internal dialogue. He will see her, walk up to her, and say exactly the right things. This is the power of cocaine. It's not the high. It's the confidence. Think of the most confident you have ever felt. Imagine feeling like this all the time, imagine what you would accomplish with no fear or regret, then, add in the bonus of never having to sleep.

If you are one of the lucky few, your heart will stop before you lose everything that makes you a functioning member of humanity. Or maybe you are even luckier in that you can afford to keep your addiction going well into your

50's, when you will want to die anyway because your tolerance has been built up so much to this magic little white powder that it no longer has any effect on you.

NICKEL AND MINE'S combined body weight was around 240 pounds. We had just downed a bottle of Vodka, and she was passing around the Yay. It was her and I, Ferris and the King of Israel. We sat on the floor of the tent. The rain creating that all too familiar sound as it pounded against the canvass roof. Making a noise that is at least a thousand times more ominous than the damage it will actually create. We felt like we were on an expedition to the summit of Everest.

I didn't know what to expect on the outside, I didn't know what the next two days would hold for me. I didn't even know where I was. We were only a couple hours in and I couldn't tell you the last time I had felt such excitement.

As my liver fought off the poison that was cocaine combined with alcohol, it released cocaethylene. Cocaethylene is definitely a drug, and most people who are doing blow are really searching out this new narcotic. The high from this concoction is one of the greatest feelings you will ever have. You keep all the attributes that cocaine gives you, but you lose all the grogginess of alcohol. With each new drink, you gain a sense of euphoria. You have the energy and charm of a coke addict mixed with the delusions of grandeur that a bottle of Vodka brings. You are the most badass motherfucker on the face of the planet and by the end of the night, every mother fucker around here will know it.

It must be about 2AM. We decide it's time to hit the dance floor. We had found each other. We were here. We were excited, and it was fucking freezing out. Freezing and wet. I had my five-hundred-dollar waterproof alpine gear on while Nickel sported her three-dollar Walmart poncho that I made her buy a few hours earlier. I expected her to thank me, but she just wasn't that type.

This was my first festival, my first taste of what this strange culture was, but before I unzipped the door, I thought back to how I got here in the first place.

Chapter Two:

Time Moves at the Rate God Intended it to

I'm not an indecisive person, I just don't like plans. It was a few days before Desert Hearts, and I still hadn't bought my ticket. I only knew one person going, and we had a relationship I was still trying to define. Were we friends? Were we going to date? She was cute, but not really my type. I finally ponied up the hundred and fifty bucks and contacted her to see if she wanted to carpool.

Her name was Nickel. I had met her a year earlier, but we had only started hanging out a few weeks ago. She immediately put me on a message board with a few other people who were also going. We chatted, made plans, and tried to figure out what the fuck to do. What did we need? Where were we going? Some old pros gave us advice, but festivals are one of those things you can't really understand until you get there.

The one thing we were completely sure about was we needed some sort of costumes. We had seen pictures of festival goers and anyone who was having fun, seemed to be dressed in festival garb. Steampunk was a favorite, but you could wear anything from a rainbow tutu to a penguin onesie, as long as you were expressing yourself in a genuine manner. Whatever that meant.

I met Nickel at Melrose and we decided upon fur vests. At the time, I thought I would regret this $140 dollar purchase. I added a Taliban-like scarf, cowboy hat, American flag shirt, camo pants and pink sunglasses to the mix. We walked out of dressing rooms and looked into the mirror.

"We match, I don't like that," Nickel said.

"You'll have to get over it," I replied.

24 hours later, Nickel would show up to my house. We packed her gear into my hatchback, and made the three-hour journey to Apple Valley California. I hoped to God she had directions, because I had no clue where we were supposed to end up.

THERE IS ALWAYS an air of mystery around these smaller fests, you are never exactly sure where they are. Vague directions such as "About 2 hours Northeast of Los Angeles" are written on the ticket, but you won't get the exact location until 24 hours before the gates open. It reminded me of old high school parties when everyone was waiting to see whose parents would be out of town over the weekend.

All the small fests want to become bigger; they often start out as annual warehouse parties or theme camps at larger festivals like Burning Man or Lightning in a Bottle. They slowly get a following, bring back their art each year while adding more, until they outgrow their space and try their first stand-alone event.

Desert Hearts started in San Diego, and I am sure has a similar story to all the rest. It's a very Americana way of disruption. We see something large and bulky and want to destroy it. Let's say Folgers Coffee, so we create a better alternative, small, warm, family like and friendly. Then you become Starbucks, and the cycle continues. This festival was like the locally owned coffee shops with three locations. They want to change everything, even though by changing everything, they will become the very thing they hate. I remember reading that African coup d'etats follow a similar pattern.

The founders will get rich, move to the Hollywood Hills, sell out in every way possible, get addicted to yay. All while a new, younger, festival plans their demise. And thus, the cycle will continue.

I'M GLAD I'M not doing this alone. It's dark, cold, and about to rain. We turned off the highway onto a dirt road that seemed to be made for pack animals, not my four-cylinder Japanese car.

"You get car sick?" I ask.

"Yeah," she replies.

Well, shit. Now I am not only worried we are on the wrong, random, dark dirt road, but I have to make sure I drive consistently enough that I don't make this girl puke. With every bump, my stomach turns, knowing I may be causing her pain and sickness. The very core of my masculinity is questioned. Man was made to protect woman so that women could protect child. I am failing at the one job evolution gave me.

"I'm gonna be fine," she said, "I should be puking, but I am actually excited,"

Nickel was the best traveling buddy you could possibly have. This was the first time we had ever been in a car together. And as I looked at her, I was sure she was just as glad to have me here, as I was to have her. Though she would never admit it, like I said before, she just wasn't that type.

Some primal instinct kicks in as we drive. All of a sudden, I feel like I am going to get into trouble. That feeling you had when you were sent to the principal's office. As an adult, you know that fear was irrational, but right now I was feeling it again.

What if we got pulled over? Would we be thrown in jail, never to be heard from again? I have to imagine the local cops hated us, hated everything this festival stood for. How much faith did I really put into the institution that is the government of Apple Valley California?

It reminded me to join the ACLU when I got home, unless I could find a smaller more intimate organization that does the same thing. ACLU, fucking sellouts.

I looked over to Nickel, she's as scared as I am. "Whatever happens, happens, fine by me," she says.

Why don't I have a crush on this girl? I thought.

I MISS BEING bored. Remember how slow time used to move when you were a kid staring out the window? It's not the feeling, it's that slow drip of time that comes with it.

Now a day, a year, goes in a blink.

We have been driving down this dirt road forever. The festival was only five miles off the main highway, and I was sure we were lost. I look down at the odometer and do the math, we had only gone two miles. I forgot how slow time could move. Three miles later, We hit a fork in the road. It was the only real landmark given in the directions. We were going the right way. Fear turned to excitement, tension into anticipation.

In the distance, I see lights. They are not white or orange. They cover the entire spectrum of the rainbow, purple standing out above all others. The lights are bright and sharp. They are pure. They are truth. They are real.

We are entering a wonderland. You are a child. You jump on a tram or monorail. You are going somewhere you have heard about but have never been, maybe it's Disneyland or New York City. The ride is long, slow, a little scary. You go through different emotions, fear, anxiety, excitement, boredom. You travel through a tunnel, it's dark, quiet, stale. Then, in the distance, a light appears. You hear the experience before you can see it. The light gets bigger, sounds cackle in your ears, you can't tell what they are, colors, smells, all the emotions that a person on this Planet Earth can experience come to the forefront of your very being. But they are jumbled, you don't know what to make of them.

There are no words to describe this experience, but it

is an experience we are lacking, it is something we need more of, we should search it out and embrace it, even if dangerous, even if looked down upon, even if people tell you to grow up and get a job. Look at them, look at what they do? Would you want to be them? What would you give up to be something else?

The entrance is where dreams are still reality, where the bitter disappointments of life have yet to take hold. It's good to feel like a kid, it's good to feel limitless and delusional. This festival may suck, this experience may be boring, maybe it's not for me, or you, or anyone. But right now, as I drive down this dark road, as I go to my first festival with a new friend, seeing distant lights and hearing distant sounds, feeling the beat of the music vibrate the very structure of my car, I feel alive. And I don't care if it's all one big lie.

We pull up to a girl straight out of the original Woodstock except for the tablet computer she is holding in her hand. The contradiction of seeing technology mixed with a sort of primal living always catches me off guard. Like when campers pull out their solar panels so that they can watch a movie on their phone.

She asks for our credentials, which has become the de-facto name for tickets. Nickel shows the flower child her wristband which has a micro transmitter embedded into it, which allows the hippie chick to scan and activate it with a hand-held computer device. I pass her my driver's license, so she can pick up my ticket from will call. One of the downsides of last minutes planning is always having to wait in the will call line. For preaching the virtue of the shared economy and the horrible thing that is money, it's amazing how these transformational festivals become McDonalds efficient when exchanging currency. It's all explained away for the greater good, but it makes me think these people don't know what capitalism is.

Hippie chick waves us through security with a smile and a "have fun," then the cluster fuck begins. I'm sure it is always this way, there is no good way to get 2000 people from point A to Point B, especially when there is no real A or B. But this being my first introduction to festival life, brings out the German engineer in me. "Tis so inefficient."

We are told to keep moving, asked if we are camping - yes we are camping, it's midnight and we are in the middle of nowhere, what else would we do! We get further away from what we think is the stage until we finally give up and pull to the side of the road. Perfect timing, just as we park, rain begins to pour down.

The raindrops thump against the roof of my car, creating that ballistic like sound that feels more like an artillery battery than tiny 5-milliliter droplets of water. I have my hiking gear in the back, and put on a cozy outer shell to keep my body warm and dry. Nickel places on her plastic poncho that I made her buy a few hours earlier.

She then pulled out a bottle of Vodka, "Let's kill this before we get started." I did like her style.

Now drunk, we ventured out into the wilderness, the

rain coming down harder and colder. For a second, I swear I felt a snowflake, but this is the middle of the desert in April.

We try to follow the crowd, but as many are going as are coming, and they seem to be going and coming from every direction. Everyone is cold and miserable, you can feel it in the air. Yet they remain friendly. People talk to us, ask where we are from, ask if we have been to DH before. The guys are especially friendly to Nickel because she is hot, and guys like hot girls. They talk to me, and try to determine whether I am her friend, or "something more."

I shine my headlamp to the ground so that Nickel can avoid mud holes, I'm assuming her shoes are not waterproof, and there is nothing worse than being in the middle of nowhere with cold feet. I am amazed time and again how useful a fully stocked backpack is, I can live out of my pack for seven days in just about any condition. I never have need of fear.

Nickel holds her booze well, but is swaying while she is walking and talking. She's not talking to me, she's just talking. I can't follow her speech at all. She really is the perfect traveling partner. She is social, and helps you meet new people. She never complains and never has to be entertained. "Whatever happens, happens." She didn't just say this, she actually lived by it.

"NICKEL?!?!?" The sound came from the distance, from behind us, someone we had just passed. "I hear Nickel's voice!" There were two of them, it was a discussion.

Nickel continued to walk, completely oblivious to the

person yelling out her name. There was only one person who it could be. "Is that the King of Israel?" I shouted back.

"Yeah, who are you!" I shined my light at him, two figures were looking our way. I had never met the King of Israel, but I had talked to him online, I figured he was the only person who would be yelling out for Nickel.

I yelled my name to him as I walked up. "Holy Shit!!! Good to meet you!" He then introduced the man next to him. "This is Ferris."

And if you haven't realized it yet, all the real names have been changed, to protect the people in this book.

We all yell towards Nickel, but she is still talking and walking. She hadn't even realized I was no longer by her side. I ran up and grabbed her. She pulls away from my touch, and turns around. Then, without any surprise in her voice she says, "oh, hey everyone." She turned to me, "this is The King and Ferris."

"I know, we're old friends." I said.

"Oh, I thought you guys had never met." She missed the joke.

Both Israel and Ferris were DJ's, neither was playing at the fest, but DJ's stick together, and they go anywhere that electronic music is playing. It was a community for them, but also a networking event.

"Where'd you guys come from?" Nickel asked.

"We're walking back to our car, going to try to get

our tent up, this place is miserable!" The King said.

We began to walk towards Israel's car, They turned off the main path into the desert brush.

"We found a shortcut," Ferris said. He had this childlike grin, it was pure and innocent. I loved this man.

I stopped, looked at them as they disappeared into the darkness. "Holy shit." I said it to myself. Had we left our car one minute later, we would have never found these two. Our night would have been drastically different. So much of life comes down to a missed look here and a wrong turn there. But in the festivals, there is no such thing as a pleasant coincidence. According to the Transformationals, everything here happens at "the perfect time." A belief I hate to the depths of my soul.

I HAVE NO clue where I am. Ferris and Israel were setting up their tent on top of the brush. The environmentalist in me cried a little, knowing that they were destroying the desert fungus that keeps this ecosystem alive. All around, I saw cars and tents being placed without regard to mother nature.

I didn't think I would ever know my way around this place, but then I thought back to my first day in a new classroom in a new school. The place always seemed so big, the other students looked so far away. By the end of the year, the room would be tiny, the strange faces familiar. Nothing changed, but the brain compresses things into tighter spaces and shorter times as we become familiar with them. By tomorrow, I would completely know the layout of the grounds.

We were in a small valley, I couldn't see the festival or cars from here, but I could see a light source from over the next hill. "I'm going to find my car." I announced to everyone.

Israel and Ferris stopped their work, they knew it was a bad idea, but no one tells you what to do in the festivals. "You were meant for that mission," Ferris said, "God Speed."

I was drunk, cold, and in terrain I had yet to master, but all my material possessions were in that car. I'd feel safer with them by my side. I looked into the pitch-black desert and used the constellations to figure out where I was. Moving opposite of Orion's belt to find the tip of the big dipper and follow it down to the North Star. It would be an epic quest.

I trust myself drunk, probably too much. I am not a stupid drunk, not the type that drives 100 miles per hour on the freeway. No, I am the speed limit plus one mile an hour drunk. I am the drunk that knows he's drunk.

As I walked down the hill, I smelled porta potties, I remembered seeing porta potties earlier. Guided by that chemical scent, I came across a colony of tents pitched on a flat rocky surface. It was a parking lot. This explained the earlier cluster fuck. There were no rules or customs here, people just did whatever the hell they wanted.

I looked back towards where I had come from. A trick

I learned in a survival book, always look back, always see where you have been. My camp was hidden behind a ridge. It didn't look like anyone was up there. On my return, I would have to look for negative space, and go against my instincts in order to find my way home.

I could get lost for hours in this desert. The entire festival was only a square mile. But in darkness, that could mean death. I am an avid hiker and outdoors man, you'd be amazed at the stupid shit that can get you killed in the wilderness. We all say we like nature, enjoy getting away from it all, but what we really mean is we liked controlled nature within the safety of maps, compass and hopefully GPS. Nature is more brutal than any drug, it takes no prisoner, and even the most prepared outdoorsman can get killed.

I continued on to a main road that intersected the parking lot colony. I saw the string of porta potties on my left, right past a V in the road. I remembered that V, I remembered those porta potties. I knew exactly where I was.

"HOLY SHIT!!! WE didn't think we'd see you again." Israel yelled as I pulled up my car.

"He always finds a way," Nickel said in her high-pitched voice as she shook her head at me.

They took me inside their now pitched tent. It was a nice setup, felt like a little home, he even put blankets on the floor to act as carpet. The King had done festivals before, and he was smart enough to know a little extra effort now, would make the entire experience more comfortable.

Nickel pulled out a bag of yay. This would keep us going through the night. Israel gave a gracious thank you to her. He always thanked people, and he always meant it. I hoped that someday I could return this kindness to him. Ferris then snorted the blow up his nose and Nickel passed the bag to me.

Funny, I had never done cocaine before, I had never done any drugs. I snorted the white powder into my nose, I felt nothing. I tasted the yay roll down the back of my throat, mixing with my mucus. It tasted good, then I decided to down a beer.

Fuck, I thought, this stuff isn't even hitting me. Then, I suddenly wanted to dance. I didn't even like dancing. But you know, I was some sort of badass mother fucker, and I wanted every mother fucker here to know it.

Chapter Three:

Pay it Forward

Nickel slept in between three Russian DJ's on a bed that came right out of a Grimm Brother's story. We were in an old dilapidated cabin somewhere in the Caucasus Mountains, or maybe just outside of Los Angeles. The cold was making it hard to think.

We had left The King's tent an hour ago, and never made it to the actual festival. We were walking towards the entrance when the rain began to pour so hard we could no longer see more than a few feet in front of us.

A thick Russian voice yelled in the distance, "Get in the cabin!" What type of weird portal had we just crossed through? "You'll be safe here!" he continued to yell.

We ran through the mud as it grabbed for our shoes. I thought it might pull us into some dark underworld, but before it did, the Russian grabbed my hand and brought me into the safety of this old building.

Upon entering, Nickel introduced me to all the Russians. She knew each one by name, and they knew her. How the fuck did all these crazy Russians know Nickel?

We had now been here for an hour. I was pacing back and forth, doing anything I could to keep warm. "Come to America, play a set, it's in Los Angeles!" one of the DJ's mumbled out as he cuddled up to another in the bed. "They didn't tell me it was gonna be a fucking Siberian prison."

There must have been ten people packed into this cabin, the cuddle puddle on the bed was not sexual, it was all about body heat. I would let those Russian DJs do just about anything to me if it meant I would stay warm. There was a Franklin Stove in the corner blasting out flame, I touched the iron exterior only to find that it was cold. Was this some sort of sick dream?

I continued to pace, wondering what my next move would be. My only thought was that of a shark, if I stopped moving, I'd die.

The old wooden structure could barely hold up to the wind that beat against it. The thuds were becoming louder, it was no longer raining, this was hail. I felt like I was in a crazy Russian Fairy tale. Not that I knew any, but only Russian Fairy could be this fucked up.

Ferris had told me there was a large fire pit by the dance floor. It was my only hope. I opened the front door, dodging the multitude of Russian curse words being thrown my way as the cold air entered the structure. I pushed through the sleet and wind, listening for the sound of bass, hoping it would guide me to the Promised Land.

My hands began to freeze, I instantly tried to warm them up by sticking them down my pants. The cold skin pushed against my legs, and I thought about a pair of mittens I had left at home. When Nickel arrived at my house, I grabbed my backpack. I leave it near the front door in case of nuclear war or zombie apocalypse. Next to the pack was a pair of mittens. I stared at those mittens sitting on the floor. They had a carabiner attached to them so that I could instantly clip them to my pack. I just stared at them. I must have stared at them for two minutes, wondering why I would ever need a pair of mittens in the middle of the desert.

I began to weigh the cost-benefit analysis of an added 1 oz. of weight, and 3 seconds of time to my trip. The amount of effort I put into this question was equivalent to what Einstein must have put into that equation he made. With all that effort, with all that analysis, I decided against bringing them. In the end, I was wrong. Had I just instinctively grabbed for those gloves, my hands would be dry and warm right now.

THERE WAS A small trail that pushed through the trees. Branches curved overhead me as I walked through it. I was now in a tunnel, moving towards the music. I had been in the rain and sleet. I had seen the tent colonies, and wooden cabins. Now I was about to enter the festival. This Desert Hearts.

Glowing lights greeted me as I stepped into this new land. I saw a giant stage surrounded by art installations. The DJ's booth looked like it was growing right out of the ground, it was made of mangled pieces of wood that glowed in the dark night.

I stood in the middle of the dance floor, and looked at the things around me. A thirty-foot yurt strewn with hammocks. It was the tree house I never had as a kid. A Main Street, full of bars, and lounges and restaurants. A lookout tower with rope ladders, and a blank canvas wall, surrounded by paint cans, where anyone could create art.

I saw the fire pit and made my way towards it, but there was not a single gap in the human flesh to feel the heat of the flame. "Oh shit! Did you just get here?" someone said, "take my spot, warm up." He physically pulled me into his position, so that I would be right against the fire. "Feels good doesn't it? Warm up, the night is young."

A friend once told me that festivals are about an experience. It's about seeing what you are made of, feeling the emotions of life in an amplified situation. Some festivals are about finding yourself. Others are about exploration. They are not always fun. That misses the point. They are about discovery. Desert Hearts was a good place for me to start. A good place to get a taste for what this world had to offer.

After I had thawed, I moved to the dance floor. I was joined by half a dozen others. It was just us few, and the DJ. Another burst of rain, but this time the wetness did not bother me. It did not bother any of us. The water felt soft against our skin, like feathers dropping from the sky. It took us all a minute to realize what was going on. We all stopped in unison, and stared up into that black night, as the white snowflakes fell down upon us.

Those around the fire, walked towards the stage,

looking up at that beautiful sight. Then we danced. It was cold and unbearable, but everyone wanted this once in a lifetime experience. Everyone wanted to dance in the snow in the middle of the desert night.

The flakes began to fall harder, the ground became white. This was not a light brushing. This was real snowfall. People shouted at the sky, screamed in joy, yelled in pain. We threw snowballs at each other and made snow angels. We wrote letters of love into the chairs that were now covered in thin ice.

Till the day we died, we would all remember that silly night, when we danced in the snow.

THE SUN BEGAN to rise and the air began to warm. The sound of tents unzipping echoed through the hills. People walked out into the cold air, looking at the snow-capped mountains, wondering what they had missed.

I walked back to my car and unlocked it, figuring Nickel would find it a good place to crash. I set up my Coleman instant tent, dropped to the ground and fell asleep.

I was awoken a few hours later by the smell of bacon and the sound of Nickel's laughing. Ferris's nose was bleeding from too much blow, and Israel had puked all over his tent. "I'm glad the dumbass forgot to lock his car!" Nickel said as she giggled. "Wake up!!!" she yelled through my tent. I smiled.

Day two was about to begin.

Chapter Four:

Introspective Bullshit

"We know your secret."

The two girls had been sneaking glances at me for the past hour. They would peek over, talk among themselves, then begin to laugh.

"What's the secret?" I asked.

"We know who you are," one of them answered.

They began to laugh. I could see this conversation was going nowhere, so I looked back down towards the dance floor.

I was standing on the highest hill above the campground and could finally see the layout of the place, my tent, my car, the wooden cabins, the road leading into town, the dance floor, the entire festival. All the mystery was now gone. It was no different than any other campground I had ever been to, except for the costumes, stage and music. It was not wonderland, it was a facade.

A police helicopter began to hover above the crowd, this wasn't the first time. They had come before, even sent troopers to the front gate. For a moment, we thought the entire party would go the way of tear gas and bullet fire. I wonder if anyone on the outside would have even cared.

This time was different, it was just a single helicopter. From this vantage point I could see there were no cruisers headed toward the camp. People began to shout at the flying metal beast.

"We love you!!!"

"Thank you for your service!!"

"Peace and Love!!"

"Try MDNA!!"

It was stupid yet funny at the same time.

I WAS HERE with the Mayor of Desert Hearts. I dubbed him so, because he wore an American flag vest. He and his friends were taking turns waving a giant American flag into the air. Just so everyone down below could see it.

There is a strong vein of patriotism at these transformational festivals. American flags and outfits are everywhere. I'm not sure where this patriotism stems from, but it is palpable.

Festivals have a sense of idealism, and America, if nothing else, is an idealistic country. The people here believe they have the ability to reshape our nation, and they know that we live in one of the very few countries that can be reshaped. America was always more of an idea than a place, and the festival goers believe they can help bend America into the perfect version of itself. Their perfect versions of themselves.

I can't help but fall in love with everything America is as I look upon this camp of debauchery. Naked people dancing with clothed people, bros hugging artists, acid induced prayer and chants. There is even free beer.

I'm sure many Americans would be disgusted by this display. But this is America. This is as American as any midwestern town, governed by Christian churches and local pride. Things that would most likely disgust the people in front of me. This is America, and that is America. All of this is our country. One could not exist without the other. I don't think I have ever loved this country more.

"WE KNOW!!!" THE girls were back at it. They looked me up and down seductively, licking their lips, and for a second, I thought about how smelly a threesome would be under these conditions. I sat next to them.

"You are not fooling us!" One of them said.

"Who am I?" I asked.

"You're a wolf!"

"Good wolf or bad?" I asked.

"I don't know yet, what are you going to do to us?"

"I think you guys are doing well on your own."

"Do you need acid?" One of them replied as she slipped her hand into her purse.

"No, I'm totally sober." I wasn't lying. I hadn't even taken part in the free beer yet.

"why why why!?"

"I've never done acid."

"You'd probably eat us up on acid."

"Would you fight back?" I asked.

"Only one way to find out."

"I am a wolf," I showed my teeth, "It feels better that someone knows." Their eyes lit up as I walked away. Leaving them to ever wonder if I actually telling the truth.

THE KING OF Israel was still lying in his tent, sick as hell. Ferris was off doing drugs, so Nickel was all that I had left. She disappeared a few hours earlier, but I was on a mission to find a familiar face. In the two days I had been at this festival, I had yet to make a new friend. I could talk to people, have some fun, but never anything more than that. I was feeling out of place and very alone.

I pushed through the dancers who seemed to be on a mix of molly, E and acid. Each had it's own characteristic in the way the user reacted. E, was just molly cut with another drug, usually a type of speed. these dancers went hard, they couldn't stop moving. The ones on Molly stayed near the back, rubbing each other, looking for love, and the acid users, they were on a spiritual quest. They worshiped the DJ. He was God for as long as he could keep their attention.

I walked among the tents that were located behind the "main street." these were community tents, it looked like anyone could walk in, but I was not sure. I couldn't tell if their services cost money, I couldn't tell how welcoming they really were. I was intimidated by them, afraid I would be yelled at for breaking some ritual or custom.

I walked around the personal tents, no one put any thought into their campsites, this annoyed the outdoorsman in me while making me respect The King of Israel even more. A few minutes of thought and each encampment could have felt like a home. I made a mental note to make an awesome camp if I ever went to another festival. Something I was doubting would ever happen.

Then, in the distance, I saw a tiny little figure staring into the sky. I could recognize that silhouette anywhere. I had found my Nickel. "Heyyyyyyyy!" She looked at me, then back to the sky, "take me over here." She grabbed my hand and dragged me towards the stage. As we got closer, she pulled back. "No, no no, that's too much, let's go over there." She again, grabbed my hand and took me to wherever over there was. "No no no, I don't know…"

"What do you need?" I asked her.

"I don't know I don't know, I don't know…. Yea the stage." And again we were off to the dance floor. "No, I was wrong, over there is right…" Then she looked at me, "I just did acid for the first time."

That explained it. There were few drugs that scared me more than acid. Most everyone who knew me, said I would hate it. It would be a 14-hour high that felt like a week. "How is it?" I asked.

"I'm, I'm not sure. everything is too much."

I looked around and realized the vibe was much different today. There was a lot more introspection going on, a lot more people staring at walls, a lot more chants. I guess day two at festivals were acid days. Day one is about fun, day two about introspection. It made sense enough.

I don't know what the acid high is like, but whenever I see someone on acid they tell me a lot of stupid shit. One of my best friends told me acid "will make you question everything about life and everything that you believe. it will make you question beliefs you don't even know you have until you know how to question everything." Seemed like some pretty stupid bullshit to me.

"Can you take me somewhere?"

"Where?" I asked.

"Just somewhere."

"I'm gonna get a beer." I said.

"That's good, I like that."

I walked into the bar, filled up my nalgene, took a sip and liked what I tasted. It was a light IPA, the citrus mixed perfectly with the desert atmosphere. It was time to get my buzz on.

"Okay, that's enough, I need to go now." Nickel eyes looked past my face as if connecting with my gaze would cause her to run away. "I appreciate your effort," she said while trying to only see me through her peripheral vision, "but now it is time to be alone. "

She began to back away, still her gaze looking past my eyes, when she was far enough, she turned around and ran, until she disappeared somewhere into the tents or maybe the desert. Who knows?

Festivals feel like the loneliest places in the world. Looking at everyone around you, makes you understand just what an outsider you are, just how isolated you can become. I took another sip of beer, Nickel needed to be alone, but I was the one who felt lonely. Why the fuck did I even come to this place? Why the fuck does anyone?

Chapter Five:

An Outsider on the Inside

It was dark. I was pretty wasted. The King was still asleep and God-the-hell-knows where Nickel and Ferris were. I wandered around, made small talk, at least as much as I could. I wore my fur vest matched with an oversized Soviet military hat. Not oversized by Eastern Bloc standards, but definitely absurdly large by the standards of any other civilized people on this here earth.

I turned down sex and drugs. I was asked to talk about spirituality and sustainability. I felt so out of place. Nothing here interested me. I wandered the desert, smelled the air, listened to the music, walked among the tents, stared at the festival goers, tried to find my place in this world.

"Why did I come here?" I said to myself as I walked through the campground, feeling the introspection of a light buzz. Was it Nickel? She was cute. I bought my ticket expecting to see other friends here, but it turns out, I had confused this festival with the much bigger Lightning in a Bottle. I met a pink haired hoola hooper a couple weeks ago. She told me about her favorites. Lucidity, Lightning in a Bottle, of course the Burn. The ones to avoid, EDC, Hard Summer, anything that seemed like a rave.

My thoughts were interrupted by a voice hailing me from an open tent, "come in, we welcome all!" He had a

Russian accent and a smile on his face.

A second head popped out and spoke with that same accent. "That hat! Is that a Soviet hat!" For a second I thought I was in trouble, but they both went into a hysterical laugh as I explained it was an authentic Soviet military hat that I bought from a surplus store.

"I remember these, it's funny, on you, at this festival, is peaceful, but back home, if I saw that, it was fearful, how times have changed, I must get a picture."

They invited me in and poured me a cup of tea. The floor was lined with quilts and pillows. People slept while the Russians served cake and drink to anyone who passed. "We call this the tea tent," the second Russian explained to me as he poured me another cup, "all are welcome here."

"Do you need a donation or anything?" I asked.

"No, money is no good here, we abide by Burner culture."

I didn't know what that meant.

"What's in the bottle friend?" the first Russian asked me as he pointed to my nalgene.

"It's an IPA."

"Friend, we don't allow any drugs in here."

"Oh, I'm sorry, can I leave it out outside."

"Yes, of course, just not in the tea tent."

"Are you guys straight edge?" I asked.

"Yes, yes, I am." The first Russian answered.

"I am also straight edge, but I drink some, and do marijuana." Said the second.

"I see," I really didn't, but I find it's best to never question people, only learn from them.

The second Russian then lit up a bowl. "Would you like some?" he asked.

"No, I am good, pot's okay in here?" I said.

"Yes, no pills or booze, pot is fine, anything natural." I thought about asking if I could bring in some grape juice and drop natural yeast into it to drink twenty days later, but the joke would probably be lost on them.

"I wish you wouldn't do that," the first Russian whispered as the second took a hit.

"It relaxes me, it's no different than tea."

"Do we have tea?"

"Yes, we have tea."

It felt like a lover's quarrel. The first Russian lifted the tea kettle and began to shake it, "it's almost empty, we won't if someone takes more tea."

"Fine! I will get more tea." This tea tent was a beautiful thing, but it was not real, it is what we wished were real. The second Russian left to get tea, but I would not see him again.

"Are you guys going to Lightning in a Bottle?" I asked.

"I think we will, we want to spread the tea tent, spread our way of living," his thick accent rolled off his tongue in a slow manner, but I knew he was lying. He was trying to manifest his reality. The power of belief, it's all you need right? I couldn't help but think how everyone wants to change the world, but no one wants to help out their next door neighbor.

A few more people entered the tea tent, I wanted some beer, so I decided to leave. I thanked the Russian for the hospitality and put my shoes back on. I walked over to the bar, found a keg and filled my nalgene to the top. I took a sip of the IPA and thought about how this has become the American beer, how everything that is good about an IPA grows amazingly well in the Pacific Northwest of America. I thought how the IPA was made because the hops allowed it to stay fresh on the long trip between Britain and India, yet an old IPA taste like a gym sock, whereas a new fresh IPA tastes like a citrusy pinecone. Age and experience versus youth and innovation. How quickly a culture can get old, how quickly a culture can change.

"THIS IS THE tea tent, not the sleep tent!" the loud Russian accent woke me up. I looked around, moved my arms, got my bearings of where I was. I had been drinking, I had fallen asleep on my back, there were others who were sleeping in here, maybe they were friends, or maybe the Russians did not like me.

"Sorry, I fell asleep." I tried to remember how I even got back to the tea tent, but was in such a flustered daze, I couldn't remember anything, I thought best to just leave.

"You started snoring too." The Russian said.

"I'm sorry, I'll go to sleep, I mean leave."

"Don't forget your hat." This reply took me off guard,

he went from unfriendly to friendly so fast. My hat had fallen off and he wanted to make sure I did not lose it.

I left the tent and walked towards the fire where I saw Nickel sitting indian style. I sat down next to her, only to find that she had passed out, Her head was in between her legs, swaying back and forth. I was a bit envious that someone could fall asleep in this position.

I walked over to the DJ booth as deep house played. In the little area behind the stage, I saw Ferris snorting coke. I wondered where Israel was, but then remembered I had checked on him earlier, only to find that he was still sick, and asleep.

I hadn't made a single new friend at this festival. I had met people, chatted, talked, but not one real friend. Not the type of person I could go explore with, dance with, walk around with. Nickel had made friends, Ferris had too… It was the drugs, I wasn't doing any, they were. They had drugs. I had none. Everything was centered around drugs, yet no one seemed to know it. They would have said it was the music, the community, the art… It was the fucking drugs, the drugs kept this place together.

I have experience with addicts, I know how they think. Not everyone here was an addict, in fact, the vast majority were not. But almost everyone here had been caught by the allure of drugs. The thing about drugs is they can catch up to you, they can become part of you, and your mind can't comprehend it until you are in too deep.

Every man understands this feeling. Every male has

been in a situation where they find that they really like hanging out with a particular girl. You will drop plans to see her, you will stop whatever you are doing for the opportunity to be with this person. She is the greatest thing ever. Then she either says something, or does something, that makes you realize that she will never have sex with you. You are not sad, you weren't in love with her, but all the feelings of wanting to be with her, instantly disappear. You weren't enjoying her company, you just wanted to get laid.

Drugs are like that too, the problem is they never say no. You find yourself at parties you would have never attended, shows you had no interest in seeing, camping in the middle of a cold wet desert, all because drugs were there. But your brain says you really like these experiences.

I used to be addicted to cigarettes, and even I did this. I would give myself cheats, if I was with a certain friend or in a certain situation, I could still have a smoke. Those cheats became daily. I would drive across town to see that old friend, put myself in those positions where I was allowed to smoke. I didn't even realize it until I quit cold turkey. Drugs make the rest of life seem so dull.

The wind began to push through the hills as the sun peaked over the horizon. It was the last day of the festival, the last few hours for Nickel and I.

I turned around to see the place where the stars still remained. I noticed a group doing the same.

"Is that Mount Baldy?" I asked in quiet voice.

"The what?" a girl answered back.

"Mount Baldy. The Crest, the Los Angeles Crest Forest."

"We're not even close to LA," she replied.

"Well it's not the Sierra's."

"The Sierra's are in like Colorado!!!" She then turned to her friends, "He thinks the Sierra's are in California!"

Her friends laughed, one of them looked back at me, "Dude, you really need to explore this state more."

We all get to live in the worlds we want to live in, surround ourselves with the people we want to surround ourselves with. Those worlds become our reality, and no one can prove us wrong. It's not a bad life.

My first festival was over, as was Nickel's. We didn't talk much on the ride home. We texted back and forth the next day, but didn't have much to say. Nickel introduced me to her friend Token. She wanted me to join her at Lightning in a Bottle. I don't think I much enjoyed Desert Hearts, but I was curious. I was bored with life and was looking for something new. Maybe that's how it started for everyone.

I had entered a new world, and the entire community seemed to know. It was like someone had signed me up for an illegal mailing list. People were now contacting me to find out where the best spots were during the weekend, where the Burner scene was, which illegal clubs were open. I played the part well, but honestly I had no fucking clue what I was doing.

You don't choose this culture, this culture chooses you.

Part II

Capturing The Lightning

We live in an age of islands. There are more islands in the city of Los Angeles than there are on the great oceans of the world. Traveling has become about exploring like places. One flies from JFK to LAX, stays in Silver Lake then moves to Williamsburg. This illusion makes you think you are experiencing diversity, when, in fact, it is just hardening your own beliefs.

People compare us to the generation that lived in the 70's, when they should look to those from the 20's. The Lost Generation came out of World War One, a pointless war where nothing was accomplished. Everything we believed disintegrated right before our eyes. So we moved to Paris. The great thinkers, the great artists, writers and musicians. This place defined the world for the next 90 years.

Now, these same people are moving to the City Of Angels. We also come from a time of disruption, not from war, but from wealth. The age of abundance. We connected the world, tore down the wall, the literal Berlin wall and the figurative wall that kept a man in Omaha from ever meeting a man for Mumbai. Our basic needs were taken care of, shelter, food, survival. We had it all. And having it all made us wonder what the point of any of it was. So we moved to Los Angeles. Maybe for no other reason than it was as far west as we could go.

Paris in the 1920's. It was a special place. A similar thing happened at Haight Ashbury in the 60's, Greenwich in the 70's. I'm sure it happened in Vienna at one point and Athens at another. Some people refer to them as Golden Ages, I don't believe they need names. This is Los Angeles in the twenty tens. Los Angeles in 2014.

Anyone who has lived in this city for long knows something is different. Things are changing. The ghetto is being gentrified by artists, downtown has been given a rebirth, tech has moved into Venice. And of course, we have always had the biggest bullhorn on this planet. All these people, all these professions have merged at this one point, at this one time, and are slowly creating something that will define us for a generation.

Los Angeles is the most exciting city in the world. It is now dominating the cultural creations of man, the music, the fashion, the technology, the architecture, the video games and the visuals. Everything is slowly coalescing in this one place, this one city... And this one city, is slowly being defined by another place, another movement. You can see pieces of it walking down any street, eating any food, hearing the music out of the clubs. The Transformational Festival Movement is shaping the one place that shapes the world.

Chapter Six:

Birth of the White Suit

I found myself traveling to one of these islands. It was my first Burner event. When the sun goes down on the warehouse district of Downtown Los Angeles, the Burners come out to play. The essence of the area changes into a dreamlike state, inhabited by the spirits of childhood memories. Business suits are transformed into elegant attire. Women shed clothes, while men increase their layers. The dilapidated buildings become mystical cities and steampunk laboratories. The shackles of our inner imagination are torn off so we can do whatever we please.

Tonight was the White Party. A fundraiser for one of the Burning Man sound camps. It took place in a large, multi building warehouse. It was just one of the half dozen parties going on in DTLA this weekend. This movement could not be stopped. Not that city hall would ever try. Whatever was going on in this city, it was only going on because of the people who were creating it. If this new world was created by inner-city hoodlums, or Mexican immigrants, it would have been shut down before it even started. But these events were being thrown, and attended by the very elite of the world. The tech industry, the design industry, and the artists who relied on these people for their livelihood. The city would never bite the hand who fed it.

It wasn't just my city that was undergoing change, I

was as well. It had only been a few days since my first festival, but I was getting this strange fuck-you attitude towards money. I have never lived beyond my means, and I have never been in debt. Debt meant being a slave, forcing me to abide by its will. But now I was walking around the fashion district of downtown, looking at hundred-dollar costumes. I didn't regret buying my fur vest or Soviet hat for Desert Hearts, and I sure as hell wouldn't regret whatever costume I bought for the White Party.

I thought about what I should wear. I didn't know much about Burning Man or the culture. A fundraiser for a camp was absurd to me. I looked at fabric and flowers. I looked through scarves and glasses. I imagined how I could turn such raw materials into an elegant outfit. I was enjoying every aspect of the process. Something I would have made fun of myself for just a few weeks earlier.

And then I saw it staring at me. The White Suit. It looked like something Al Capone would wear during the prohibition era as he wiped a splotch of blood from his sleeve. It was so perfect, so original. No one at the festivals ever wore anything like this. I added a black scarf and white fedora to the outfit and looked at myself in the mirror. The clothes do make the man.

I bowed to myself and said, "People never dress for the occasion anymore." At the time, I could have never imagined how this $150 dollar purchase would change my life.

THE DOORMAN FELT around my legs and under my arms looking for contraband, not that he would find anything, I only had my keys and ID on me. These parties may be illegal, but the organizers are not stupid. Professional security guards pat you down and go through your bags before you are allowed to enter. They will never check so closely that they might find drugs - plausible deniability for the event's producers - but they will definitely make sure you don't have any weapons or booze - safety and bar money being equally important.

As he turned me around and checked my shoes, I started thinking about High School. Sitting at the lunch table on a Monday, hearing about the party I was not invited to. You know the one? Where all the popular kids and that girl you had a crush on were? But not you, you were sitting at home, or at a friends, doing boring normal stuff while all of them were living in a real-world version of your favorite television show.

I grew up, and nothing changed. The high school parties turned into VIP guest lists, red carpets and bottle service. Again and again, I was left out. A giant "Do Not Enter" sign above the door that led to the life I wanted.

But now I was about to enter one of these doors. Right now, I was about to go to that place I had always wanted to go. Here I was in downtown Los Angeles, at the single best party going on in the city, maybe the world. Walking through dark alleys, avoiding the cops, entering an unassuming door. Movie stars didn't know about this. Rock stars were sitting at home watching reruns. They envied me. For this night, I would be at the most badass place on the entire planet. It felt good.

The security guard gave me a nod of approval as he pushed aside the curtain to let me in. I looked around, trying to figure out the layout of the event. To the left was a bathroom, the line ran 20 deep. These parties always lacked restrooms. Warehouses were made to store stuff, not hold employees, which meant most buildings only had one or two toilets. The really smart event planners would order half-dozen porta potties to make up for this.

In front of me was a very large bar with a very limited selection. Beer, Water, Vodka and Redbull. Each the same price, water and Red Bull being the best-selling items. A large sign above the bartender explained that all proceeds from the bar would be used to fund their Burning Man camp. By attending this party, I was helping to fund the next party. It was a self-financing system.

Past the bar was the main stage, the heart of the club. It was psychedelic even without drugs, I started feeling dizzy and high even though there was nothing in my system. The music became deep and powerful. A parade of white totems came out from behind the stage and made their ways through the crowd. They looked like octopuses on sticks, moving up and down as they pranced through the warehouse. These were the symbols of the camp. Corporate logos for people who hated corporations.

This single room would rival any club, located in any

mid-sized city in America. Yet, here in Los Angeles, it was nothing more than a large party, thrown by a group of friends, who were using it to fund a much larger party out in the middle of the Nevada desert.

The absurdity of it all was quickly lost on me, as I realized I had absolutely no clue what to do here. The music was so loud I couldn't talk to anyone. I didn't want, nor know how to dance. I looked at the friends I came with, they were standing in a corner, having fun doing nothing. As they had all eaten edibles before they had arrived.

I remembered the few high school parties I had attended and how out of place I felt. I always feel out of place. This was Desert Hearts all over again.

I HAD BEEN hanging around for an hour, when my pocket began to buzz.

"Where are you???" The text read from Nickel.

"Where are you?" I replied.

"Security line."

I couldn't wait to see her. It would be our first time together since Desert Hearts. I ran back through the party, to the front entrance, waiting for her to appear, silly smile on her face, skinny body looking hot, ready to give me a giant hug.

She peaked through the curtain and instantly saw me. She walked up and said "hi" in the same manner you would say hi to a roommate you saw every morning of your life. The King of Israel pushed through a few seconds later, a smile and giant hug greeting me. Why couldn't he be the hot skinny Thai girl?

Then another young lady ran up and hugged me, "I've heard so much about you!" she said. "I'm Token? Remember? From the message boards?"

"Token!" I smiled and hugged her back, she was supposed to have joined us at Desert Hearts but had to cancel at the last minute.

"So, you going to Lightning in a bottle?" She had been messaging me this all week trying to get me to join her and Nickel.

"It's too expensive," I said.

"Life's short!"

"I don't think I'll enjoy it, It's far and I don't know anyone there." I said.

"You know us!" Then she hugged me again. "Maybe you'll find something there, what would you pay to find something?"

"A lot," I replied while thinking the naiveté of the young reminds me why I am alive.

"I'm not saying you will, just what would you pay?" She asked.

Token's eyes looked old for her age. She had the eyes of a soldier. Hardened soldiers have the eyes of children. People, who have seen humans do the types of things we never want to believe, look at the world in a childlike way. Maybe it's the only way of dealing with it, or maybe seeing the worst forces you to ignore the little things. Token shouldn't have those eyes, but she did.

"I'll think about it." I said. Israel looked distracted. "Want me to show you around?" I asked.

"That would be awesome."

I lead The King through the club, and it occurred to me, not a single person here was being paid - security guards being the only exception. They were doing all of this for no other reason than they wanted to create something for Burning Man.

"Do you know who's running this party?" Israel asked.

"No, I know it's some sort of fundraiser," I answered, "honestly, it makes no sense to me."

"Never try to make sense of Burning Man, that's a mistake everyone makes." How can something not make sense? Burning Man was a festival, maybe it was bigger and better than Desert Hearts, but I knew what festivals were. "This party is run by Abundant Sanctuary, they are one of the largest sound camps at The Playa." He said.

"What's The Playa?" I asked.

"It's just another name for Burning Man, but specifically, The Playa is the desert. So Abundant Sanctuary has a camp that is on the side of the city, this allows them to position their speakers directly into the desert, meaning they can be super loud without bothering anyone. They hold this insane White Party on Wednesday, it's like the best party at Black Rock City."

"What's Black Rock City?" I asked.

"It's just another name for Burning Man." I remembered hearing that China had a lot of hells, I guess Burning Man had a lot of names. "I'm looking for some of the leaders of the camp. I want to introduce myself."

I was new to this scene, but I knew what Israel was doing. He was playing the networking game, and he was doing it all wrong.

"Did you try the silent disco?" Israel looked over to me.

"What's that?" We were walking through the group of crazy people dancing to the imaginary beat of the DJ.

"Hand over your driver's license to the booth, they will give you a bluetooth headset so you can listen to the music."

I had seen the dancers before, but I had assumed they were all just rolling balls. For all the talk of spirituality, this place was run by technology. This was a brilliant way to have a dance party in a place with noise restrictions. Think of the ingenuity, engineering and programming that went into such an installation. This place, this party, this is what happens when the best and brightest of the world want to have fun. These are not a bunch of homeless hippies who hate capitalism. This is capitalism. It was beautiful.

"If I could just get my music played on their channel," The King said.

"Music has a funny way doesn't it?" I said.

"The Internet was supposed to give us all opportunity, but it seems the more opportunity we have, the harder it gets."

"Funny, it has just made the gatekeepers more powerful," I replied.

"Well Van Gogh died penniless and insane," he said.

The King of Israel bumped into a mutual friend of the camps. A fellow DJ. I could tell the King was intimidated. Israel introduced me, but I quickly excused myself, so he could have his moment with the man. I hoped he would get his break. He deserved it.

I walked up to the balcony that overlooked the main stage. Men and women were cuddling and making out. The booze and molly lowered their inhibitions. It's funny how we do that, use drugs to give us an excuse. I knew it was all bullshit, but I still envied them.

Chapter Seven:

Fuck the Police

We used to pack big chests full of clothes and supplies to cross the great oceans. We traveled far and slow. We experienced places viscerally. We were always present, because we had no other choice.

Now, traveling seems like a chore. We get on a plane, complain about the money, time and legroom. We want to get where we are going, never appreciating the actual experience of getting there. Then it ends, and we share our adventure on the Internet. Instead of changing who we are, we travel to change the way others perceive us to be.

Traveling to festivals seems to bring the adventure back. Maybe it's because the entire experience is such a mystery, or perhaps it is because you have enough drugs in your car that you could spend the rest of your life in prison. I found myself practicing the speech.

"No you may not search my car."

"I have nothing to hide."

"I don't need to give a reason."

"Am I free to go?"

"Am I being detained?"

"This is amazing, see this means something," Token was looking out the window at a sunshower. We decided to take the coast up to the festival and were lead through a canyon road that looked like a technicolor version of reality. "It's a cleansing, this is going to be the greatest festival experience I have ever had."

The festival life was pulling me kicking and screaming. People plan for these events months in advance, I bought my tickets three days ago. So far, this culture was nothing more than a strange peculiarity to me, one I wasn't even really enjoying. But like the self-destructive girlfriend who you continue to give a chance, I kept going back.

We took a right off the canyon road onto an old country highway. I think we may have entered Oklahoma during the dust bowl. We drove past a burned out old main street, and an abandoned farm. These towns must only survive on speeding tickets, because there were more police cars than people here. Their red and blue lights shining against the massive empty fields, giving us short bursts of vision into the reality of the place.

"It looks like a rave!" Nickel said.

I turned the music down, thinking this would somehow protect us from being pulled over.

"You need to lose the Anxiety," Token told me.

"Sorry," its amazing how one person's anxiety can change the energy in a room.

We took the last turn before we entered the festival grounds. Two police cars on each side of the entrance. I was expecting they would wave us down to check our car, but instead they waved at us to have a good time. Fucking Pigs.

We were arriving on a Thursday night. The festival didn't officially start until tomorrow, this would mean no lines and easy access to the camping area. I always liked getting to events early, I enjoy seeing the sausage made, it makes you feel like you are part of something.

"IF A STOWAWAY is found, everyone in the vehicle will lose their tickets." A giant sign read above the entrance to the festival.

"You guys have some Tetris like packing skills," the gate checker told us as she looked into our vehicle. A deep masculine pride arose within me, at my ability to fit the most amount of stuff into the least amount of space. We were pointed to a dusty barren field and assigned a parking spot. We had no clue where to go, where we were allowed to camp, or where the festival was.

"Let's kill a bottle of Vodka and check this place out," Nickel said. It was a good plan, a fine plan.

"No," Token objected, "Let's kill half a bottle of vodka and put the other half in our nalgenes, so we can explore and drink." It was a better plan. Well done Token, well done.

Lightning in a Bottle started out as a small birthday party in which nature and music were celebrated. It remained a private event for five years, but kept growing in size. It finally went public in 2004 and is now often referred to as the poor man's Burning Man.

20,000 people will gather on this dried-out lake bed

this year. Not the actual lake bed, but the giant buttes that overlooked it. A deep ravine lined with paths separates each one of these landmasses. It made the place feel like an ancient city, built before modern amenities, the type you would find in the middle of the Italian Alps. These natural barriers created distinct districts and cultures, all out of the laziness of man not wanting to hike up and down these hills.

On the side of each ridge was a sign with a non-offensive word such as "Love" or "Create" or "Unity." I felt like I was exploring an old 8-bit video game, each ravine felt like a different stage and I feared I would end up in an area where the monsters were too strong for me to defeat. I was there with new friends, a small group of low-level adventurers. Token and Nickel and I. I wondered if we could make it to the end of the zone. Would we be able to defeat the final boss? Or must we keep adventuring until we leveled up and learned the proper spells?

Every great adventure starts with a quest, I hadn't been given mine yet, but I felt like I was on the verge of something special.

I COULD NEVER last long in museums, the greatest works of art mankind had ever created surround me, and I couldn't understand how anyone enjoyed them. Paintings weren't made to be stared at. They were made to be experienced. My brother was a classical painter. He could look at a painting, analyze the brush strokes, see what was going through the artist's mind. He'd sit there and start sketching.

Museums were made for artists, not people like me.

As I lugged seventy pounds of gear down, then up the ravine towards our camp, I made a mental note to spend the 50 bucks on a car pass next year. This was the third trip we had made, and we were already exhausted. Lightning in a Bottle was going to test our willpower and strength. This place was huge, and getting around took effort.

I set up my insta-tent and we placed all the gear inside. The Vodka had now been killed, so we moved on to a bottle of Rum. There are not many things more fun than exploring a festival while intoxicated.

Long strings of paper lanterns floated above our heads. They were attached to wooden posts, creating a sort of road through the camping area. I felt as if we had entered a new village in ancient Japan. I half expected to be accosted by a pair of Samurais asking for my papers, and wondering what a group of white people were doing in their country, except that I was the only white one in my group.

The camps along the sides of the road were more like shops and restaurants than tents. The purveyors of each establishment would greet us and ask if we would like to enter.

We crawled through the entrance of a small yurt, the door only about three feet high. We were handed headphones and given a set of cards that instructed us to perform different acts. "Make a funny sound," "scratch the side of the yurt," "talk with your mouth closed."

There was a microphone in the room that picked up the sounds of our actions and filtered them through some device that created music. The headphones were high enough quality that they drowned out the outside world. The four of us, around that small table, inside that small yurt, were now in our own wonderful world. There is a bond that comes from creating things together. We thanked our host and continued on our way.

"I bet that's Israel's renegade stage," Token was pointing to a group of dancers near the edge of one of the cliffs.

"What's a renegade stage?" I asked.

"It's not supported by LiB, they can get shut down."

"Why would they do that?"

"Mostly politics," Token answered.

When I was a child, it seemed important to be cultured. It was important to learn a little about Mozart and Monet and that guy who made the Thinking Man statue. You didn't enjoy it, but as your mom dragged you to the county art museum, you knew you were building the foundation of something that you would be able to pull from in the future.

At some point, the cultured began to look down upon the uncultured. A divide was created and the "working man" began to hate the "thinking man." The thinking man started to believe that being clever was more important than unclogging your toilet, and the working man starting believing that anything that was not practical was elitist.

But here, people respected the carpenter and electrician. They were put on the same pillar as the artist and the intellect. This was interactive art, you were not a passive participant, you were part of the experience. Art was not separate from the community. Art was the community.

What I was witnessing was something that was lacking in my country. This was the reason that culture used to be valued by the working man. He may not understand that giant copper statue which was so admired by the critics, but in some small way, the grooves of the metal, the changing color of its surface, the craftsmanship that went into creating the great work of art, inspired him to be better. So that when he made that spice rack for his wife, he put a little more effort into it. Creating something that was both functional and beautiful. Maybe not as beautiful as the great artist's work, but it was more than it would have been.

Every time he entered the kitchen, he would stare at that little wooden trinket that he had built with his own hands, for the woman he loved, and he would stand a little taller. Have a certain type of dignity that many of us are lacking today.

We begin to walk towards analog music. It is so out of place within this world of electronic sounds, that it pulls us towards it. The sound of a fiddle, a banjo, someone singing Bluegrass. Up yet another ravine we enter a whole new world, a world of the American Wild West. There is a saloon here, a grand Ol-Opry like stage, a general store, and a giant house with four wheels that can drive anywhere within the Festival. The banjo player stops his song, and begins to preach his word. "We believe in the values of conservatism!" He yells to the audience. "Real instruments, practicality, and booze. We don't want any of those hippies, drugs and sex here at our festival!" Everyone in the audience cheers. "That is why I am declaring right now, my intention to run to be the next mayor of Lightning in a Bottle!"

Beer cans are raised to the air, and I realize, I know this story, it is playing out right in front of my face.

"MY DEAR FRIEND, it is so good to see you." Fernando said in his thick, unidentifiable, accent. "Here at Fernando's, we stand for love, we shall be opening shortly."

Fernando was the three-time mayor of Lightning in a Bottle. I had known him for ten years, but had just recently learned of his secret LiB life. His real name was Rubix, we had worked together in film, and I only knew him as being a hard-working producer and director.

"Remember to vote for love," He pinned a campaign button upon my jacket in such a suave manner that I almost forgot the whole affair was pretend.

It all started simple enough. A few years ago, Rubix decided to attend Lightning in a Bottle. He put on a pair of heart-shaped sunglasses and an American flag vest. He called himself Fernando. He stood for love. His message spread until he declared himself Mayor of Lightning in a Bottle.

But a man named T.C. Worthington would not have it. He was a fiddle playing conservative who hated what Lightning in a Bottle had become and wanted to bring back the values of whatever the opposite of love was. This is America, and we have elections. Fernando won in a landslide.

It was like taking Halloween to an extreme end. What started out as fun and play, had turned into a full-fledged tradition within the festival. Fernando's Tent had a stage, dance floor, burlesque show, shops, and casino. Lightning in a Bottle took notice and fully sanctioned their once renegade camps. They now ruled the afterhours scene at the festival.

I gave a deep bow to Fernando and said, "I am so grateful to call you friend." We shared a nod of understanding, and I walked away.

TOKEN AND NICKEL left me, now I was on my own to explore the last of the festival grounds. I climbed down one of the hills trying to find my way to a distant yellow shrine. I slip and fall, ripping my hand open, blood gushing from the wound. Nothing about this place is safe. Fernando's tent would never pass an inspection. There were no safety ropes up and down these cliffs. People spun fire while high on acid. You had to be aware of your surroundings. You had to take responsibility for yourself.

When was the last time I felt unsafe? Everywhere is safe, you never really leave the confines of society. We go through three layers of security to get our passports stamped. Jump on an airplane that has gone through rigorous inspections; never travel anywhere where we are in any real danger. It makes you wonder what the point of it all is.

I remember when I was a kid, staring at power lines, the type that are held up by those old wooden poles. They have ladders built into their sides, being constructed before the invention of modern utility vehicles. built back when electricity still felt a little fantastical.

The poles always had two sets of wires that lead into the ground. I always assumed these wires were collecting electricity from beneath me. The only protection from electrocution were the metal sheaths along their sides, that didn't go so high that I couldn't reach up and touched those wires of death, not that I ever would, I wasn't insane.

As I got older, I learned about grounding, and that you would need to touch both a positive and negative wire in order to be in any real danger. I'll never forget testing this out for the first time, touching one of those wires, wondering if I would be able to feel any of the electricity run through my body.

Now, as an adult, knowing about lawyers and lawsuits, company liability. I intuitively know that there is no danger from these metal cords. I can deduce that they are actually there to give the old poles more stability, and the reason wire was used is purely logistical. They were already laying wire on top of those poles, might as well use the same component to hold them down. No company would ever allow itself the liability of exposed live wires.

I live in a safe world. I don't have to worry about anything. I am sheltered and taken care of, always. Fun...

I was nearing the giant shrine, a yellow beacon reaching for the sky. It must have gone up seventy feet. It was calling the festival goers with its strange sound. It was a living instrument that seemed to sweat music. This bizarre off tone that made you feel uncomfortable for finding it so beautiful. People sat indian style in front of this weird building and worshiped it. Hoping that it might talk back, tell them something of importance.

I walked up to the structure and touched the side, only to realize it was a giant trash heap, made of old cans and splintered wood. Garbage was turned into a church. The recycled shrine. It looked over the ancient lakebed, like a lighthouse over her crashed ships. We were on the edge of one of the cliffs, and in the distance, I saw a city being created.

What was this place? I knew it was a festival. I knew it was about music and art, but this was like nothing I had ever seen before. The world collapsed in on me, and I imagined we were creating some new great colony in a brand new world.

The lights coming from the tents gave a hint at what lie beyond that great dark void that was the dried-out lakebed. The movements of people wearing el wire and LED lights, gave the whole place a feeling of blood running through the veins of a new creature.

I couldn't help but feel unimportant. Small. No matter what I had achieved or done, I was always peering into my friends and heroes world. I looked behind me and saw the giant stages being erected in the distance. Tomorrow there would be thousands of people standing where I was. But right now, I felt very alone.

Chapter Eight:

Don't Hate the Player

I'm sorry, I know this shit costs money, but for all the talk of being anti-consumerism and the evils of capitalism, why the fuck is everything so expensive? It's not just the four-dollar cup of coffee and ten dollar burrito, but also the fifty-dollar footsies and hundred dollar led hoodie.

These people are not anti-capitalism anymore than they are anti-democracy. They just don't know what those words really mean. They are willing to pay 10 dollars for some alternative treatment, because they think the treatment works, and that the pharmaceutical companies are lying to everyone. They hate religion ripping off old people, but have no problem shelling out their hard earned cash to a spiritual adviser who tells them "If you believe hard enough, you will achieve it." These holistic remedies and new age sages make them feel as good as an ice cold Coca-Cola makes me feel on a warm summer night. Both are equally absurd. However, my Coca-Cola only costs fifty cents.

They listen to the foreigner in a white robe who tells them about the laws of attraction, while ignoring the businessman who built his company from hard work and practicality, because, honestly, they could never achieve what the latter did.

THIS IS WHAT the inside of a cat feels like when it purrs. I could feel the musicians walking around us, banging their tambourines, rubbing giant metal kettles and beating drums. The vibrations shook my body as Token grabbed for my hand. Our eyes were covered with a black mask so as to deprive us of our senses, but the overpowering smell of 50 human beings who have not showered or changed in two days made this an impossibility. We were lying inside the music therapy tent. The shamans were releasing our inner energies with the healing power of sound. It was supposed to reinvigorate our spirits, or some kind of shit.

"I want to thank everyone for letting us experience this with you," the leader of the group said. "Feel free to take off your eye masks when you are ready, there is no rush, our next show won't be starting for another ten minutes."

I couldn't help but think the word "show" was a slip up by the shaman. Token pulled my mask off and gave me a giant smile as he continued to talk, "when you turn in your eye masks, please feel free to give us a donation. The suggested amount is twenty dollars. "

Twenty Fucking Dollars!? Token and I looked at each other with the unspoken understanding that neither of us would be paying twenty dollars for this procedure. We threw our eye masks on the ground and snuck out a side entrance, so as not to look at anyone in the eye as we made our getaway. .

"Wasn't that amazing!" Token grabbed my arm like a

girlfriend would, and began pulling me towards one of the larger tents.

"It was an experience," I said while my only thought was, 'Twenty Fucking Dollars!?' I probably shouldn't expand upon this, but I can't help myself. A bunch of natural healers, trying to change the world, create a recrudescence of spirit through the power of sound therapy, was charging us twenty dollars? There were probably fifty people in the tent during the five-minute show. A thousand dollars for five minutes, makes for $12,000 dollars an hour of the expected donation. Don't get me wrong, almost no one paid this donation, but just the nerve of it. It went against everything I had known about what these festivals stood for, it was so transparent, so against everything that was preached, yet I seemed to be the only one pissed off about it.

We stood outside a giant shoeless tent where people practiced yoga. Token contemplated joining them, but decided she would rather dance. I still couldn't get over the twenty fucking dollars. The Do-Lab charges 260 bucks for tickets to this event. The headliner was Moby, and I am sure he got paid well, but very few people came to LiB because of a big musical act, they came here because it was LiB. The Mayor of Lightning in a Bottle was not being paid, his opponent in the election was not getting paid. The people who made that amazing sound yurt were unpaid. Everything that I had seen, that I had loved, was put on by the actual campers, yet it was the Do Lab making all the money.

I'm probably the most capitalistic person walking

these grounds, I love that people can make money off of such a spectacle, so why was I the only one whose stomach was completely turned off by such apparent greed?

I went off on my own. I stood by a large wooden temple, a man in a white robe was speaking to the audience about "living in the Now." A woman asked the preacher a question about animals, it was a loaded questions, "How can we the human beings of the planet earth learn to respect animals?"

He gives a strange answer that the audience eats up, he tells us that animals are actually smarter than we are. That a dog never thinks of anything more than being a dog. The lady then asks her real question.

"How can we get human beings of this planet earth to respect animals enough so that they don't kill and eat them."

He answers again, "It is not your place to teach Human's of the Planet Earth how to act, you must change yourself and in doing so, hopefully they will change themselves and learn to respect living things as you do."

I fucking agreed with every single syllable of his answer, yet I hated him, hated her, hated this tent, hated this fucking festival.

I walked past a series of garbage cans, a "No Trace" sign hung above them. Looking at it made me cynical. Seeing the cars drive through the campsite, people stomping through the desert, having no clue what no trace meant. Just words on a sign, no true ethos attached, no understanding of what it really meant to be no trace.

Why would people spend so much money to be here? The average camper must have spent five hundred dollars on gear and gas and tickets. That's a lot of money, even for someone with a good job. What was I not getting?

ALL ELECTRONIC DANCE music sounds exactly the same, but people have a strong allegiance to their favorite genres and DJ's. Nickel and Token spent most of their time at The Woogie, a stage that was always the stage that was furthest away from where I was. I had to find them and talk to them.

The Woogie DJ sat in a round pod that was placed within the branches of a massive tree as he played deep house. I don't know the difference between deep house and house, or even the difference between house and anything else. But it seemed to consist of elongated bass percussions that overlapped one another. Not that I know what the fuck I am talking about.

As I search around the stage for my two friends, a random guy goes crazy, he pulls out a knife and tries to slash people. The veil is lifted, and the reality of human nature is on display. Everyone backs away. Some run. Some cry. Some scream.

Police come from nowhere. They jump on the man and quickly subdue him. An ambulance and cruisers come to their aid within minutes, checking on the festival goers, and offering any assistance they may need. Then they are gone, and everything is back to normal.

I hear no talk of the bravery of the law enforcement, I only hear about a bad energy in the air that must have caused a man to go crazy. Someone must have manifested this anger with his bad attitude. And I think fuck, maybe it was all my fault.

I spot Nickel and Token dancing alone. Everyone dances alone here. I stand next to my two friends and try to fit in. They both give me a smile. "Will you guys take care of me tonight?" I say as I try to determine why anyone enjoys dancing.

"Us? You trust us to take care of you?" Nickel says without looking at me.

"This is a bad idea, I know." I say.

"What's going on?" Token says. She wasn't looking at me either.

"I think I am gonna roll for the first time tonight."

"We're both on Acid right now, but we should be coming down by then," says Nickel.

"I'll wear the white suit."

Token asks a stranger to take our picture, we smile and pose. We act silly and make it look like this is the greatest party since V-E Day. After receiving the camera back, we choose the best take, apply filters to completely erase whatever was left of its reality, place a caption on it about how much fun we are having, then share this picture on the Internet with all of our friends, so that they can be envious of our amazing time - here in this smelly, hot, dust filled dance floor, playing bad electronic dance music.

Girls wear makeup to enhance their true selves, giving us an ideal that we can never live up to. Now we put makeup on our experiences. Our travel magazines have become better than the real place. I looked over to Token, there was a tear in her eye. "You okay?"

"Yea sorry, I was just thinking about my brother."

"You guys close?"

"Yea we were, he committed suicide last year."

Chapter Nine:

Releasing the White Suit

I don't know who lives in the enchanted forest or what lies beyond. It must be a special place. Little ferries hover above the trees. They stay still and silent. Their only purpose is to guide our way as we venture through, illuminating the sacred place as we talk and hug. The ferries are so kind and giving, asking for nothing in return, their joy comes from knowing that we can see, that we can better experience the place because of them.

I do not know what is beyond the forest, I can see lights peering between the branches and leaves. A slight roar of music flowing like an unseen wind. The lights move, they are colorful, so colorful I imagine I can taste them, like a ripe piece of fruit. They are red and green and purple, but these names do them no justice. They cover multiple senses and make you thirst for others.

I understand the forest now, I never did before. I had been wrong, so wrong. It wasn't about anything that I had imagined. This festival was not what I thought. I was wrong. It was just about play. That is all. Is there anything more natural to humans than play?

R*emember when you were a kid, every new Street was like a whole new world. It's kinda like that.*

-some sort of poem I wrote while staring at Christmas lights hanging above a picnic table.

"PEOPLE DON'T DRESS for the occasion anymore." I pulled off my white hat and gave a slight bow to a cute passerby. In a land full of ferries, and furries, steampunk and LED, I stand out above all. I am wearing The White Suit.

"May I take your picture!" the passerby asked.

"Of course," I said.

We pose as her boyfriend snaps the camera. It wasn't the first time someone had asked for a photo of the White Suit, and it would not be the last. As I walked from stage to stage, people bowed and waved to me.

"May I call you The White Suit?" A girl wearing a panda onesie asked me.

"I like that, reminds me of an Anime character," I said.

"You are awesome, you are an Anime character!" she then kissed me on the cheek and skipped away.

I was walking underneath the string of lanterns when a friend of Token's yelled out to me.

"The White Suit!!!" He said, "Are you rolling balls yet!?"

"No, I was hoping for Token and Nickel to be with me, they are asleep. they were tripping all day, then smoked a bowl and passed out." I said.

"Just go for it, something happens, you come back here, we will take care of you." I looked him over, he had blue hair, no shirt, and a banjo around his neck, I'm pretty sure he was also on acid.

"Should I be worried?" I said.

"You are going to love it."

It's amazing how excited people get for you to do drugs for the first time. I imagine it's like watching an old favorite movie with a friend who has never seen it. You get to re-experience it through their eyes.

I stared at Token's friend. I don't know why I put my trust into this topless blue haired man who played the banjo, but if I couldn't trust him about drugs, then who could I?

"Fuck it."

I walked over to the nearest porta potty and entered. I put on my headlamp and shined it onto a small Ziploc bag that contained my stash. I looked around this commode, wondering how people at the fests functioned without headlamps.

I pulled out a purple pill that had a thumbs up symbol stamped against its side. I looked at that pill, it looked like a piece of candy. Pills seemed dangerous to me, years of learned behavior from taking medicine from the doctor I guess. I felt like this little pill could kill me. I remember talking to one of my tech friends, he believed the reason tech people weren't afraid of pills was because their parents had been giving them Adderall since they were nine years old, thinking their ADD and borderline Asperger's was something to be fixed.

I put the little colorful orb into my mouth, took a swig of water, and swallowed. It was done. I had just crossed the Rubicon, and it didn't even feel like a big deal.

PEOPLE FUCKING ENJOY this feeling? It's all I could think. I was dizzy, I had anxiety, my body temperature was changing, and I had already drank about a liter of water since I dropped the pill. I had to fight every urge within me not to just go lay under a tree and fall asleep. Why would anyone want to have this feeling? Why the fuck was this the most popular drug in the dance scene!? Was I really that different from everyone? This is what rolling felt like?

I was at the main stage watching Moby perform. I expected him to play his own music, but he was doing a normal DJ set. He looked like he was having fun as he conducted the audience through the rhythm being programmed on his controller. I looked around, wondering if everyone was feeling the way I was. It was like asking for a piece of candy, only to stick a sour ball into your mouth.

I was out of water, and I could barely fill my camelbak. Everything was just harder. I had to keep moving. I saw the recycled can shrine in the distance, and figured that was as good a place as any. If I stopped moving, I'd die.

I watched as the Transformations, high on acid, tried to find meaning where there was none. Chanting to this holy shrine, hoping it would talk back. Maybe it did. I must have known 20 people at this festival, yet Token and Nickel were the only ones I ever saw. Where was everyone? I needed a fucking friend! I needed to tell someone I wasn't doing good, I needed someone to hold my hand. I was so lonely, here among all these people, so lonely! I needed to be touched and hugged... FUCK!

I began to walk back to the main stage when my feet started lifting from the ground, I started to fly, just a little bit, you know, like the astronauts on the moon, every step is twice as high as it should be. I could feel the wind against my ankles, pushing me side to side as I bounced, like a sail on a boat.

I knew drugs were about escape. I knew ecstasy was about getting away from it all, but who the hell wanted to get away from it all like this? Influenza helps you escape life too. It overpowers all of your problems, but the new problem was even worse. Were people really this fucked up? Had humanity fallen so far that it would rather embrace this sickness than live in the real world?

By the time I made it back to the main stage, I could no longer control my feet, they were now bouncing with the music. I must have been jumping 10 feet into the air with every new electronic sound. I started flapping my hands, thinking I might be able to hover above the audience, but it did not work. I wanted to dance. I wanted to dance alone. I wanted to embrace this suck that was being all alone among thousands of people rolling on this horrible drug for no reason that I could understand.

I walked into the middle of the audience, moving

with the music, my legs were getting lighter and lighter. I felt myself losing control. I hate that feeling, I hate the feeling that I can not coordinate my thoughts, speech and movement. It was an utterly awful feeling. I couldn't wait for this high to go away, I couldn't wait to be myself again.

I watched the stage and effects. It was an amazing stage, LED screens shown brightly behind the DJ booth, silhouetting him. Then the LED lights started to move, they were moving back and forth, They were changing their depth. I had no clue lighting effects could even do this. I had never seen such an elaborate stage. The lights became brighter, the colors became thicker. They were the most beautiful lights I had ever seen. I fucking wish I hadn't taken this stupid drug so I could experience them in a lucid state. How the hell did they make the lights so beautiful?

Then, what? The stage started changing shape, but it was so organic. The screens started moving backward and forward, but almost at the same time. It was like watching a 2-d movie then putting on 3-d glasses. But I was already in 3-d, how the hell were they doing this? I half wanted to send the production crew an email that instant to congratulate them on breaking all the laws of optics in their stage design.

I turned to my left, the Woogie stage was about half a mile away, I wanted to see the lights pushing through that giant tree… But I stopped as my eyes gazed upon the Shrine that was at least a football field's distance from where Moby was playing. It had moved, it was closer, a lot closer, it was bigger too. Except it wasn't. It was the same distance, just bigger and brighter, and closer, but not.

Wait, it wanted to see me. I don't know how a building can want to see someone, but it wanted to see me. It hadn't changed distance, it had changed the amount of presence it had in this universe. It was getting bigger just for me, just to tell me something.

As I walked towards it, it stopped calling, it was guiding me, not calling me, it wanted me to get away from the main stage, it wanted me to come towards it so I could have a new vantage point on the ravine below. Up and down those pathways that linked the two districts were people walking to the different parts of the festival. But they were not people, they were fellow players. Most of them were in well-seasoned groups, but not me, I was all alone. I knew this mission. I had played it before on my old Sega Genesis. I had to put together a team. I needed a well-seasoned group so that we might explore some cave just outside of town. It was a dangerous cave, but if we were sure of heart, and had faith, we might be able to fight to the end, where a wizard lived. He would give us a great prize.

I stepped forward, as I got closer to the edge, I realized the other teams were not all human. They took on human shapes, but like, elves or gnomes or hobbits, they were different variations of our species. They wore magical gear that lit up with their powers. Some of this gear increased wisdom, other gear allowed them to fight better. For some reason, I thought of my friend Wolfgang. I knew he was here. I imagined he had a hat they gave him charm and boots that increased his charisma.

I walked down that gorge, past a small renegade camp, and made my way up to the Woogie stage. I did not make much eye contact, I didn't know if we were all in this together, or if the other teams were my enemies. However, I was smart enough to understand that I was a lowly level one, and anyone here could take me out with a single swipe of his sword, or some sort of flame ball wizard spell.

It was hard to determine what was far and what was near, I intellectually knew the stage was close, but it looked miles away. Before I could think on this, I had realized it was now right in front of me.

I decided to explore the city that surrounded the stage, I walked into an art installation and was handed a pair of 3-d goggles, no 4-d, I was already in 3-d, no 5-d, that's right, I had already crossed into the 4.

The installation was amazing, the paintings reached out at me from the walls. The ground moved like waves. And in that moment, I understood. All of this was built for me, not me, but people like me, people rolling on molly, experiencing acid, dancing on G. It was all about increasing the fun. It was fun. An entire industry, worth billions of dollars, was built around these substances. All to enhance each person's high. I guess it was no different than a pub. Except that this blew the shit out of watching a football game while drinking a fancy craft beer.

My mind remained lucid. I could still think, I could still

feel, I was still exactly the person I always was, just the best version of that person.

The fake trees surrounding the Woogie stage were lit up in brilliant neon colors, they were so vivid, I tried to figure out how much of the light was coming from the actual LED's and how much was my imagination being altered by the drug. It was like the taste of a sweet juice after a long hike, your mouth is so dry that the flavors seem to penetrate each and every pour inside of it, replacing that salty dryness with delicious goodness. The lights were like that, but for my eyes.

The trunks of the trees looked like they were reaching for the stars, jutting up thousands of feet, or maybe ten, I didn't trust my senses anymore. They created a canopy high above the dance floor, and I wondered what it would feel like to climb to the top, to look down upon all these fellow players. Was I the hero of this game? I think I may have been. Whatever the case, I had lost track of my mission. I was still trying to figure out what I was doing here, at this festival, at this, Lightning in a Bottle. I walked to the stage, then back to the dance floor. I walked from tree to tree. I explored the new senses. I had fun figuring out what was real and what was not. I guess it was all real though. I shouldn't lessen my feelings by saying they are fake.

I remember when I was a kid, my grandparents lived out on the Chesapeake Bay. They had an orchard in their front yard, an old shed and an old fishing boat in their backyard. Inside the house were a series of little storage rooms, they had a couple attics, you had to walk through one of these attics to get to my grandfather's office, my grandfather was so old that he never climbed up to this room anymore, it was this ancient office that time had forgotten, I walked inside and felt like an explorer opening up a mummy's tomb for the first time. His desk still had paper and pens on it, there were old books next to it. I traced my finger through the dust that lined the wooden desk and made a picture, instantly feeling bad about disrupting this peaceful place.

I wonder how big these rooms would be if I went back today, I wonder how big the yard would be. I wonder if I would be amazed at all by that old house, if I would explore it, try to figure out my place there. We live in this giant fucking amazing planet, surrounded by giant fucking amazing things, and we just go about our day, never realizing that we live in the most amazing time in the history of forever.

I was a kid. I was playing. I was exploring this house, this neighborhood for the first time. I had been so wrong, I had been so wrong about everything. This drug was not about escaping, it was about living, it was about reminding you what it was like to be a kid again, what it was like to play. Life is so good and so few of us seem to realize it. I wished the world could feel what I felt.

It didn't last long, the main effects wore off in about an hour. I still felt good, content, and happy, but I was now myself again. I was now alone in this giant festival. I walked across another ravine. I now had my bearings and could see Fernando's tent in the distance. That red tent of love.

It's a strange thing to be content with the friends you have and yet still seek out new ones. The problem with old friends is that they are old, they are set in their ways. If you decide to take on a new calling, a new life, you will have to sacrifice many of your relationships. As I walked into Fernando's tent I saw faces I barely knew, people I had bumped into one or two times. These were not good friends, but if I were to keep exploring the festivals, I had to get to know them, I had to find camaraderie somewhere within this tent. I was satisfied with my friends. I had the greatest friends in the world, yet here I was, in a place that none of my good friends would ever venture, or even understand.

And then I was greeted. "Welcome to Fernando's Tent of Love," she said. It was Elache. My heart had a special place in it for Elache. She didn't recognize me at first. I pulled off the hat and bowed.

"You seem to always be there when I need you." I said.

"Yea, okay... Oh hi?" She replied, she was acting weird, probably tripping, "I'm really glad you are here." She said it in a stern and frank way. But I could tell by her body language she meant it. She was just fighting something off. She gave me the most she had at that one moment. Aren't we all trying our best?

She was my mission. She was the princess I needed

to find. I remembered, she gave me this mission a long time ago, I just hadn't realized it was a mission until right now. I smiled, and then walked inside of her castle.

The place was bustling with energy. It felt like an illegal casino operating within the confines of post World War II Berlin. Fernando was on stage, making his plea for votes, while a DJ played deep house behind him.

I saw Wolfgang in the corner. I had only known Wolfgang for a few months, but I very quickly learned to respect his style. He was a good man who had the ability to connect different types of people from different areas of expertise and help them combine their knowledge into something new.

I looked to a large cage in the middle of the room and saw Avalon, who was Wolfgang's girlfriend. She was hooping to the music, I hadn't realized that she was a hooper. I didn't know her well, but she had a scientific mind and I always enjoyed talking to her. I once heard her give a speech on the benefits of Psychedelic drugs, and for the first time could understand where she was coming from. I wanted to grab her, hug her, and explain that I finally understood. But ours was a young friendship and I hadn't determined our boundaries yet. This entire festival would now be different, this entire experience started now. I was no longer alone.

"HOW HAS YOUR festival experience been?" I was grasping for his name, he was one of those people you saw everywhere but didn't know anything about.

"It's been really good," I answered, "yours?"

"That's so great to hear," He was wearing that smile people in cults always have. "My festival has been good, it has been good." He nodded his head as he spoke. He creeped me out.

I had moved from Fernando's Tent of Love to Worthington's old timey town. It was nothing personal, Fernando had my vote, but the band performing here were close friends with the crew I had just seen. Everyone was now showing up. As I looked at this group, I could not imagine these people anywhere but in the festival world, well and Venice beach. I tried to picture them hanging out with my suburban friends at a local sports bar, rooting for their college in a football game, but my imagination was not strong enough.

Then I noticed the guy with the creepy smile, was still staring at me, waiting for some sort of reply. He finally gave up, hugged me and said, "It's so great to see you here."

I DON'T KNOW how old I was, and I don't remember the year. It could have been 1982, or it could have been 1986; time is like that when you are young. But at some point during the decade of the 80's, I heard the sound of a synthesizer for the first time. It was magical, not magical as an adjective, it was literally magic. This was a new sound, if someone went back in time with a synthesizer, they would have been burned at the stake. A new instrument was created. Basically, anyone who played a synthesizer during my childhood was the koolest. And right in front of me, this feeling of awesome was back.

I expected The Tale of the Sprinting Fox to play EDM music or a normal DJ set. I could not have been more wrong. They were the reincarnation of my favorite bands from the 80's. They were not a tribute band, they were not making fun of the music from that era; they were that era. They had mastered the sounds of the decade, and I was in love after a few short seconds.

I had briefly met the lead singer once before. I had my normal social anxiety and remember having an awkward exchange with him. I saw that he was playing at this festival, and I made a mission of myself to go.

It was the type of music you could sing along with after hearing the first verse. We jumped, and sang, and danced to the beats of 80's synth. It was an amazing time. The best night I had yet to experience in the festival world.

The two musicians stayed in character, looking straightforward, being stoic as they played. But at one point, I saw a smile creep across the lead singer's face. How could you not smile at the sight of all your friends? He yelled for everyone to come on stage, so we danced and sang to the last song.

It was one of those nights where you find yourself out with the popular kids. Somehow you get accepted into their group, you go to a party with them then end up at someone's house for the night. You imagine waking up on Monday and having a whole new life, with a whole new group of friends. From here on out, everything would be different.

The set finally ended. I bowed to the singers and looked to see where everyone was headed. But they were gone. Just like that. They didn't even leave together, they all went their separate ways.

I saw two familiar faces. It was Dostoevski, and Nabes. I did not know them well, but I had met them once before. They were the only hope I had for the rest of the night. "You guys headed anywhere?" I asked.

Dos looked at me, confused, and then answered, "eventually," he then gave me an uncomfortable laugh. Nabes forced a smile while she grabbed for Dos's hand and pulled him away. I was reminded how special nights with special people can quickly evaporate into the reality. I was not part of this group.

Holding my pride in, I smiled and began to walk away. Feeling that feeling I had felt too often at these festivals. Trying to figure out this world and never seeming able to crack it. I sat down underneath a tree. I looked at my White Suit, the best-dressed person at all of Lightning in a Bottle. How could I feel so out of place at this place that was made for people who were out of place? Even here. If festival life had done anything for me, it had caused me to be brutally honest with myself. I constantly found myself in cultures where I didn't belong. When I was a kid, I tried to be an athlete and was always a failure. Year after year, I would play football, run track, and year after year, I was always the worst player on the team. Why did I keep pushing it, why could I not face the realities of the things I was not made for?

I was good at a lot of things. I had a knack for math, an understanding of music. But I never chose the life of my natural abilities. I always fought against them. I never much liked the people who were good at the things I was good at. Maybe that's a lie, I just found their lives to be so boring, and no one could ever say my life was boring.

How could I have friends, how could I make a life like this work for me? I could never be satisfied. Never, no matter what, I would never be satisfied. The loneliness overtook me. I did everything I could to keep from crying. What the fuck was I doing with my life? And why the fuck did anyone come to a place like Lightning in a Bottle?

The sun began to rise and I walked back to my tent, might as well sleep, I didn't want to, but there were no answers to be found here. As I neared our camping area, I saw that small little girl bouncing towards me. Nickel had a smile on her face as she waved in my direction. It was now 7AM; she had been asleep for a good ten hours.

"Sorry!" She said to me while she laughed.

"I tried to wake you guys, you were out cold."

"I'm gonna go find Distrikt!"

"They're in a Ravine near the main stage."

"How was it?" She asked.

"I'll tell you later" I said, "I guess we'll probably be hanging out a lot now."

She smiled and cocked her head. "See you in a few hours." I turned and watched her walk away. She was the closest thing I had to a friend in this entire strange world.

Chapter Ten:

In the End, We're All Going the Way of Universal Entropy

"Be careful! There's a dinosaur running about!" It was six in the morning and a girl was running towards me as she tried not to spill her beer.

I looked behind me, seeing a man wearing nothing but tighty-whities and an American flag, slowly stalking me, like a tiger would his prey. I caught his eyes, and he went into a full sprint, tackling me into the ground. I was unprepared, I was expecting a hug, but soon I found my head being bashed into the hard dirt. He stood up over my body, let out a scream and ran off to his next victim.

A random passerby began to give me a slow clap, "You are fucking awesome." It felt good to be called awesome, it always does.

The girl who warned me, grabbed my hand and pulled me up. "I'm so sorry, I gave him a shit ton of acid and accidentally projected the spirit of a velociraptor onto him."

I WAS PACKING up our camp while Token and Nickel finished off the rest of their drugs. There is nothing worse than having to tear down your gear after a weekend of partying, and I thought they would appreciate my little gift to them.

These festivals are about moments. Small little

experiences that you would never have in the outside world. Like a childhood day, once the sun goes down, everything is reset. A new day is a new year. Constant death, constant rebirth. You can live a hundred lives in a single week.

I heard music in the distance, only to be greeted by giant metal cords reaching up to the main stage. They must have been a hundred feet long. A musician standing at their base, caressing them, like you would a naked body. Electricity snaps off the lines, complimenting the sunset that we were now worshiping. It was a giant electronic violin. It made a surreal sound that played in unison with the angelic voice of a woman who sang to that giant ball of flame millions of miles away. It was one of the most beautiful things I had ever seen in my life.

"I'm not doing any drugs this year, I decided to live with my emotions." I was sitting in Fernando's tent as Wolfgang interviewed different artists from LiB. People praised the girl for staying sober, talking about what guts it took to live in the festival world in your normal state of mind. Experiencing life for what it actually was. She looked sad and defeated. I wanted to hug her.

I met a girl, it was an instant connection. She held my hand and walked with me. We talked all night as I thought this may be something that would last. A few hours later, she left, without a word. I have no clue who she was.

It was the last night of the festival. I was completely sober. I decided to greet anyone who entered Fernando's tent with overwhelming positivity.

"Welcome to Fernando's, thank you for making this place so special!" I said.

"Excuse me, you have just made the room more beautiful, thank you so much for joining us at Fernando's." I said.

"You, yes you, you are fucking awesome, thank you for being awesome." I said.

"We are honored to have someone like you enter our party! I am so grateful for who you are!" I said. I would never forget the feeling of seeing the joy on the people's faces as I spoke.

I thought I would spend the night alone, I could not find anyone. The King of Israel spotted me. He introduced me to all his friends. We wandered around until the sun rose. A random encounter with the King made for a great night.

I found myself in the sound yurt. The artist who made it remembered me. We talked and laughed. We created music with each other. I thought that everyone should make music together.

I headed to my tent for the night, but Nickel had just

woken up. She grabbed me and forced her musical tastes on my tired body. Going from stage to stage until she found something that she just "felt." It was torture and joy at the same time.

These were all just moments, no roots, nothing came from them. No seed was planted. No bodies were buried. You have to be almost emotionless, and just experience it all for what it is. The fun will go away, the love with go away, but so will the hurt and pain. Except for the sound yurt girl, we became very close friends.

Chapter Eleven:

The Loss of a Friend

We had our first real meal in four days at one of those side of the road diners that don't exist in the big city. Our bodies redistributed its energy towards our stomachs so that we could digest the giant calorie laden pile of slop. Our internal engines went into overdrive, as our core functions shut down, we could barely keep our heads up as we drove across the old highway towards Interstate 5.

"James Dean Highway?" Token read the sign on the side of the road.

I recognized this place. We were crossing the intersection where James Dean had died. We were not driving on the actual road, after the accident they made a new road, a safer road. I looked to my left and saw what remained of the original. The bits of tar were still there, grass growing through them.

An American Icon died here, he was 24 years old. Twenty fucking four. He accomplished more in his 24 years than I will in my life. And he was dead. I wondered when he would die for the second time, the time that the last living human being who remembered his name passed away.

We made it back to Los Angeles, and dropped Token off. Nickel and I were now alone together. My original festival buddy, She was quiet. I was exhausted, and then she spoke.

"Do these festivals ever change you?" She asked.

Nickel had never spoken to me like this, our relationship was as skin deep as skin deep could possibly get. "I don't know, I'm not sure." I answered.

"You know how I always wander, always meet new people, just do my own thing," It was true, as soon as she found herself getting close to anyone, she always pulled away, she always found someone new, "I'm not normally like that."

"What do you mean?" I asked.

"When I go to a concert, really when I do anything, I always stick with my close friends, I have never been alone before. I just felt like changing."

"I didn't know that," I knew that she had been in an 8 year relationship, they had recently broken up. You never know what is going to happen when life doesn't turn out the way you thought it would. Seems like everyone was going to the festivals for a similar reason. We were all trying to find truth, maybe that's why I kept going as well, maybe I was no different from anyone else. "I don't know, I just want to change myself," she said as I pulled up to her house. Then she told me one last thing, "thank you for everything."

It is one of the great joys and tragedies of life, that you never know who will be there tomorrow. Nickel grabbed her gear and left the car. She gave me a half hug, she was still that type. She was a good friend, like a little sister to me. I watched out for her, wished her the best. She went off to travel the world, find herself.

I never saw her again.

Part III

The Fraud Economy

"For the next five days I am asking that you trust our process, up until this point, you have been trusting *your* process. How has that worked out? For five days, trust us, you have nothing to lose. If it fails, you have only lost five days of your life. But you will not fail, this process works. I am proof of that. The person who referred you here is proof of that. The process works."

I couldn't help but think, I knew this process, I had read about it many times, from books on building cults, to those on creating a winning political campaign. It always came down to the same philosophy; create sheep by making them think they are wolves.

Chapter Twelve:

I Wish Everyone Was Open Minded Like Me

The VP invited me to dinner to announce her engagement. She had only known the man for a few months, but I strongly approved. He was against her type in all ways, exactly the type she needed.

I once thought this girl would become my best friend. We had similar tastes and styles and liked to do similar things. We had spent many a night together, talking until the sun came up. It was one of those relationships that made you feel like you were back in high school. Back when the world was yours for the taking.

The night would end with her storming out of the restaurant while yelling at me and making a scene so large, that the other guests would laugh as the door slammed behind her.

The waitress gave me a reassuring smile, and all I could think, was this entire adventure had started because of her.

Four months earlier...

Memories are weird; they come and go; they feel more like parts, or chapters. Time is irrelevant and one thing doesn't always lead to another. Sometimes you connect the dots later on, going forward and backward. I guess what I am trying to say, this may not be the way it happened, but it is the way I remember.

I was in an ugly room with one hundred and fifty other students. I guess we were students. They would probably call us candidates or future leaders. On stage was our trainer.

"I am going to tell you how to achieve your dream," he said, "I'm not saying you will actually succeed in achieving your desires. I am just offering to send you on the path that will make anything you want possible. Following that path, is up to you." This was why we were here, we wanted the answers to life, we wanted to accomplish things. We were capable of more than we had become.

Three months before that...

I sat at the 4100 milking a beer. Looking out the windows made me feel like I was somewhere in the mountains above Nepal. It's funny how the brain can do that, you enter a new room and you are in a whole new world. We were on the side of a cliff in Silver Lake. I had entered off of Sunset Boulevard, but all the windows looked over the cliff. The city no longer existed.

I looked down at my phone and read the text again. "I need to talk to you." The VP wanted something. I could tell by the choice of her words.

"I NEED to talk to you." The VP never needed

anything, she had too much pride for that word. She might use it to manipulate someone. "I need you to do this for me" but this was her wanting something. Here, ME was the most important word, not NEED. She was desperate. She gave me all her power. She admitted to needing something, really, truly, needing something. Maybe it was manipulation. She could play me like a fiddle. She knew I would help her, but she was also afraid. I was the only person she had.

I replied back that I would call her, but she insisted we meet. She chose the 4100. She knew this was my favorite bar. She knew I came here when I moved to Silver Lake, I came here when I broke up with my ex, I came here when my sister moved away. She knew what this place meant to me.

I watched her as she pushed through the curtain that acted as the door to the bar, rubbing her hand against the colored drapes that lined the walls. "Heyyyyyyy!!!" She said with that giant warm smile of hers. She was looking extra hot tonight, her breasts seemed larger than normal, maybe she was wearing a push-up bra, or maybe she finally had the surgery. "Two of whatever he is having, and two shots of whiskey," she yelled over to the bartender who was mid pour for another guest. "Down your beer, let's do a shot," she told me.

Like I said, she could play me like a fiddle.

"SOOO I'M MOVING out of Al's place." She had been dating Al for about a year, he was rich, and the VP liked rich guys. I don't say this as a criticism; it was actually a strength of hers. She liked money, and rich guys liked trophy wives. It was a better arrangement than most couples had.

"I'm sorry," I replied, "I was hoping it would work out." This was true, though I never thought it would. Al was the type of rich guy who owned a Rolex watch and Maserati. You know, because that is what rich people do. I'm sure he had a Ducati collecting dust in his garage as well. He didn't look for that classic car he had wanted since childhood. He owned well-made, beautiful things, because they were well made and beautiful. As soon as he realized the VP was a trophy wife, he would try to change her, but the VP wasn't the type you could change. Maybe that's why we remained such good friends. I accepted her. She accepted me.

"Here's the thing," she said. "I'm subletting my place, and you know I'm still broke because of everything last year. The movie, and I'm still paying off the surgery."

The VP was a cancer survivor, I felt like an asshole for forgetting. It was probably the most defining thing that had ever happened to her, and I hadn't even thought about it. It's so easy to forget that we are all fighting a hard battle. Her bills were enormous. It was almost enough to make a socialist out of me.

"You know when I came over the other night, it was the happiest I had been in a long time. I miss my old friend. I need someone like you in my life. I know this is big, so I'm just gonna say it. Can I stay with you for awhile?"

What was I going to say, no? She was like a sister to me, and honestly, I missed my old friend too.

Chapter Thirteen:

Regression to the Mean

The VP was the lowest I had ever seen her. I began to worry about her sanity. She was at the age where every breakup meant you would forever be alone. This was her life, and then she would die. She was getting dangerously close to believing in reality, and I knew that would kill her. She found a group.

I had recently taken up cooking. I have this habit of taking on new hobbies every six months. I don't plan on it, it just happens. I was steaming chicken, experimenting with how it would tenderize the meat. I was home alone; I was always alone now. The VP never got home before 2AM. The house seemed strangely empty without her there.

I could hear the front door rattle. The VP peaked her head around the corner a few seconds later. "May I?" She asked as she looked at the chicken.

"Here you go," I said as I handed her a piece.

She bit down into the meat, smiled, a genuine smile, "what the fuck! That is delicious," she said.

"It's steamed," I remarked, "crazy right?"

"That sounds disgusting."

"I know right?"

"Hey," she stared directly into my eyes, The VP never backed down, and I knew she was about to ask for something "so I know you have probably been wondering where I have been going all night." I hadn't been. She had joined a "Large Group Awareness Training Seminar Group," or LGAT as they were formally called. She had told me about a group like this years ago, it only made sense she would join them now.

"So I joined this group called Romney," she explained.

"Oh?" I said.

"They have really helped me a lot. I know you are not into all that New-Age stuff. But it's not New Age. It's about transforming the way you think. It's really scientific, you'd probably like it."

"Thanks, I'm not interested," I said.

"Here's the thing, it's a bit pricey, and there are multiple tiers," I couldn't stand when people asked me for money, my body tensed up as the question came. "I know this is a really big favor, but I want to hold a fundraiser for my class to help people out, and I was wondering if I could throw it at your house?" I breathed a sigh of relief, maybe these classes had changed her.

The VP knew how to throw a party better than anyone I had ever met. I was honored that she would use my house. "It's yours, just let me know when," I said.

"Thank you so much," she said, "I just want to say, you've always been there for me. I think of all the people in my life, and you are always there, as the others go."

"Of course," I gave her a kiss on the cheek, "let me make you dinner." I said.

THE PSYCHOLOGICAL TERM is, "Regression to the Mean." We all have our average attitude towards life. Some people are more happy, some more sad. But no matter what happens, you will return to your baseline. Whether coming down from the high of winning the lottery, or coming up from the low of losing a loved one. You will always regress to your mean.

Humans look for a reason, and people and organizations know this. You join a self-help group at a low, and you will rise up to your average. You will then give credit to the group for getting you there, never realizing you would have gotten there on your own. A billion-dollar industry, built on a psychological effect.

"I KEEP THINKING, there are three things everyone should do with each other," I said as I took a sip from a bad IPA.

"What are they?" Lego asked, a smile on his face. I had only known him a couple of days, but I loved this man. The VP had met him a few weeks earlier at Romney, and it was instant love. I hoped she didn't blow it, I had never seen anyone treat her the way Lego did.

"One is spinning." I said.

"Spinning?" He looked The VP in the eyes and squeezed her tightly, "why spinning?"

"Give me your hand," I said as I spun him around. "Dance, should always precede friendship."

"Okay, and two?" He asked.

"Two is making music together, either tapping on the table, singing, making sounds, whatever. Creating something together bonds people in ways words cannot. This was part of human culture for one-hundred-thousand years, we must not lose this."

"What about three?"

"Three is eye contact," I was a bit tipsy, but the type of tipsy that makes you sharper and more energetic, "Look at your partner in the eye, ask them a question, let them answer in full, then tell them exactly what you heard. Nothing is more powerful than listening, nothing is more powerful than being listened to."

"I'd like to do three with you," Lego said.

"No," I replied, "I might fall in love with you."

"See, wouldn't he love Romney?" The VP smiled at me then turned to Lego.

"You would," Lego told me.

The party was a hit, my house had never looked better. I was a few beers in and sick of talking to people, so I walked up to my balcony and sat alone, soon to be joined by another of the Romney zombies. He sat next to me, then offered me a joint.

"I'm good," I said. I looked down on to the party. People were glancing up to me, like you would when a friend was sitting next to a girl he wanted to ask out. I felt like this was all some sort of planned intervention.

"You know, I used to be a fuckup, I was a pothead,"

the man now sitting next to me said while he smoked his joint, "this group changed my life." Sometimes people's self worth comes from converting others, I wish I knew the reason why. "I was at a low, and after I took the basic course, everything started to change," I almost interrupted him to explain the psychological phenomenon behind what he was experiencing, but even I know it's a dick move to tell someone the science behind their faith. "They teach you how to think different, be a leader, achieve your dream," he said.

"That's great to hear," I said.

His confidence was raised by my feigned interest; a slight smile crossed his face. "My family used to have money, then we got involved in this pyramid scheme. You probably heard about it on the news. I lost everything. But now, I am practicing what this group taught me, not only in the basic class and in advanced, but now I am in the leadership program. My life is back on track. I'm no longer smoking pot every day and soon I will be rich again. Romney taught me how to do that."

"I'm really happy for you," I said, wondered how much money he was now spending in this new pyramid scheme.

"Sign this card, I'll take it in tomorrow." He pulled the card out of his pocket with such ease that I imagined he had placed it perfectly in-between the slots of his wallet right before he sat with me. It was the type of move a Carney would make on his unsuspecting mark.

I took the card out of his hand, immediately knowing this was a mistake. It had some questions on it, and a pledge to join the group. "No, I won't sign anything," I said.

He was taken aback, "Why not?"

"I don't need a reason not to sign something." I said.

He paused for a second to gather his thoughts, "that attitude is what's holding you back in life."

So now he was just an asshole. This was a classic tactic used by used car salesmen and bad real estate agents around the globe. ABC and HPS. Always Be Closing. High-Pressure Sales tactics. These are very effective forms of selling that tap into the deep human insecurity that makes losing hurt, more than winning is fun. In short, being wrong about something sucks. It works like this:

"Sign the dotted line and all your dreams will come true." The salesman says.

"How will my dreams come true?" You say.

"I can't tell you that, unless you sign the dotted line."

"I don't think I am comfortable with this."

"You don't want your dreams to come true?"

"No I do, but that's a lot of money."

"Isn't your life worth such a small price? Don't you value yourself?"

"Yes, but I don't want to throw away money."

"You only live once. What do you have to lose."

"How do I know it works?"

"It worked for me, don't you trust me?"

If it's true, your greatest dream may be realized. If it is false, you lose a bit of money. But it doesn't stop there, once you pay, your brain will turn on itself. Your brain assumes that quality goods cost money, and because you spent a sum of money on this good, it will now assume it is quality. Cult building, luxury good marketing, and unwinnable war fighting 101.

"I'm actually doing very well in life, and you seem like a loser," I told him.

"Now you are defensive," he said. I knew I shouldn't have called him names, he was probably trained for this. So I stayed quiet, sometimes it's the best thing you can do. He continued to talk. "Look, I can tell you this, my life began to turn around when I signed that card."

"Kool," I said.

"What breakthroughs are you looking for?" He asked.

Breakthroughs? Who talks like this? "I don't know what that means," I answered, knowing full well what he meant.

"A breakthrough is something you can't even conceive to be possible at this moment," he said.

"If I can't conceive it, how can I even tell you what I want my breakthrough to be," I asked.

"Because you do know. It's something you want, but your perception is holding you back, what is the dream in your heart that you don't believe you can achieve." I stayed quiet. "What about work? If you could have any job, what would it be?" He asked.

"I would probably start a tech company." I said

"See, Romney can help you with that. What's holding you back"

"I actually just founded a startup, I have my dream job."

"Oh," I don't think he understood the joke, "that's got to be stressful. I'm sure you need support. They can help you with that."

"I have a great co-founder, he is one of the best programmers in the world." I replied. "We're having a lot of fun."

"What about your family? It must be hard juggling work and family." He said.

"Oh my family is great, my dad was an entrepreneur, honestly this whole thing has made us closer." I felt like he was reading from a card that listed the ten most common stresses a man has in life.

"You have a girlfriend?"

"No," I answered.

"Why not?"

"I really don't want one, I'm having a lot of fun being single right now."

"That's perfect for you," he moved in to whisper to me, "the girls there, they are so fucking hot, and their inhibitions are down. It's a perfect place to meet singles."

So he was now a complete douchebag as well? Did he not think this would offend me? This fucking sexist pig, loser of losers. There is nothing worse than someone who is so pathetic that he thinks he is a winner. I checked out, losing all respect for him. He will live his life, always thinking he is right, always criticizing those who actually do things. This organization did not teach him to transform his thoughts, it taught him to harden his beliefs to such a point he thought he was open-minded.

Everyone began to leave, the VP pulled me aside. "What if I paid for you?" She said.

"I'm really not interested," I replied.

"You have bailed me out so many times," she said, "let me do this, if not for you, then for me." I knew these classes were expensive and I knew the VP was still broke, I couldn't take her money.

"Thank you, but no." I said.

"It would mean so much to me." And I swear she started to cry.

"Well I have always been interested in LGAT's," I said.

"What's an LGAT?" She asked.

"Nevermind," I said, "I'll join." What was I going to say, no? The next day I filled out the card. I was now part of whatever the fuck this thing was.

Chapter Fourteen:

The Real Money is in Religion

"So I see you filled out your card," the young voice on the other line told me. "I just wanted to go over your answers so you can get the most out of the experience."

I was lying upside down on my couch, rubbing my hair against the tile floor as we talked. "Do you work for Romney?" I asked.

"Oh no, we're all volunteers here. The program just helped us so much that we wanted to give back."

"Well I hope you can read my handwriting."

"I'll be fine I'm sure." She didn't even give me the courtesy laugh. "First, I want to enroll you into having a great experience, and I want you to know that I am here to support you on your upcoming transformation." Normally I would have hung up the phone right then. "Okay, so let me see, you are seeking help in two things?"

"Yes, that is correct," I said.

"The first is, brewing beer. What do you mean by that?"

"Well I am an avid home brewer, and I am always looking for other beer lovers to talk to," I said.

"Oh, I like that, it is very specific. The more specific you are with your goals, the better we will be able to help you." She continued, "Second, I see you need programmers?"

"Oh yea, I started a tech company this month, and we are looking for an IOS and an Android programmer."

"Oh that's great, you are a connector. We have a lot of tech people involved in Romney. I love that you know exactly what you want!" She was genuinely excited about every answer, she reminded me of the wiz kid who raised their hand to every question in school. I could hear her flip the card over as she started to read from the back. "So now I would like to talk about your breakthroughs. I see you didn't write much here."

"I only need one breakthrough," I said.

"Am I reading this right?" She asked.

"You tell me."

"You wrote down that you want to know if God exists?"

"Yes, that's right," I said.

"Could you explain that a bit?" She asked.

"Oh sure. So I used to believe in God, and then I lost my faith a few years ago. And you know, as I think about it, knowing if there is a God is a pretty important thing. I mean if there is a God, then we must have a purpose in this world. And if there is not a God, well then, there is no point to anything, so why not just do whatever the fuck we want. I mean if you really think about it, it's the only breakthrough that matters."

Her tone changed, "wow," she said, "This conversation just took a turn. First, I want to thank you for showing such trust in me to say such a deep and personal thing. You are a very special and beautiful human for doing this. I want you to know, Romney will give you the support you need. I am so excited for you, on the last day, you will get your answer. I am so happy that you are going to have such a large breakthrough in life. I promise you, when you are done with basic, you will know the truth."

I hung up the phone. I was in shock. There was no doubt in her voice. She believed every word she said. What the fuck was I about to get myself into?

YOU EVER NOTICE successful people usually lack charisma? They spent their time learning how to do real things, instead of learning how to talk about doing real things. If your mind immediately jumped to Steve Jobs, remember, he was not charismatic, he was just the most charismatic person in an industry that lacks charisma. Politicians are the one exception. But politicians are not trying to be successful; they are trying to make you believe that you are right. This is why I don't trust people in suits; If you have to wear a suit to look professional, you probably have no clue what you are talking about.

I was in a beige conference room at an airport hotel. This room was not pretending to be anything except for what it was, a beige conference room at an airport hotel. There was a piece of tape on the carpet at the base of my chair. We would be moving the chairs a lot. I knew this technique from film production, we would always mark the floor, so we could move things in and out of set more easily.

One hundred and forty-nine other people surrounded me. The room was filled to capacity. There was an ethnic man sitting on a chair at the center of the stage before me. He wore a bad suit. I hate bad suits even worse than I hate suits. If you are going to dress up, might as well do it with style. He stood up as music began to play, music that made Christian Rock sound edgy.

There were no bold choices here. No bold colors, no bold music, even the smiles seemed calculated in their lack of passion. There was no soul in this room. The only thing worse than a man in a suit, was a man without any soul. It was like the white boy from Omaha who tried to be a rapper. Even if he spoke the same words and had the same voice, he would never be as powerful as the black man who grew up in the hood. I was an inner city oppressed minority compared to a room like this.

The doors closed, and the music stopped. The people in here were scared, that type of fear that fills a classroom on the first day of Jr. High as you wonder if all the rumors had been true. The man in the bad suit stood began to talk. "I will be your trainer for the next five days," He had an accent, of course he did. "You are all here for different reasons. Some of you joined because you were looking for meaning, others want change. Most of you found this program through a friend who went through transformation."

I turned around, at the back of the room was a long desk of people who looked official. All wearing bad suites, all sitting with good posture as their eyes followed the trainer like zombies looking to their king. But they weren't official, they were trying to be official, they were mimicking what they thought confident people looked like. They were pretending. Real confidence is relaxed. This confidence was contrived.

"Some of you do not want to be here, you were pressured by a friend," the trainer continued, "but whatever the reason, I want to congratulate you all for coming. You have already taken the first step to your transformation. This program works, whether you are here of your own volition, or because you feel you have been forced here. Whatever the reason, it will work, as long as you trust the process. I ask you all to trust the process, give into this process. For the next five days, trust us. What do you have to lose? It's 5 days. I guarantee, in five days, you will understand the truth. On the last day you will learn why your friends and family are so excited for you to be here."

Carrot and the stick, it was high-pressure sales all over again, but it made no sense. We were here. We bought our ticket. Why was he still selling?

"I want everyone to stand." The trainer looked over the room, making sure everyone obeyed his words. "Over the next five days, I am asking that you take a pledge for the process. You are to abstain from drugs, liquor, and marijuana, anything that is not prescribed by a doctor. You are to be sitting in your chairs at the start of the class. We will give you a one-minute musical warning. I know Los

Angeles has traffic, but you will find a way to be on time, if you knew your future depended upon it, you would be in your chair. If anyone disagrees with these rules I ask that you now sit. "No one sat. "Good, now let the process begin."

This was an authoritarian power play. It used our instincts against us. When a human being takes a vow, it takes that vow seriously. The vow becomes more important than the action. These tactics were used in the early days of the communist uprising, they were used by the Catholic inquisition, and are still used by cults around the world today. The trainer was hoping someone would break this vow, he would use that person as an example, it would show that breaking a vow was akin to treason against the tribe. The brain would then assume that we were a tribe, and it would create camaraderie within this group, while giving the trainer the status of Alpha. He was teaching these people to be sheep, while giving them the costumes of wolves.

AFTER TALKING FOR what seemed like the longest talk anyone had ever given in the history of all mankind. The trainer said, "Now we shall do our first exercise."

I looked to my left, there was a man dozing off. I could see him forcing his eyes open, trying to stay awake for the trainer. He looked like he could be my brother, there was something about him that was just so familiar.

"I want you to find a partner, and for ninety seconds, you are to stare into their eyes as they tell you how they came to be part of this group. I want you to then spend ninety seconds to tell them what you heard. You are not to break eye contact. Then switch roles."

After the exercise was finished, we were instructed to use the tape on the floor to place our chairs back into position. The ingenuity of this simple hack amazed more than one in the audience. A microphone was passed around as people talked about their experience.

"I feel more connected to my partner than I do to my own husband," the first lady stated, "he has never listened to me that way. I didn't know this type of connection could exist."

"Maybe you should try this with your husband," the trainer replied.

"I wouldn't even know how to ask it."

"You are the only thing holding yourself back," the trainer stated.

I found myself feeling bad for anyone who spoke. Had they really never done anything like this? Was the room full of people who had never tried to break out of their shell? Tried to be introspective? Tried to improve their lives? Or maybe they were just pleasing their chieftain?

We took a short break. I hadn't smoked in a year, but I needed a cigarette just to stay sane. I stood at a corner with a cute, busty girl puffing away as she talked.

"This is my third transformational group," she said, "they all follow the same exact pattern. I don't know what's wrong with me, they don't seem to change me in any way, and my family just doesn't get it." We finished up our cigarettes and headed back into the conference room.

The music began to play and I took my seat. I saw a woman limping across the room, another woman got up to help her grab a chair. The music ended.

"You!" The trainer yelled "Why are you not sitting?!" The woman was confused, she had no answer. "You took a vow, did you not?" The trainer asked.

"Excuse me?" She answered.

His tone turned the room into children, people act the way they are treated. "You took a vow, you said you would be seated by the time the music ended."

"I was helping a girl into her seat."

"And now you have excuses, is this how you live your life?"

She stood there, searching her thoughts for the correct answer, as if there was any other than, "fuck off."

Another student yelled, "I saw the whole thing, she was just helping someone."

"If you're dream depended upon it, you would have been in your seat on time. If your life depended on it, you would not have been late. Or maybe not, maybe that is why you continue to fail." The trainer said.

It was pathetic, and everyone ate it up. I should have stood beside the woman, yelled at the trainer, telling him that if breaking a vow to help another human is considered wrong, then sign me up for hell. But he owned the audience and I would just look like a fool. He confronted people like me a hundred times, he would know exactly what to say. In a room like this, a good argument will always beat an actual result. It was a power play, nothing else. I would make my own at some point. Just so I could look myself in the mirror at the end of this entire farce.

THE WORLD IS a hard and vicious place, it is also very beautiful. You must embrace this hardness to find the beauty. This room was about avoiding it. Maybe the best advice for these kinds of people.

I looked over to that man who could have been my brother, and my eyes could not look away. I knew him. Where had I met him before? Was it Cheshire? It was. I didn't know him well but I liked him, I respected him. He was smart, very smart. He also built real things. Video games. We met each other at a convention. I didn't know it at the time, but he and his girlfriend of fourteen years had just broken up. He wanted a family, kid, a normal life. She left him. Just like that, she was gone and his whole perspective changed. I went through something similar at the same time.

The class ended. I had four more days of this crap. I wanted to say hi to Cheshire, but I saw him run into a fast-food joint. I purposely took my time to jump on my motorcycle, hoping I would catch him when he walked out. Turns out, he was parked right behind me.

"Cheshire?" I said as he walked by.

"Hey," he had a strange cadence, you could never

tell his intention, I wasn't sure if he was confused to see me, or angry at me for interrupting his night. "How are you?"

"I wouldn't expect to see you here." I said.

"Yea, I had a bunch of friends do it, figure it can't hurt."

"The VP enrolled me." I caught myself, "I can't believe I just fucking said enroll."

"Everyone's into this shit, I don't know what the fuck I'm doing." I loved his honesty.

"Yea it's just a week, I think I'm more interested in the audience than the trainer." I said.

"I'm mostly bored as fuck," Cheshire replied.

"See you tomorrow brother." I said as I put my helmet on.

The White Suit, Seeing Cheshire at Romney. Moments that forever change your life, if you let them.

Chapter Fifteen:

Making Life Winnable

I was beginning to feel like a forgotten POW trapped in this room. I was trying my best to embrace the reality of this situation, but could not find a reason to go on. The teachings were the most basic psychology, mixed with the most basic understanding of Eastern religions, mixed with a weird corporate campiness, and it was boring as hell. I found myself dozing in and out of reality when the trainer said, "We are now going to play a game," It was like hearing the sounds of my country's troops approaching. I perked up. I became alive. I love games.

The trainer's assistant revealed a scoreboard with the title, Red versus Black. I had never heard of this game, finally something I could sink my teeth into. "I will not repeat the rules, so listen carefully," the trainer said. "We will split this class into two, everyone to the left of me will go into the adjacent room, everyone to the right of me will stay in this room."

I was on his right, I quickly assessed my team. I saw Wolfgang, we had just met, and I liked him. I was looking for Allies. I would make sure we would win this thing.

"Each team is to pick a leader." I was going to be that leader, this was my chance. "The game is simple. There are six rounds. Each round you choose a color. Red, or Black. You will not learn what color the other team has picked until both of you have chosen. Every person on the team must vote. The color is decided by the majority rule."

It was a math game. If one team chose red and the other chose black, the red team would get one point. If both teams chose black, both teams would get one point, if both teams chose red, both teams would lose one point.

My brain went into overdrive, I knew this was a prisoner's dilemma game, we had to pick red, we could not lose as long as we chose red every time. I could feel my pride rise. I had been a math genius since I was a little kid. My team was lucky to have someone like me in their midst.

"The goal of the game is to get the maximum amount of points." Wait, this was not hard math, this was incredibly simple math. That was the trap. This was not a prisoner's dilemma game, it was just constructed to look like one. They were playing into my pride. I didn't know how to beat this game, but I knew what Romney would never want me to do. What they would never expect me to do. I knew why they had made me take that vow, and I knew why they were doing this. This game was stupid. It was about shaming us into their way of thinking.

"Now, let the game begin, everyone to my left, please leave the room." Two men in black suits escorted the other side of the room out. I jumped up onto the stage, joined by half a dozen others who wanted to take their position as chieftain. I stood silent, as they tried to force their approach on my team. They talked loud. Their stance became big. They did everything you learned in leadership school, but they forgot the most important rule. In the end, it is about results. Before that, it is about making everyone on your team feel as if they have a purpose. People need to feel safe with you. People need to have dignity.

I heard a quiet voice from the back. A meek small man was trying to make his opinion known, but none of the other leaders noticed him.

"This is the approach we will take!" One of prospective leaders shouted out as others in the audience tried to speak over him. It was one giant cluster fuck of masculinity and feigned importance. I did the only thing that would stop this nonsense.

"Shhhhh, Shhh Shhh Shhh..." The entire room instantly fell quiet.

"Did you just shush me?!" One of the potential leaders screamed in my face.

"Yes, there is someone trying to speak." I pointed to the quiet man in the back, "Everyone here will get to speak, we have plenty of time. There is no need to talk over each other. We are all in this together." The other's on the stage looked at me, they stayed silent. It became primal, I could feel their confidence shrink, as the confidence of the audience grew.

The quiet man spoke up, "I just had an idea for voting, we can just sit and stand, I think it will make voting much easier. I can take the roll if you would like."

"I love that idea," I said. "That's so much better than what I was thinking. Please, take the roll from now on, thanks so much."

A frantic voice yelled, "We are running out of time! We have to vote!"

"We can take this vote in five minutes if need be," I said, "he gave us forty five minutes and we will use most of that time to decide our strategy. I promise you, deciding our strategy is the most important thing."

One by one, the people who joined me on the stage began to walk off. I grabbed one girl's hand, "would you stay, I need your help. Can you take the score." Her eyes lit up.

I knew what we had to do, we had to pick black down the line. It was the last thing Romney would expect, so it had to be the right choice. It made absolutely no sense. But I knew I was right.

Person after person had their say. I pointed to a large man in the audience. He was smart and understood game theory, "I just want to point out, there is no way we can lose if we pick red," I looked to the audience, they were nodding and agreeing. "It's actually the only way, it would be silly to pick anything else, we just have to hope the other team picks black at least once."

In any other situation he would be right. Here, he was wrong. How could I get my team to go against everything they believed? "I completely agree," I said. "And that is why I think we should pick black. Look, this is a stupid game. Those people in the other room are our friends. There's no trick here, hope they choose black, hope we choose black.

This isn't a game, it's luck. I say we try for the tie. "

I thought I would be booed off the stage. People yelled at me. They actually yelled. Said that Romney was about leadership, and I was teaching them how to lose.

"Everyone listen up. I'm going to say it right now." Then I made my move. "Fuck Romney. Fuck our trainer. Fuck this game. I want to tie, or I want to lose. You know why? Because I will feel good about myself if I do. I want to look in the mirror at the end of the day and know I was there with my friends in the other room." I looked to the trainer who was now sitting at that long desk against the back wall. "Who the fuck cares what they think? This is about me, about you, and about our friends." The audience was silent. I had won, and I knew it.

We took a vote on who should be our leader. It was unanimous.

I WANTED TO make sure we had the votes. There was still a strong faction on my team going for the win. I would not call for the tally until I was positive that I had half the room on my side, even if this meant no vote would ever be taken.

The arguments went on, but they stayed cordial, no one talked over anyone else. I had set the groundwork for a well-functioning team. One person stayed on the clock while another passed around the mic. The more people I had helping me, the more allies I would create.

In the corner, across the room, I saw a young lady

crying. It was one of those cries where your whole life had just been shattered, and you knew it. The last exercise had been about childhood, about what your child self would think of you today. Would they be proud of what they became? I guess she wasn't.

"Everyone stop." I didn't say it loud, but they listened. I stepped off the stage and walked toward the girl. I knelt by her side. "Are you okay?"

"I don't know," she answered.

"I bet there are a lot of people here going through the same thing."

"I don't know why it hit me so hard."

"That's how it works sometimes." Then I stood and looked over the room. "I think this person needs some love, anyone here want to show her some love?" Three people came over. They sat with her. They hugged her. And then I was yelled at.

"Why are you wasting time?!" someone screamed.

"Really?" I said. It wasn't a lone voice, a dozen people began to reprimand me. My heart broke, but I saw the opportunity. "It's a stupid game," I said. "There is someone crying here. A friend, a teammate is crying. You would rather win this game than help that friend?" I looked back to our trainer, thinking this was his fault, people can be manipulated so easily, we want to be accepted, and he set the stage by calling out that person the other day.

"How much time do we have left?" I asked.

"Twenty minutes," the clock girl announced. Her

answer scared everyone, we were running out of time, and now their leader, the person they had unanimously voted on, was going to ruin it all for them.

"I want to tell everyone a story." The air was sucked out of the room, my team hated me. "I do extreme hiking. I have always been outdoorsy. About fifteen years ago a group was hiking up Everest, and on the side of the path, just thirty minutes from the peak was a dying man. The leader of the expedition explained that nothing could be done for him, he was already too far-gone, and if anyone stopped for him, they would not be able to summit Everest. Think about that, It was a lifelong dream for these people to summit the highest peak in the world. An expedition costs about seventy thousand dollars. You have to spend three months on the side of the mountain, acclimating your body to the elevation. Humans were not supposed to be in places like that. It's hell, three months of hell. And now you are low on oxygen, exhausted, near the peak, and you see a dying man. No one stopped for that man, not a single person. And I remember deciding at that moment, that if I were ever to be in that position, I would stop for my fellow human, even though there was nothing I could do for him, I would hold his hand and sit with him. I would miss my chance at greatness, he would still die, but I would do it, because that it the way things are supposed to be."

Everyone stayed quiet. I made eye contact with our trainer. I looked at him for 30 seconds. Then I looked over to the crying girl. "May I take the vote?"

She did not speak, but her lips moved, they said "thank you." And then she nodded.

I looked to my audience, "We are now voting on the first column, if you vote black, please stand!"

The vote was closer than I expected, but those who stood, stood with pride. The final outcome was black.

One of the black suited, Romney assistants stormed into the room and yelled, "HAVE YOU MADE YOUR VOTE!" The drama made it hard for me to take serious. I smiled and looked to my team, letting them know we were above such showmanship.

"We vote black," I said.

"YOUR VOTE IS BLACK? IS THAT CORRECT?"

"Yes," I said.

"YOUR VOTE IS RECORDED, TEAM A HAS VOTED BLACK. TEAM B HAS ALSO VOTED BLACK!" And we cheered.

"We're on the same page! We can do this!" I couldn't hold back my excitement. Everyone was excited, you could feel it in the air. This is why winners win.

Vote after vote after vote, black after black after black. We looked at the board, that black board. We were all proud. I was proud. I was proud of my team, I was proud of myself. Who cares what we were supposed to do. Who cares what the real way to win was. We set out to do something and we had won. It felt good, if for no other reason, than that was the way it was supposed to be.

"I WANT EVERYONE to think about what you are feeling right now." The trainer looked at the final score, speechless. "In all my years, no one has ever beaten Red versus Black. In all my years." He seemed angry. "To win the game, you had to get the maximum amount of points. Both teams, were on the same team. You won."

I had beat them. We had beat them. The other team had beat them. It meant nothing, but it was what I needed to do.

"I don't want you to feel good about these results. I want you to think about them. Think about how you live your lives. I think you were trying to prove something. Take your break, you have thirty minutes." The trainer sat down.

I walked down the street by myself, pumping my fist. The air was cool, and each breath felt good. I returned to the class and saw Cheshire sitting alone. I sat next to him. We nodded to each other but did not talk.

As the break came to a close, my teammates walked up to me, thanking me, explaining how much I had taught them in such a short period of time. I guess for a few minutes, I became the chieftain. I noticed people were doing the same to Cheshire. We both looked at each other. Knowing the answer to the question we were about to ask.

"Were you the leader of B?" I asked.

"Yea, were you A?" he replied.

"Yea."

"Good job," he said.

"You too." That was it. We both looked down, then away, and then we smiled. We knew we had beaten some sort of fake system. We had won, we had fucking won!

Chapter Sixteen:

On the Last Day, We Were to be Transformed

This was the moment we had all been waiting for. This is why we came here. Why we lived through those five days. This was the promise we had all been given. If we could just make it to the end, we would know the truth.

"I am going to tell you how to achieve your dream." The trainer said, then he wrote three words on the chalkboard.

"Have > Do > Be."

"This is how you have all been living your lives. You think having something will cause you to do something, which will cause you to be something. This is the American dream. This is the human condition. This is why you want that big house and car. You believe having will change you. Now it is time you learn the truth." He rearranged the words.

"Be > Do > Have"

"You must BE your dream before you can have your dream. Living as if you have your dream will allow your dream to come true." Great advice for losers, I thought.

"I am not saying you will actually achieve this dream, I will just give you the means to do so" The trainer said, "you will learn to live the life of being instead of having. You might not be up to the challenge. That is your choice. It takes bravery and strength in order to live this life. Up until this point, you have only learned to survive. We will teach you to live. We will teach you your potential." And then he said it, "it is in the advanced course, you will be transformed."

It was a sales pitch? The entire seminar was one giant sales pitch?

"If you sign up today, we will offer you a special. You will be allowed to take the course for just eight hundred and ninety nine dollars." I looked to the audience, they believed every word. They were reaching for their wallets. They were begging to be lead.

I looked at the board. The truth was right there, it was right in front of everyone, and no one noticed. No one saw it. It was right fucking there! I wanted to yell and stand. How could I be the only one who saw this beautiful truth?

"Excuse me."

It was a quiet voice from the back of the room.

"Excuse me?"

The trainer saw him, "Yes?"

"What about Do, Be, Have?" the voice said. He saw the truth as well, and he had the guts that I did not.

"No, you can either be something, or have something. Do, Be, Have is not an option."

"Sure it is," he replied," it's the only option. You can't just BE something without doing something."

"You are falling into your old trap, your dream doesn't come from doing, it comes from being," the trainer said.

"No, I am not. I am not talking about having something. You do something, then you be something. Than you are something." He realized it just as he said it. "You are something by doing. You are nothing by being."

"You can't just do something without being something, you must be, you must live the life you want to have before you have that life."

"That's the trap, being is the trap. We've all been there, we have all been 100 percent sure of our capabilities only to find out we were not up to the task. We've done the opposite too, thinking we were not up to the challenge, only to be thrown into the deep end and succeed. You don't know what you are made of until you do."

"It was your perception of being that created that success or failure, and it is in the advanced course you will learn to hone that ability."

"That's bullshit."

"There's no need for anger."

"I'm not angry, I'm stating a fact. That is complete bullshit. There's another name for someone who tries to be something before they do something."

"And what name is that?" The trainer asked.

"It's called being a fraud."

"WHAT DO YOU want to get out of the Advanced Course?" The incredibly attractive girl asked me. This was the final sale, a one on one with a Romney representative as they tried to talk you into taking the advanced class.

I gave the same answer I gave for Basic. "I grew up very religious," I told her, "and recently I lost my faith. I don't believe in God anymore, and I really want to know if he exists. I can't seem to find a reason to do anything if this is all there is."

She looked at me with caring eyes. "You will find your answer in Advanced. I found everything I needed. I used to be shy, I couldn't talk to people. But now look at me, I am training to be a leader, all because of Romney."

Maybe this was the future we had created. The fraud economy. Based on frauds teaching others how to be a fraud. It reminded me of a friend who told me about a get-rich quick book that I should read.

"How do you know it works?" I asked.

"Well it worked for him! He has 3 houses, a private jet, he travels the world by yacht!" He said.

"How did he make his money?" I asked.

"Oh, well, he wrote this great book on how to get rich. People bought it up and he made millions." My friend told me.

My dad once told me that what I call dreams, used to be called hobbies. You can't fail at a hobby. But you cannot live it either. It's not the people who follow their dreams who become successful, it's the people who convince you that your dream is livable. It is not the Yoga instructor who gets rich, it's the person who sells them their certificates to become a Yoga instructor. The musician does not get rich, it is the school who teaches them how to make music, actor's don't make money, acting coaches do. Websites, companies, and people feed off our talents. To the cowards go the spoils. Everyday this fraud economy grows, the wealthy feed off the dreams of the poor. Soon, that will be what being rich is. Making people believe they can actually be celebrities, have the perfect life, live like they are the exception. The heroes are fools. They run into battle and die, while these assholes get rich.

I looked at the young girl, with love in my heart and compassion in my eyes. "I will never find God, I will never know whether God exists."

She couldn't believe my answer. "Yes you will, you will see, in Advanced, you will see."

"No I won't."

"You will."

"No, I won't, I think I am going to have to live with that for the rest of my life. And it is absolutely wrong for you to spread such hope to people"

She was sick to her stomach. "How can you say that, how can you be so negative, I don't understand. If you believe in something strong enough you will be able to manifest it." I saw her self worth diminish, not because of anything I said, but because she had failed to get me to join

Advanced.

We believe in the lies because the truth hurts too much. It hurts too much to know you are exactly where you are because of your abilities. You are where you are because of what you have contributed to humanity. You are where you are because of you. No manifestation will change that. You don't have your dream, because you were not good enough.

Nearly 70% of the class signed up for the advanced. The frauds had won, the hero had failed, the coward got the money.

Chapter Seventeen:

Cheshire and I Become Friends

"You headed to Abundance tonight?" It was a text from Cheshire. After the last day of Romney, we promised each other we would stay in touch.

"I saw the invite, what is it?" I replied.

"It's an EDM event, a lot of my friends will be there." He said.

"What is EDM?" I asked.

"Electronic Dance Music lol!" I almost asked what Electronic Dance Music was, but thought the better.

I STOOD OUTSIDE the Hollywood club, not sure where to go. There were two lines, each line was populated by an entirely different type of person. Line one looked to be rich kids of oil barons, line two seemed to be filled with people who worked for the circus. My social anxiety paralyzed me. I crossed the street and hid around the corner, waiting for Cheshire to show up.

"Oh, hey dude! Great timing!" Cheshire said as I walked up to him, oblivious to the fact that I had just spent the last twenty minutes peaking out from a bush hoping he would show. "I didn't realize that this was a Burner crowd, I would have dressed up," he said.

I had heard of Burning Man, it didn't seem like something Cheshire would be into. I always imagined it was a bunch of hippies and drug addicts. "Burning Man? You go to that?"

"Yea, of course," he said. "There's a huge tech influence up there, that's how I got involved."

We were waved into the club by the doorman. I was surprised at how friendly he was, doormen usually give off an air of assholery. Cheshire was greeted by a dozen friends. I didn't know anyone, and upon seeing this, he began to introduce me to person after person. You can tell a lot about someone by how well they introduce you to a new crowd. We walked through a series of vendors selling weird clothing and gear. Cheshire grabbed a pair of glowing fox ear and placed them on me.

"They were made for you," he said.

"How much are they?" I asked the vendor.

"Forty Dollars." The price was shocking to me. I placed them back on the counter and walked into the main hall.

"That seems really expensive," I told Cheshire.

"It's actually not, it's very Burner specific, people spend a lot of money on this stuff." Everything about this was ridiculous to me.

We walked onto the main dance floor. The outer walls were surrounded by tables inhabited by rich kids who could afford the two thousand dollar bottle service. The actual dance floor seemed to be a lot more fun. An aerialist hung from a sort of hoola hoop tied up to the ceiling while costume clad people danced underneath her.

A man dressed up like an ancient gypsy came up and hugged me, it took me a minute to recognize him. It was Rubix. I hadn't seen him in a year. I had worked with him in film.

"I didn't know you were in the festival scene!" he said.

"I don't think I am," I replied.

"It will be your home soon." I didn't say it, but this would definitely never be my home.

His eyes were dilated, everyone's eyes were. Everyone was weird, they acted off, they must have all been on drugs. The term "club drug" finally made sense to me. I had been around people who smoked pot, did shrooms, but I had never been around this. Everyone was so damn happy, they all hugged and rubbed each other as if they were dating, there was a sexuality in the air, and it seemed to have no Male/Female boundaries.

Cheshire was straight edge, his only vice being copious amounts of caffeine and Adderall. He knew people here, but he seemed as out of place as I was. I could tell he had anxiety problems. This explained the weird cadence he had. He didn't know how he was supposed to act.

I walked back and forth between the main hall and patio. I bummed smokes and made small talk. I didn't know what I was supposed to do here. Back and forth. Back and forth. Back and forth. Back and forth. I remembered doing this in summer camp when I was young, seeing people talk, seeing people play, always wondering how they did it. I just wanted to build things. I would walk from one part of the camp to the other. My counselors would get mad at me and tell me to make friends. So I hid. I would find myself in a corner writing, or whittling wood. Now I was an adult, and still had my same insecurities. People don't change, they just adapt.

I noticed a cute girl following me with her eyes. She finally walked up and grabbed my shoulder. "Hey, excuse me." Her cadence was a little funny. She was uncomfortable in her own skin. She was extremely cute and very awkward.

"I know you don't I?" I asked.

"Yes, we met last week in Romney, "she said. "I just wanted to tell you something... I know this is your first time in this group... I've been there..." She struggled with her words, and I realized this was a brave act, to stop me and comfort me. This was hard for her to do. It's a beautiful thing to see someone push against their own instincts. "I know it can seem really clicky, but that's just because we have all been through a lot together... I just wanted to let you know... I am really glad you are here. I want you to keep coming out."

It was exactly what I needed to hear. It was the firsts sense of humanity I had felt since I entered this place. It was like she read my mind. Putting me at ease. Putting my awkwardness and strange emotions at bay. She was a brave, beautiful girl.

"What is your name?" I asked.

"Little Heart," She said.

"May I call you L H?"

"Elache? I like that," she said.

...Back in the now

"This program has changed everyone I know, every single person had their lives changed through the advanced course. Do you really think you are that different from everybody else?" The VP yelled at me.

Here on the day she announced her engagement, all she could think of was recruiting me into her club. Maybe I was that different. What she didn't seem to understand, what no one ever seems to understand, is groups have a self-selecting processes. Whether it is kickball, pottery class or LGAT's. They attract like-minded people. The word "transformational" filtered out certain people. Writing down your breakthroughs on a card and taking a vow, filtered out others. The location, the cost, the method, until they were left with their mark. Funny, the festivals had similar filters, but I kept giving the festivals another chance.

"Aren't I the proof that this works? Do you think I am lying to you?" She said.

"I had problems with the group," I remarked, "I don't believe you can manifest your destiny, I don't believe you can be before you do."

"And how is that working out for you?" She replied, she was now getting mean.

"Really fucking good," I answered. It was true, ever since I had started focusing on the next step, on doing something. Funny, I spent most of my life trying to be, it had only been recently that I focused on the do. My life was not some magical perfect ride, but I was going in the right direction, actually enjoying the adventure.

"Oh please, you wear your depression like a badge of honor," now she was getting personal.

"That's because it's the single most defining thing about who I am as a human being, and it is hands down the greatest accomplishment of my life." She knew about my past. She knew what she was saying.

"If you take advanced you will be able to fix that for good." I was reminded why I had kept my condition a secret for most of my life.

"I lived most of my life thinking that way, and it almost killed me." I told her.

"You obviously didn't, if you had, you wouldn't be in the place you are. You can change yourself, you can manifest a better you."

"No I can't, I will never get over it. I lost 13 years of my life because I was told I just needed more faith. I was told that people would pray for me. I was told to trust the process and manifest a new reality. It wasn't until I started thinking the exact opposite that I learned how to manage this. It wasn't until I threw that all away, that I actually started living a good life and making real accomplishments. You think it's so easy, it's not, it's hard."

"No, it is easy, that's the great secret to life, it is easier than you can even imagine," she said it with a sort of religious zeal and passion. She was right, life was easy, it was easy if you only wanted to live in the now, it was easy if this is all there is. "I believe I can manifest a better world, I believe by spreading my love, this world will become a better place. I believe my dreams will come true if I live like I already have them."

I couldn't take it anymore, so I got mean myself. "Yea, because doing something never helped anyone," her face dropped, I must have hit a nerve. She stormed out of the restaurant.

Part IV

The Most Honest Place on Earth

The girl's faces contort as if they were about to orgasm while the men grind upon their half naked bodies. They have that same funny half smile that a porn star wears while two overweight men are fucking her; at least the porn star is being paid. Bottle service in this room can cost over twenty thousand dollars. Maybe it's the drugs.

Oh, we aren't at a festival, we aren't in the middle of some dried out lakebed, or God forsaken forest. This is not transformative. This is not Burner or tribal. This is Vegas. And we are about to experience the largest rave in the world, where some three hundred thousand people converge in a drug, light and music carnival for three nights. Dusk till dawn, in the middle of the Nevada summer.

This is EDC.

I wonder if I am the only sober person at the club, I also wonder if I am the only person who knows how to build something with his hands. Not everyone can be a rich kid living off his parent's money. Some of these people are familiar, they are techies; I recognize their social anxiety. Their analytical brains deducted that this must be a fun place. Why else would it be so expensive and filled with such an array of beautiful women? But it doesn't feel that fun. Maybe it's the drugs.

These were the kids who were always on the outside. People like me. Now they can afford a table at the hottest club in Vegas and feel like somebody, now the girls will come to them and drink their drinks and snort their coke. They are masters of this universe.

There's something wrong with their eyes, you can sense it. These were the kids who got beaten up and made fun in High School, all while trying to live out their parent's fantasy of getting into an Ivy League or Stanford. Nothing has changed, the jocks still make fun of them, but now they do it on the social network that the people in this room created.

The music is EDM, playing to the most primal instincts of us human beings of this planet Earth. Up Up Up Up Up Up, Turn down the bass… Boom. Forcing the emotions of the dancers, making them move in rhythm, it is never a surprise, everyone knows what is coming next, it creates a community among them, it must be what it was like back when we told stories around campfires.

It seems both very human and very alien at the same time. I find that I envy it. I see female after female that I wish were mine. I wish I could afford a ten thousand dollar table and invite girls to dance on it with me. I'm not sure why girls come here. Are they having fun? Of course they are, how can you not have fun while you pop pills that release copious amounts of serotonin? I wish life were nothing more than drugs and dancing and half-naked girls. But is this the end game? Did we work hard and create and build for this?

Many of the guys will get lucky, the girl's inhibitions are down, which is right where the guys like them. I guess if you are held accountable for drinking and driving, you must also be accountable for what you do with your body while intoxicated. However, the male instincts in me want to protect every girl I see. At least I remain human.

We forget about the outside. This room is now our home and Vegas is our world. We all need a break from life sometimes. I think of moments of pure joy; dinners with friends are just as pointless as this spectacle.

I have to leave, I tell my group not to worry about me, but of course they won't, they won't worry about anyone, or anything for the next ninety minutes plus. They are too busy being amazed by bright colorful lights, and how good human touch feels.

I walk down The Strip. I look at the ridiculousness that is the most ridiculous thing humans have ever created. The city of Las Vegas. A country song begins to play against a sixty foot, LED projected American flag. "We have everything we need," the twangy voice sings, "here in America, we have everything we need." We have everything we need. It's true. This is America.

Chapter Eighteen:

Fuck EDC

We want to believe in the lies, the truth hurts too much. Think about it for long enough, and you are bound to ruin the rest of your life.

I was 37 miles from Las Vegas. I know I was 37 miles away because I was entering the parking lot of Primm, a giant, family-friendly casino on the border of California. Driving down the I-15 through the Mojave, in the middle of the night, Primm looked like an Oasis in a sea of ink. I imagine it will be the same feeling my great grand kids have as they stop at the halfway point between Proxima Centauri to get a chicken-fried steak at some diner in the Oort Cloud.

There are two Casinos in the city of Primm, "Primm" and "Trucker Petes." God only knows who actually stays here. Gamblers who can't wait the extra forty minutes to make it to Vegas? Families looking for a cheap alternative? It's a certain type of Americana that is very foreign to an American like myself.

Every time I drive to Vegas, I stop at Primm to fill up on gas and get a cheeseburger. It's this little tradition I have, it feels like the last bastion of civility until I cross the boundary into the absurdity that is The Vegas Strip.

I pull up to the Carl's Jr. It's closed. We're just outside of Las Vegas and a fast food restaurant is closed. My only other choice is McDonald's. I hate McDonald's, but it is three in the morning, and this may be the last chance I have to eat tonight. I pull up to the intercom and am informed that they are switching over to their breakfast menu and will not be able to serve for the next hour. What type of a fucking country do we live in where I am turned down for service at the most inclusive restaurant in the history of mankind? I haven't even reached Vegas and I already want to turn around. Fuck EDC.

Whenever I near The Strip I have to emotionally prepare myself for the illusion that is the largest concentration of hotel rooms in the world. You always feel closer than you actually are, it's something to do with the size of the buildings and how your brain determines distance. Not the height, but the girth. Buildings don't look like this anywhere else. My destination is Rio, it looks to be about a mile away, but I know it is closer to ten. I chose The Rio because it was off strip, and because I get free rooms there - free not being the best choice of words.

I toss my keys to the Valet and walk up to the registration.

"Checking in," I tell the lady behind the desk.

"Oh, wow, you are checking in late." she says, I pulled up around 4am.

"Yea, I get free rooms here, so I always book an extra night before I come and an extra night after I leave, so I can check in early and leave late." This is the thing about Vegas, they don't care if you game the system, it was a system made to be gamed. As long as you don't cheat, or bother the people who are gambling, you can do anything you want.

She has a look of fear on her face as she begins banging on the keyboard. "Excuse me," she says, then walks away.

I look at the Casino floor and begin to judge the degenerates that have nothing better to do than play blackjack in Vegas on a weekday morning.

She comes back. "I'm sorry, our system is acting weird, it's down or something." She leaves again and I know exactly what happened. I was checking in so late, that their computers had assumed I had canceled my trip and failed to inform them. Why would I? I had a free night, and would gain nothing by doing so. They gave my room away to some lucky bastard who showed up to EDC, only to find out that every hotel in the city was booked for one of the largest events in the world. Fuck Las Vegas, EDC, this country and everything in it.

Now her head down as she walks up to the computer, she begins typing again, she's avoiding me, she's embarrassed, doesn't know what to do. Probably been dealing with assholes all week. Probably has a boss, who has thrown this whole thing on her. Where the fuck is her boss anyway? He should be out here. Piece of shit coward.

"It's okay," I say. "Would you mind if I left my bags here?" She looked at me confused. "You see, I want to go gamble and get shit faced," I say, "I'm here for EDC, dusk till dawn, so I want to reverse my schedule. If you'd just cut me a break, hold onto my bags so I don't have to walk up to my room and drop them off. And I want you to know, why I love the fine establishment that is the Rio. I know Caesars owns other properties here in Vegas. And if by chance, you can't find a room here, I will gladly move to another casino. I like all your properties equally."

I swear a tear began to form in the corner of her eye, "You have no clue," she said, "you leave your bags here, someone will come find you when your room is ready. Thank you." She gave me a smile, I gave her a wink. Then I walked over to the blackjack table and became one of the degenerates myself.

Everyone told me I'd hate EDC, everyone except for Cheshire, it was his favorite fest, "It's just sexy," he said. Maybe everyone was right, and Cheshire was wrong.

At around seven in the morning, a hotel worker came up to me and informed me that my room was now ready. He handed me a small envelope that contained my keycard, room number, and a bunch of coupons that I never took advantage of. I was now completely drunk and trying to figure out where the hell I was headed.

"Twenty-o-one sir," the worker said.

"Like the movie," I replied.

"Yes sir."

I slowly walked over to the elevator and stared at the numbers on the control panel. 2001. Twentieth floor, well nineteenth really, they were always missing that number thirteen. Top floor, what a view, I thought. I pushed the button marked 20, and it did not light up. Maybe the light was broken. I hit it again, and the door did not close. Of course the elevator would be broken. Have I mentioned that EDC could go fuck itself yet?

I began to stumble through the giant metal doors, hitting that plastic flap thing, which kept them from slicing guests like me in half. For a moment, I thought about the amount of faith I put into that cheap piece of plastic every time I tried to catch an elevator, and what this said about how little I valued my life. Then another man entered and hit floor 19. The button lit up, and I thought fuck it, I can walk up one flight of stairs.

Now on the 19th floor, I found myself wandering across the giant lanes of hallways that traversed one of the largest hotels in the world. I walked to each end, but the stairs only headed down. What the fuck was up with the architect who designed this place? I finally gave up and entered another elevator, hitting the 20, only to find that it also was broken. Fuck!!

I began to exit the elevator when I realized the astronomical odds of having two elevators broken at the same hotel just for one floor. I knew how to use an elevator. This was something I had done thousands of times in the past. I remembered when I was a kid, I could always make my elevator go to the floor I needed, why could I not do it now? I was shit-faced drunk, but I knew how a fucking elevator worked.

"Room 20, room 20 01. Top floor?" Holy fuck I thought. There was a small slot in the side of the wall, a little plaque underneath it, I squinted my eyes and read the text. Insert Keycard for penthouse. I did, the 20 lit up.

The doors opened and I walked into the hallway of the room. Not the hallway of the hotel, the hallway of my room, which was nicer and bigger than the hallway of the hotel. I looked across the hundreds of feet of marble towards the windows, which gave me a perfect panorama of the Vegas Strip.

"Oh Fuck!" This was not an "Oh Fuck" of joy, this was an Oh Fuck of complete and utter fear. How much was I being charged for this room? I ran through the hallway, to the kitchen, past the dining room, bar, living room, and every other room from the board game Clue, until I reached the study where I grabbed for the completely generic white phone on the desk and panic dialed zero.

"Hello sir, what may I do for you?" The friendly man on the other line said.

"Yes," I said, "I just got to my room, and it seems a little... big."

"Here at the Rio every room is an executive suite or better."

"Yea, this seems a lot better than an executive suite."

"Well, maybe you received our normal suite?"

"I've stayed here before, and I have to say, this room seems to be a little larger than your normal suites."

"Maybe our deluxe suite? It has a nice little side room."

"No, I would say this is larger than your deluxe suite as well. I just want to make sure I am not being charged for this room."

"Let me see, it looks like you have been comped sir. You are free and clear"

"For this room?" I asked.

"Yes"

"This exact room, you can confirm this?"

"Ahh I see now, looks like someone gave you an upgrade. I don't know the name of that suite, it's not a listed room, it's only available for very special guests."

"So I am not being charged for this?" I said.

"Of course not sir, have a great week here at the Rio."

I love this country.

"WHAT THE FUCKING shit shit?!?!" It was The Little Mermaid, I had an extra ticket for EDC so we made a deal, she'd pay for the room, and I'd cover her ticket. Well fuck me I guess. "What the fuck am I paying for?" She yelled out.

I ran through the hotel room as I pulled a robe over my almost naked body, and tried to determine where the echo of her voice was coming from. "We're comped." I yelled.

"Like free?" She yelled back.

I finally found her in the dining room, "yeah."

"See, manifest your destiny," she said. More like manifest your hundreds of hours at the blackjack table, I thought.

She began looking around the room, not at the room, but for something very specific in the room. "Where's the mirror?" she asked.

"Mirror?"

"You know, like a little serving tray, but it has a mirror on the bottom?"

I had never realized it until just now. Every nice Vegas suite always had a small serving dish with a mirrored bottom. It was like the time my crackhead friend explained to me that those little rose glass things they sell at every truck stop in America, just happen to be the perfect size for making crack pipes.

"Here it is," she said, "underneath the vase, love that placement." She began to tap some blow onto the mirror and cut it up into two fine lines. "We need debauchery in a room like this," she said as she snorted coke. Then she pulled out a chocolate chip cookie, "it's an edible, I eat exactly one eighth now, and one eighth when we hit the parking lot. I should be evened out in about forty minutes."

Evening out was one of those terms that would have made no sense to me just a couple of months earlier. Drugs are highs and lows, and your body has a natural ability to mix the two to hit a strange equilibrium. This way, you can have the mellowness of pot, and the energy of cocaine. The empathy of molly with the flow of G. To people like the

Mermaid, evening out was a scientific process where drugs were measured in exact quantities.

She closed her eyes only to jump up twenty minutes later. "I'm good," she said, "lets get the fuck to EDC."

THERE WAS NO sense of adventure on the road, no sense of fear, there was no unknown. We were in the city of Las Vegas, stuck in traffic, EDM music blaring from every corner of the highway as the cars shook.

People rolled down their windows and held hands, until the entire road became one giant unity chain. They traded small ornamental wristbands across the lanes in what seemed to be a sort of EDC ritual. This was pure excitement, pure joy. People came from all over the world to be at this place. People counted the days until they were here. Together, we would all be dancing underneath an electric sky.

White people dominated the transformation festival scene. This crowd was darker and more optimistic. On this road, headed to this party, nationalities and ethnicities did not exist. Everyone was just a friend. A fellow human being. This was the America that America dreamed to be. The shining light on the hill, the state without a nation. We were, in this moment, the capital of the world. We were E D C.

Chapter Nineteen:

Underneath the Electric Sky

The transformational festivals were a series of emotions and realizations. You experienced the entire canopy of life. Joy and sadness, excitement and fear. You learned what you were made of, you were forced to look both inward and outward. So far, EDC was different, it was nothing but sharp instances that I had no time to reflect upon. That was until this moment, standing in line, sneaking drugs into the event. Pure terror.

I had snuck drugs into LiB, but that was different, driving through a ticket line where the only concern was extra passengers. Here, every single person would be patted down by security before they could enter. Police stood at the ready just looking for a reason. This was Nevada, the state of contradictions, funded by out of towners throwing their kid's college money away, while voting for the core values of Christianity. We don't mind your vices as long as it keeps our taxes low!

I was about twenty deep in the patdown line, at the point where men and women were separated into two different groups. Women were only to be patted down by female security guards, whereas men were patted down by both sexes, because men don't give a fuck.

I had hidden my stash in-between my toes, figuring that even if my shoes were taken off, no one would ever grope my feet. I went through the scenarios in my head, if they asked me to take off my socks, I would yell something about living in a police state and walk away.

It was enticing to pass a group of cops while doing a very illegal thing. It was fun. I wonder how much less enjoyable the festival circuit would be if everything were lawful? Does illicit activity make counter culture counter-culture? If everyone lived the festival life, would counter culture consist of people sitting around the TV, watching the big game?

I looked around at the three hundred some thousand people trying to enter the same place, and thought if there was ever a zombie apocalypse, I would want EDC to handle my safe zone. We were in constant motion. This was unlike any line I had ever been in. The first checkpoint was the ticket and ID station, you didn't actually have your ticket and ID scanned, you just lifted them up so that the security guard saw that you were prepared. If you had no ticket, you were guided to the will call line, if you had no ID, then you were going to have a long sad existence in a Las Vegas hotel room for the rest of the weekend. The next checkpoint was the actual ID line; each person's ID was scanned to make sure they were of age. Each line turned into ten separate rows in a sort of reverse bottleneck.

After this, you reached the pat down line, the guys line always moved faster than the girls' line, so right past this gate was a waiting area, where you were allowed to wait for your significant other. There was a sort of fear in each guys' eyes, hoping that his sweetheart would get past security. It does take a certain kind of skill to hide your drugs when all you are wearing is a bra, fairy wings, and a tutu. Finally, your ticket was scanned, and you were allowed into the festival.

Looking at this perfectly planned logistical nightmare gave me respect for Insomniac Events, the company that produced EDC. I could tell by the way they organized this line, that they loved their attendees. I felt like I was being hosted by a family that wanted to share its traditions with me. I felt respected.

I walked up to the seventy-year-old security guard, and he began to pat me down. I caught him looking at a near nude, female attendee, and wondered what was going on in his mind. He probably fought in some war on the other side of the globe just so the younger generations could do this.

I removed my backpack, coat and emptied my pockets. "That's okay," he said, "you don't have to do that." He did a very quick search, making sure to only check the parts of me where I would never actually hide drugs. Then he quickly passed me through. God bless it, it was all just a show for the lawyers. Plausible deniability! "Look your honor, we frisk everyone who enters our party, we make it clear that drugs will not be tolerated. In fact, we won't even let light gloves in for reasons that no one has ever seemed to understand!" Topless girls covering their nipples with pasties shaped like MDMA pills, wearing nothing but faerie wings and glow in the dark bikini bottoms are fine, but light gloves are considered drug paraphernalia. I wished we lived in an honest world.

My ticket was scanned, and I walked through the final gate. "HOLY FUCKING SHIT!!!" I yelled, as I was hugged by half a dozen other festival goers waiting for their girlfriends, we jumped and danced to the quiet bass that was shaking the huge cement barriers behind us. We still had not entered EDC, we were now on the other side of those giant walls that separated us from whatever lay on the other side. The only way in, was a familiar tunnel, a tunnel you have crossed through dozens of times, the tunnels you find in every stadium, in every city in America. They separate the fans from the concessions, the field from the outside world, you from your team. They are always exciting to cross through, never more so than now. With every step into that concrete cave, EDC became more real. The music became louder, the screams became higher, and the lights became brighter. It was a near-death experience, except we were walking towards life.

As soon as we were on the other side, we paused and stayed silent. Our bodies shut down as they tried to understand this new world. A few seconds ago, you didn't know anything like this had ever existed. Now you were here. The electronic beats felt like a kind of vibrating syrup that changed the very air inside this giant venue. The lights shined into our pupils, the smells into our nostrils, the voices into our ears, and once again, we were children. We hugged and we kissed, as two playmates might. Oh the places you'll go.

Twelve gigantic stages, each of which was, bigger, better and more elaborate than any stage I had ever seen. Hundreds of thousands of people, moving in unison, colors dancing up and down the pathways. It was the most obnoxious, big, bright, absurd thing I had ever witnessed in my life. And I had just left the Vegas Strip!

At this moment, in this city, at this festival, I was witnessing the most honest place on this planet. EDC was about happiness, about fun, it was about love and furry things. It did not pretend to be anything it was not. People were here to do drugs, dance, listen to music and maybe get lucky. Each one of these senses were amplified by this festival. You want love? Then lets all run around in lingerie and pasties. You want to dance while high on molly? Why not do it on a giant ferris wheel while fireworks go off above you. You want music? Let's put the top DJs in the world, on the most grandiose stages ever conceived, rear projectors' morphing the backgrounds into a 3d fantasy that would be a psychedelic trip even if you were just high on life.

We were no longer on Earth, we were on EDC. Sex, drugs and EDM. The fucking Electric Daisy Carnival.

"YOU HAVE NO candy to give me?" I knew rolling made candy taste more flavorful, but I had never been asked for any before.

"I'm sorry, I don't." I said. I was standing underneath

a giant glowing daisy near the Kinetic Stage, the largest stage of the festival. The flower was only a few feet off the ground, it's skin had glowing veins of light flowing through its white petals. Two hulking owls stood above us all. Their digital eyes watching our every move as they flanked the DJ above the crowd. There was something about them I did not trust. I knew they were nothing more than massive, engineered structures, but they seemed alive.

"How can you come to EDC without candy?" I had just met this man, and I was thrown off by his insistence that I feed him.

"I didn't even think about it," I said.

"It's okay, I have extra candy for you."

"I don't really want candy."

"Of course you want candy!" He then grabbed my hand and made a peace sign against it. "Do you know plur?" He said.

"I have actually never been more confused in my life," I replied.

"Like this, peace," he made a peace sign, and touched his two fingers to mine. "Love, you have to make a heart." We shaped our two hands into a heart. "Unity" he pushed his hands into mine, grasping each other, "respect" and then our fingers collapsed into a single fist. He pulled his homemade bracelet off, and rolled it over to my wrist. "See it never leaves our grasp, it comes from me and goes to you, and then off to another who lives the plur life."

PLUR AND TRANSFORMATIONAL. These are the mottos of the two very different festival circuits. Festivals like LiB and Serenity, were transformational, where spirituality reigned supreme. The rave culture of the Electric Daisy Carnival, lived by "peace, love, unity, respect." Plur.

Plur is young and naive. Transformational is old and hardened. There was almost no crossover between the two cultures, the one exception being young programmers who have a lot of money and want to get laid. The drug of choice for Transformationals is LSD and DMT. For Plur, it is MDMA with a side of GHB.

I don't know how kids fall into the rave culture, I know it starts young, usually early teens. I think adderall may have a lot to do with it, popping prescribed pills that make you feel good when you were still a kid, took the stigma out of taking the much more potent pills that make you feel even better as an adult. I can only imagine an insecure teenager taking E for the first time, having their insecurities drowned out by serotonin and dopamine, becoming confident and social, talking to the opposite sex, kissing the opposite sex. Pretty much being the exact opposite of what a teenager is. It must be transformational before you even knew what transformational is.

It's no wonder this became a significant culture. A cash-cow fed by methylenedioxy-methamphetamine. What would a world look like if everyone treated everyone the way they did when they were rolling balls? It would look like this. It would look like EDC.

Whether through the introspection and world changing concepts of the "Transformationals," or the overtly sexual energy of the "Plurs," the festival goers spent between ten and twenty bucks on their pills, and the event planners then charged between 200 and 400 bucks to make that pill more effective. It was another derivative of the fraud economy that was taking over the world.

I WAS LAYING on the track that encircled the festival. The Las Vegas Speedway they called it. I thought about the racecars that drove on this track. I wished they were here now, circling all of us in their giant metal behemoths. Driving hundreds of miles per hour. I smelled the leftover oil from their engines. I swear I could still feel the heat coming off of their tires. My leg was vibrating. I wish it would vibrate forever, but it only came in fifteen-second spurts. It had been at least a minute since the last one, and I wondered if the feeling would ever return. It did, but again, only lasted a few seconds. I then remembered there was this technology, someone could send you a message of 160 characters from their handheld personal computer device. This message would fly up into a local signaling tower, then send itself to some switching station that may be hundreds of miles away, maybe even in space. It would then somehow find your own handheld personal computing device and cause it to vibrate. This was to let you know, you had a message waiting for you.

I pulled out my phone and looked at the last two

texts. They were from Raygun. "We just go through security," followed by, "Holy fucking shit!! Are you here!! What the fuck is this place!"

She was with her boyfriend Jasper. This was her festival, the first taste of this life. Up until this point, I had only experienced festivals with those from within the scene, but Jasper and Raygun were friends from the default world. My two lives were starting to intermingle. This was an uncomfortable place for me, I like to compartmentalize my experiences.

I texted back, "where are you?"

"Giant male and female bathroom signs, near entrance."

"How will I find you?" I replied.

"Look for the totem," she texted.

"I haven't been putting the time down." I replied.

"It doesn't matter they are working." We always timestamp our texts at festivals due to poor service.

"What the hell is a totem anyway? 3:14am" I texted.

"Big green sign, Jasper will be shaking it and dancing. 3:15am" She replied.

I looked up to the sky and saw that giant daisy from before, but now it must have been twelve stories up. It took me a second to realize it had been moving, but so slowly that you would never notice. I don't know why, but it reminded me of a mime I once saw. life works like sometimes doesn't it?

A giant green sign that read, "Help! I've lost my tiger

Hobbes," was dancing in the air above the crowd of people near the restroom entrance. I had seen these signs, or totems before, but it wasn't until this very moment that I realized their dual use. You could make a statement, while making it easier for friends to find you.

I ran up to Raygun and Jasper and gave them a strong hug, pointing at the sign as I squeezed them tight. "That right there is a game changer! This green dancing beacon tells me that I will never be alone again."

"What the hell is this place!" Raygun was in a sort of shock, her mouth was open as she looked upon this thing that she didn't know could exist. "Just, what is it?!?!" She yelled. I think she was also rolling.

"What's up buddy?" Jasper said. He had one of those friendly voices that was always welcoming. "So I hear we fucked up by not sharing rooms with you." He was wearing a panda hoodie, he wasn't the only one, it was a popular choice at EDC.

"Who cares," I said.

"Did you get our schedule?" He asked. I couldn't imagine having a schedule for a festival, but Jasper and Raygun had actual DJ's they were here to see. They had real plans, you know, like the type of people that make an agenda for Disneyland.

"Yea, I got it," I said.

"Anyone you are looking forward too?"

"I could give a fuck, all sounds the same to me," I said.

"You have to look at it like classical music," he said, " to someone who doesn't like classical music, it all sounds the same, it's boring. But when you get an ear for it, you can recognize the subtle changes, how a DJ forms the emotion and energy of the crowd, and the crowd becomes a single unit, they create a tribe."

Bullshit I thought.

I WAS TRYING to dance in the back of Circuit Grounds when I saw a look of fear come across a young girl's face as she stared at her phone. She grabbed her partner and they began to run away, weird. Circuit Grounds was a giant, partly enclosed stage at the far end of the festival. The music was tolerable, but I still had no clue how to dance to it. While watching my fellow dancers, I saw the look of dread come across another festival goers face as he broke out into a sprint. Then it began to happen all around me. It was like they had been warned of a nuclear missile launch and only had ten minutes to get out of town. I looked to Jasper, thinking he may know what to make of this, only to see he was also in a state of fear.

"Shit! I lost track of time." He said as he grabbed Raygun and pulled her away, he then turned back to me, "Come on!! We have to get to Cosmic Meadows!"

We ran across the Las Vegas Speedway on our way to see Knife Party, an EDM group who played music that sounded like every other EDM group, except it was louder and more obnoxious. I didn't know much about Knife Party, but the one thing I did know, was that people who liked Knife Party, really liked Knife Party.

As we began to near the stage, Raygun pulled back from Jasper, "it's too much, it's too much."

Jasper scanned the the grassy field that gave Cosmic Meadow its name and saw a patch of bamboo in the far corner, "There!" he pointed to a small elevated dance floor just outside the main stage. Close enough to see and feel the action, but not so close as to be, "too much."

I looked at Raygun and thought that Ecstasy should probably be called "Innocence." Raygun was now a child being protected by her man. She was peeking, the point where the drug becomes its strongest, and she needed someone to keep her away from, "too much."

"Does this work for you?" Jasper asked as he pulled Raygun into the bamboo.

"Yes, this is very good," she said.

I looked down to my phone and saw a dozen missed calls from Cheshire. I quickly texted him back, "where are you?"

"Jive Joint," he replied.

I had seen the Jive Joint when we had first walked in, I stood up on the dance floor and looked towards the entrance, it was less than 100 yards from our position.

Another text came from Cheshire, "I'm not doing good." followed by, "CB2 or something, don't think it was, everything weird." I had never even seen Cheshire take a sip of beer and now he was tripping out on the designer hallucinogen 2CB? "Puppy here too. She is dressed like a cat," he texted. Cheshire had been dating Puppy since just before Romney. She was a beautiful young Chinese girl. Vibrant with multiple hobbies and interests. The last thing you want when you are on a major rebound.

I texted, "Let me take care of you brother. We at the bamboo, it's quiet and safe here."

"I'm on my way," he replied, followed by, "I don't see you."

I looked to my left, Cheshire was standing maybe six feet away, staring forward. I grabbed him by the arm. He looked confused.

"I feel like I walked far, really far, but really fast." He said. He didn't look me in the eye.

"You're not far. Where's Puppy?" I asked.

"I thought it was safer this way," he said. "I lost Puppy's molly. She's going to kill me."

"I think it will be okay," I replied.

"I'm having anxiety, I don't know what to do."

"Let's go find Puppy." I said.

"She's so fucking hot. She is all dressed up. Everyone keeps hitting on her. Why does she have to be so fucking hot and awesome? Why can't she be hot and not awesome?" He said.

"Let's worry about it later." I said.

I introduced Cheshire to Jasper and Raygun, but the mixture of Knife Party, MDMA, 2CB and everything else, made this an uneventful moment. I was disappointed that some of my favorite people didn't realize they had all just met a bunch of amazing other people.

"We need to find Puppy. Time no longer works" Cheshire said.

"It's only been a few minutes," I said.

He grabbed my shirt and looked me in the eye, "How do you really know?"

We walked towards the Jive Joint and I scanned the crowd looking for a small Asian chick dressed up as a glowing white cat, realizing this would be an easy task anywhere else on the planet. Cheshire began to walk up to different girls, touching their faces while quietly asking, "Pup?"

After determining that only one of the three girls dressed as glowing white cats around the Jive Joint was of Asian descent, I used my deductive reasoning skills to conclude that it must be his Puppy.

"Puppy?" I said while I kneeled next to her.

She looked up from the grass and began to purr. "I don't know you," Then she planted her face into the crotch of some guy sitting indian style next to her.

Cheshire saw this and kneeled next to me. He pushed his face up to hers, "Puppy??" She clawed him a few times, he clawed her back. Cheshire looked up to me, "I think it might be her."

"Do you know this girl?" The man whose crotch she nestled in said.

"Maybe." I replied.

Cheshire continued to inspect the human cat. She was Asian, dressed like a cat, high on something, she seemed to recognize him. "Purrr purrr?" He said.

"Purrrrrr," she answered.

He looked at me again, "I'm pretty sure it is her."

"Thank God, she got some fucking issues," said the man, "What is she on? And do you have any more?"

"I'm all out," Cheshire said, "thank you for protecting her." Cheshire then licked the man on the face and cuddled up next to his Puppy. They pawed and purred at each other. A couple made in heaven, and I knew it would never last.

Chapter Twenty:

The End of Honesty

Three nights merged into one. They did not seem like separate chapters. It was more like watching your favorite movie over and over again. EDC was fun, it was a ride, you don't get off of a rollercoaster and ask yourself what you learned. You just feel it.

There were only a few hours left, and I wanted to make it to the main stage to find some friends. A Kandi Raver walked up beside me and joined me on my mission.

I looked over to her, "I like your wings," I said.

"I'm a fairy," the Kandi replied. Notice it is spelled Kandi with a K and an I, not with a C and a Y. I had just learned this, I don't know why it is spelled this way, maybe it's because Kandi Ravers still have a touch of annoying adolescence left in them.

"Do you live in the stars?" I asked.

"No I live in the clouds, actually the second cloud to the right."

"Oh not the second star and straight on to morning? Like most fairies?" I replied.

To an outsider, this conversation may seem silly. However, when both of us are rolling on E, you just go with it. Understand, we know none of this makes sense, it's not supposed to. It's small talk, we feel the words roll of our tongues, and vibrate against our lips. We don't have to explain ourselves. If you think this is obnoxious, just remember back to the last time you flirted with someone you had a mutual connection with. Your words did not have to be logical. You were just playing and laughing, and it felt good. It's okay to play.

"I can actually, if you take the ladder from my house you can climb up to the stars," she said.

"Oh that's awesome, so you get to live in the clouds, but can visit the stars whenever you want?" it was so exciting, I wished I could live in the stars.

"Yea, you should come, you are welcome anytime, I like to have people at my fairy house!"

"I want to see your fairy house, but I like the stars a lot."

"I'll show you the way. The ladder is hard to find, but it is there, just hidden behind some of the white mist that splashes off my cloud. I promise, it's super beautiful, the colors up there are so vibrant against the white."

"Do you have a boyfriend?" I asked.

"Yea, I'm super in love with him, he never comes up to the fairy house though."

"That's okay, you have to respect everyone's process," I replied.

"I know that, and he knows that too and that's why I am super in love with him." And then she disappeared, but I hoped to see her again.

A lot of people hate Kandi Ravers; they are pretty much the exact opposite of what a Burner is, and maybe this is why. Kandis are young and naive. They use ecstasy to search for meaning in the same way a Burner would use LSD. They have not grown up and are trying to figure out how. Burners have already gone through the realities of life and are trying to become young again. I don't know where or when Kandi ravers and Burners cross, but I have to imagine one may turn into the other, just as adolescence becomes adult or "Night You" has to wake up to "Morning You."

A MAN WEARING a suit that would be more appropriate at a Versailles tea party stood upon the stage before me. "We are all headliners," he was lip-syncing to a booming voice that beamed through the speakers above the main stage.

It was over-the-top theatrics, which felt very appropriate at this festival. "We are all one," he said. Fireworks launched into the sky and lasers shot through the audience. The entire dance floor took on a sheen of green and purple.

Maybe I should have started at EDC. It was topical and fun. It allowed you to experience all these emotions in a controlled, comfortable setting. The world of the Transformations was rough and trying, this was nothing but puppies, fireworks and cleavage. I was having a blast.

"We are going to change everything!" The man took off his hat and bowed to the audience.

This is the future, a medicated future of play and

debauchery. We were changing the world, but would we like what we changed into?

We are all headliners. That is what EDC was built around, that is what EDC stood for. This was our place. This speedway in the middle of the desert was our home, our planet. People came for the music, but they stayed for the community. This is what it feels like to be surrounded by four hundred thousand people who have zero judgment in their hearts. People who love and respect you for who you are, unconditionally. The power of drugs and music. It's no wonder people confuse this place for Utopia.

Insomniac Events could teach us all a lesson. Every city, state and neighborhood can learn something from this spectacle. They care, and it shows. They genuinely care about what they are doing, and the result is palpable. In this world of "get rich quick" and "if it feels good do it," they put the people and music first. Maybe that's all it takes, giving a shit.

I MADE A mission to find some friends. They were somewhere near center stage, holding a totem with a giant dolphin pinned on the top. My phone had been buzzing for the past twenty minutes, yelling at me to come find them.

"YOU CAN NOT MISS IT!!!!!" The last text read.

I already passed three different giant dolphins totems. I imagined groups of people all over the world having a similar conversation.

"What would no one ever think to put on top of a

totem?"

"A dolphin?"

"That's perfect!!!"

I turned around and saw yet a fourth Dolphin totem. It was not them.

"WTF DUDE?!?!? Where are you? Just look for the dolphin!" Yet another text came in.

I looked over the crowd in search of yet a fifth dolphin totem, when everything went quiet and dark. The DJ stopped playing. The lights went out. It was just us, the giant owls, that giant daisy, and that booming voice who had been our constant friend for the past three days.

"Las Vegas... Insomniac... Welcome to the magical hour of EDC 2014." A slow ethereal lead synth began to play underneath his voice. "Together, underneath the electric sky."

I am not a spiritual person, but in this moment, I could not help but believe in God. We all knew what this message meant, it would be the last set of the festival.

"We are the children of generation now! We are connected! We are all equal! We are free!"

People began to cry, and then hug, strangers embracing strangers. This was it. They had waited an entire year for this weekend. Some had waited their entire lives. They had all made it through this together, and now it was about to end. The music became angelic, the harmony rose in tempo and pitch as the lights behind the DJ booth lit up to reveal the silhouette of the final performer.

"This is it. This is the moment we celebrate the ending." The audience was not quiet, but they were calm. Then the announcer said one last thing.

"We are E.D.C!" Dash Berlin began to play and this giant tribe of human beings started to move in unison. It was the merging of two contradictory feelings, joy and sorrow. A giant display of dichotomy right in front of me. I had to leave. I had to get out. I had to finish this experience with Raygun and Jasper by my side. Cheshire and Puppy were back in Vegas, the Mermaid was nowhere to be found. I was again alone, but this time I would end in the company of friends.

I ran down the speedway, looking for the Cosmic Meadows, looking for my friends, running up behind them and hugging them as they squeezed me back. We jumped and sang to the last minutes of the last set. The DJ's seemed to be as excited as we were. They kept thanking us for making their dream of playing EDC come true. We were all headliners.

The sun rose. The stars disappeared. "Thank you so much, you will never know what this means to us!!! I can't believe we just played EDC!!!! Thank you!!!!" They were holding back tears as the mics went silent, and the power shut down. In an instant, it was over.

For three nights, in the middle of the desert, in the middle of the summer, EDC is the most honest place in the world. This cannot be life. But life can sometimes be this.

Part V

The Edge of The World

It's that in between time when you are neither awake nor asleep. Not the moment when you are trying to fall asleep, when you can't determine what is real and what is fantasy. This is a third state. You are in a trance, but you are completely aware of that trance. Your thoughts and ideas feel like they are coming from somewhere else. As if a spirit is hovering above you, giving you both the process and outcome of something that has yet to be created. You close your eyes. Images and sounds become reality. You are possessed.

That is what happened, the music continued to play. It had been a week since EDC, and the music was still in my head. I had hated Electronic Dance Music, and now I loved it. It was all I listened to. Whenever I closed my eyes, it was there, it was as real as if it were coming from my headphones. Songs I had never heard before, sounds that I did not know existed. It was beautiful.

Then the music stopped, and I had nothing to show for it. I didn't know how to write it down, I didn't know how to play it. It disappeared as quickly as it had come. I was given a gift, and I gave nothing back.

Chapter Twenty-One:

Life After EDC

"The internet fucked everything up didn't it?" I had just met this man, but he was pretty much the most interesting person I had ever talked to in my life, or maybe it was just the bumps of cocaine he was feeding me. "I don't mean video games, or even the news, it could be social networks. It's okay to keep up with the Jones if you live in a neighborhood of twenty people, but six billion? No one can compete with that? One winner out of all of humanity? And he probably got there because he was some rich kid."

I was at an illegal cocaine club in a high-rise above downtown Los Angeles. Whatever you are imagining, is exactly what it looked like.

"Hell, I could move out of my neighborhood and I doubt anyone would even notice. We used to have welcoming parties for anyone new to the street. Now when someone moves out, it is like a weight is lifted off my shoulders. I made it through those years without having to get to really know them."

Everyone is friends with the guy who has blow. A security guard started walking my way. I was sitting on the floor and I thought he was coming over to yell at me, then I realized, I was at an illegal cocaine club in a high rise above downtown Los Angeles.

"We don't know how to create anything anymore, we

look at the shadow of community and just mimic that."

In the corner was a giant black man with a woman on each arm. They looked like hookers. The man was wearing a vest, top hat and striped black pants. This was the club's dealer. These people really existed.

"Sometimes you have to embrace the suck," I said, hoping to be rewarded with another bump.

"What's that supposed to mean?" He replied.

"A marine told it to me while hiking, sometimes life sucks, but if you embrace the suck, it's part of the experience."

"I like that," he offered me another bump, I guess I had done well.

When hanging out with people who are deep into the drug culture, you quickly realize you can never know who they truly are. Their personalities change so drastically from night to day that you have to accept that someone who is your best friend one moment may not give a fuck about you the next. For all I knew, this man I was snorting coke with, worked in middle management at some local bank. You never ask. It's just part of this life.

I DON'T KNOW when it happened, but I was now in. I had been exploring the outer edges of the festival life, but now everything I did revolved around this culture. I was still an outsider, but I was an outsider from within. I was accepted by the community.

The Uber driver dropped me off in an alley just

outside of Venice. "What is this place?" The driver asked.

"It's an illegal club." I replied.

"Those exist??"

"This is Los Angeles, everything exists if you know how to look."

The Burner's were taking the warehouse parties to the next level and erecting illegal clubs throughout the city, they were burner friendly, drug friendly and served liquor until sunrise. The music and performances at these clubs rivaled anything Vegas could create. I had to give the hippies their due. They were monetizing their lifestyles.

I walked into the warehouse and looked up to the half dressed lady swinging across the ceiling on a Lira, a word I hadn't even known a few months ago. It's this hoop that is tied to the roof by a series of silks so people can do circus like performances on it.

Elache was tonight's DJ. Little Heart had started spinning, and was quickly gaining a following. I looked at her. She never looked happier, maybe she finally found her place in this world. Lasers swept over the crowd as four beautiful women danced on the stage. Everyone in the audience wore a costume; tonight's theme was Alice in Wonderland inspired. I don't know when this became my life, but I couldn't think of a better life to have.

I walked towards the smoking area when I was stopped by a familiar face. "Oh my gosh!!" a lady ran up to me and hugged me, "I haven't seen you in forever, how have you been?"

I knew her from Romney, I forgot her name, but recognized her, "How are you?" I said.

"I've been doing so great, I graduated the leadership program and I'm now taking the advanced leadership program. Everything I ever wanted is now possible."

She believed she was on her way to having her dream, and I thought for a moment, that's actually as good as the real thing.

I walked past a pair of fire spinners and spotted Cheshire hanging out with a random Asian girl. I guess him and Puppy broke up again. "I don't think I have met you before?" I gave her my hand and introduced myself.

Cheshire hugged me and began kissing my cheek, then whispered in my ear, "thank you so much for not doing what all my friends do and insist they have met my generic Asian date before." He then meowed and pawed at my face.

My cocaine high was wearing off, and there is nothing worse than losing that feeling of euphoria. It's not that the new feeling is bad, it's just the previous feeling was so good that you can't imagine going on without it. I still had no clue how to buy drugs, friends always provided me with mine. So I did what any self-respecting man would do when he needed some blow.

"Boy I sure could use some cocaine right now!" I said in an obnoxiously loud voice, and just like that, a random guy from the crowd turned to me, he came up by my side and pulled out a bag of yay. I guess finding a dealer was easier than I thought. "How much?" I asked. He looked at me like a child would, so I rephrased it, "what are you charging for your yay?" I said.

"Bro, you don't need to pay me, we're all friends here." God bless him, the only thing a coke fiend likes more than coke, is sharing their coke with others.

"What's your name?" I asked

"Rashconicov," he said, "just call me Rash." A man in a long trench coat, lined with orange LED lights, came up beside him. "This is Dimitri," Rash said.

"Good to meet you," Dimitri said while he pulled out his keys to take a bump. The three of us proceeded to talk non-stop for the next two hours, a normal night for three guys and a bag of blow. What was not normal is we continued to talk even as the cocaine high wore off.

A bit later, two more people joined us. It was Dostoyevsky and Nabes. I saw Dos off and on through my festival life. I remembered the awkward exchange we had at LiB when I was feeling very alone. It felt like a year ago, in reality, it had been less than a month. Sometimes friendship is just about timing.

Dos hugged Rash and Dimitri. They were old friends, the type you don't see in Los Angeles. He then came up to me, "Cheshire told me you work in Tech?" He said.

"Yea, I run a startup, I used to work in film," I answered.

"I do too," he said.

"Film or tech?"

"Used to work in film, now tech."

"Nice."

"What did you do?" He asked.

"Kinda have the classic story," I said, "started as a PA, slowly worked my way up, was a department head, then second, then AD and on to producing and directing."

"Why tech?" He said.

"I guess because I actually am trying to make a difference now." I said.

"Sorry, have you met Nabes," He pulled his wife against his body.

"Hello," She said in a thick Spanish accent. I knew their story. They had met in Argentina, fell in love, got married within a couple of months. Dos saw something he wanted and went for it. A trait I respect in a man. Doing everything with conviction, fuck all if you fail.

"How are you," I asked her," you know we met briefly at LiB."

"Oh, sorry," she said, "I don't remember meeting you." Damn she was cute.

The five of us continued to talk business and the changing landscape of the startup scene in Los Angeles. Dos believed the festivals were affecting the tech world in ways, which would transform everything. Three months ago, this would have sounded insane to me, but now, I was thinking he might be right.

"This is the best thing going on in LA isn't it?" I asked.

"I think it is, it's been going on for awhile, but it's different now, I think the seeds are about to sprout." He told me.

"It's funny," Dimitri said, "even now, almost no one knows about these parties, these people, what we are creating."

The sun rose, and the four of us continued our conversation on a hike up to the Hollywood sign. I finally went to bed at about 2pm, with texts from them all telling me what a pleasure it was. I referred to them as the Russian Mafia. And just like that, I was their friend.

Chapter Twenty-Two:

The Facilitator Economy

With the Russian Mafia by my side, I went head deep into the illegal warehouse party scene. Cheshire brought me into the culture of EDM, populated by the tech rich, who could afford the hundred-dollar tickets and thousand-dollar tables, and it was Wolfgang and Avalon who continued to introduce me to the mindset of the Transformationals.

I ENTERED THE small mansion off the boardwalk of Venice Beach and was instantly turned off by the energy I felt in the house. It reminded me of Romney, or a multi level marketing event. The living room was taped off to keep the attendees out. I stepped over the barrier and walked through, figuring it was the safest place to stash my motorcycle helmet and gear. I pulled a book off the counter, the cover was a picture of our host standing in front of a sailboat with his hands held out wide, visually replicating the "this could all be yours" look. The title read, "How to market yourself in ten easy steps." As I flipped through its pages, I wondered why so many of these kind of books had bad cover photos. He was either an idiot or a genius. One part of me thought, well if a guy wearing a bad suit that has no clue how to photoshop a picture can become rich, so can I! The other part of me thought he was self-selecting his marks.

I left the room and walked into the study where a couple dozen chairs were placed. I saw Wolfgang and Avalon in the corner. I ran up behind Wolfgang, kissing him on the cheek, an Introduction I learned from Cheshire, it was both a great ice breaker and an alpha move at the same time. I bowed to Avalon and made small talk with her. Our friendship had been slowly growing, and I respected her more by the day. It was that true type of respect, where you listen, even when completely disagree. She had started giving talks around the city on the medical benefits of doing psychedelic drugs. These drugs are powerful and can be dangerous. But I had seen benefits in the people who used them in controlled circumstances. Life-changing benefits that I could not ignore.

We took our seats and the man from the cover of book now stood before us, he began to speak, "I was taking my annual sabbatical on the mountainsides of the Andes, high above Peru, when my journey began." I held back every urge to stand up and leave that instant. "On our way out we diverted our route and found ourselves within a small village inside the Amazonian Rainforest. There I met a shaman who shared a drink called ayahuasca with me. How many people in here have tried ayahuasca?"

Almost every hand in the room went up, and I thought, I must have been in the only room in the United States where I was the odd man out. "Okay, for the three of you who have not tried ayahuasca, it is a liquid form of DMT." Let me stop for a second, DMT is coming, and it is coming strong. We don't know much about this drug except that it is already inside of us. It is released in our body twice, when we are born, and when we die, and if that doesn't make you curious about something, nothing will. I think whatever LSD was to the generation of the 70's, may be what DMT is to our generation.

"Ayahuasca is used by the Amazonian people for many of their rituals, and it may hold the key to everything that is the universe..." He stopped for a moment at this hyperbole, looked towards the audience, "Am I exaggerating?" No one who had tried it, disagreed. "I saw truth for the first time. I was transformed." Big words I thought. "Now, I come from a scientific background. I know that DMT occurs naturally in mammals, so I wanted to search out a way I could have this same experience without the aid of a foreign substance. Then I learned about psychedelic breathing."

His assistant began to pass around facemasks as he explained the basics of the exercise. To breath with our diaphragm as strong and as hard as we could, something I was familiar with from my choirboy days as a child. He turned on his stereo, which began to play a guided mediation. We placed on our masks as the voice instructed us to breath harder. The voice became louder as music erupted from every corner of the room. The room was now dark, and we were all there was, this music, this voice and the sounds of our breathing.

After five minutes, my lungs froze with that cold

sensation of pain that overtakes a muscle when it needs a break. If this is what a psychedelic felt like, then I hoped to never have the feeling again. People began to wail and cry in the room. Yelling and grunting. I tried my best not to judge their experience, but I did not succeed. These fools, trying to find meaning where there was none. However, I did not give up. I kept pushing my lungs to the brink. I never give up, I always fight, why do I always fight? I thought about my life, and how I got into this room, hyperventilating with a bunch of rich kid hippies. Was this it? Life? What all these people didn't understand, all these people looking for their dream, is that they had already failed. Just by saying "I want my dream," means you have failed. This is who you are. If this is not your dream, you have failed.

By age 9, I was going into math competitions and winning without trying. I looked around at the people in those rooms and hoped I would never become them. They were boring, I didn't want that life that was handed to me. So I rebelled and went as far away from it as I could. I became a jock. I was a runt with a bad heart, but I worked non-stop until I made varsity. I was always the worst player on the team, the slowest runner in track, yet I kept fighting for that life I was never meant to have. I hated myself for failing. I went from being extremely good at something, to extremely bad at something. Why didn't I take the easy way? Why didn't I take the low hanging fruit?

I think of those DJ's performing in front of hundreds

of thousands of people. They were probably math nerds who understood patterns so well they could create songs that make us dance. Outside of that booth, they are nothing, probably afraid to ask someone on a date. To be as good as they are, they had to dedicate their lives to that one thing. They can't have their dream, it is impossible to have both. My dreams as a child, my dreams as a teenager, my dreams as an adult, they are all different. They contradict each other.

The music stopped, all I could hear was the breathing. It was like finishing a run, slowing down your oxygen intake, becoming normal again. I pulled off my mask and looked around, I didn't recognize the emotions people were experiencing. They seemed tired and alive at the same time.

"Who would like to share?" The host asked. A dozen hands went into the air. Of course, they did.

The first girl didn't even wait to get called on, "I was flying through the sky, then dolphins came to my side and began to guide me, and I saw an angel and the angel and I started to talk." Person, after person, after person, shared their psychedelic transformation. They couldn't wait to sign up for his classes. Me? I experienced nothing. Even in this room, I was the weirdo.

Thirty minutes later our teacher ended the class, "Thank you so much for letting me share this experience with you," he said. "Earlier, I used the word shaman. Some people say priest, or coach, or trainer. But the actual practitioners of this technique call themselves facilitators. They are helping you to facilitate the power you already have within you."

My mouth opened wide. He said the word I had been searching for this entire time. This was not the fraud economy, it was the facilitator economy. And in an instant, I understood it all, I was in on the great secret. I saw it everywhere and I finally understood it exactly. It reminded me of something a business coach once told me, "the gold miners didn't get rich, it was the people who sold the gold miners their shovels."

"OKAY, WHAT THE fuck was that shit?" I was walking down the Venice boardwalk with Avalon and Wolfgang.

"What do you mean?" Wolfgang asked.

"All we were doing was hyperventilating, there is no way everyone had those experience." I said.

"You didn't feel anything?" He said.

"No, nothing, other than a burning sensation in my lungs."

Avalon had been walking silently, staring at the shop owners pulling down the metal grates as homeless people began to set up their tents. There is no place on the world where rich and poor live as close together as they do in Venice. "You've never done acid before have you?" She said.

"No,"

"Shrooms?" She asked.

"Nope."

"That's why," she explained.

"What do you mean that's why? Why would doing acid allow me to hallucinate by breathing hard?"

"It's a few things, first, we started by setting our intention, we created an intention to what our experience would be. Then, we already knew what a psychedelic trip was, so our intention could mimic this trip."

"Aren't you a scientist? This sounds like magic."

"I'm not, I promise. Drugs can open up things that you didn't know were there. Okay, a simple example. You hear a song, and it does nothing for you. But then you see its amazing music video, and you now love the song as part of the full experience. You don't even have the ability to separate them."

"Don't smells bring back memories for you?" Wolfgang asked.

"Yeah," I said.

"It's similar, it's not the same, but it is similar."

"You've been learning how to cook right?" Avalon asked.

"I've been doing a new recipe a week." I said.

"And when you eat now, you can taste things that you couldn't taste before right?" It was true, my brain could separate the different flavors, it made them more robust. "You had to learn how to cook in order to do that." She said.

"That actually makes sense," I said.

"I wish you didn't have to put the word actually in there," she replied.

"You know, since I did E, I look at lights different, I don't know how to explain it, but when I see Christmas lights, I feel like I know their secret."

"Now you are understanding, it's about expanding your mind. But not everyone is open to it," We came to the area where the boardwalk turns to sand, where the houses go from a million dollars, to multiple millions. We all looked down that strip of land, knowing that it meant nothing and everything at the same time. "You need to do Molly too." Avalon said.

"That's just pure MDMA right," I knew the answer, but sometimes you ask questions you know the answer to, I don't know why.

"Yea, I think you'd go deep, your different."

"I don't know about that."

Wolfgang spoke up, "You're on a mission, it's admirable."

I was a bit embarrassed by this compliment. It was a high compliment coming from these two. "Thank you." I said.

"You have to do LSD soon," he said.

"It scares me."

"Just set your intention, go in with a positive attitude, and if it gets dark always go back to that intention. LSD can be really powerful. You might just find what you are searching for."

"I've been told that a lot lately, it hasn't happened," I said.

"Keep fighting," Avalon said. I began to laugh, one of those uncomfortable laughs that reminds you that all humor comes from pain. "What is it?" She asked.

"Trust me, I won't stop fighting, I never do," she smiled and I couldn't help but think how all of these people had come into my life at this perfect time.

Chapter Twenty-Three:

You Have a Good Life

"I dated this girl once, we were so happy, we would just lay on the couch all night watching movies. Love is the most powerful drug ever." I told Raygun as the cold air pushed against my overheating body. We were sitting on the back patio of a sleazy rave club in Hollywood. It was totally plur here, not a Transformational in sight. "Then, after about four months, I realized this is all we did. I was that guy who never went out. So I started forcing us to do stuff, we went to shows, we traveled. She was a horrible traveler, we would fight all the time, she always wanted the nicest hotel rooms and the best restaurants. We were never as happy as we were on that couch. Then we broke up."

"That's sad," Raygun said. She was rolling hard.

"I need to go on a trip, I need to get out of here, something doesn't feel right," I said. "I know some people hiking Yosemite, I think I'll meet up with them. Then maybe I'll go to Seattle and catch up with a friend."

"You have a good life," she said as she caressed some sort of furry bear thing.

"I don't think I do. I don't know. I can feel this battle happening in my body," I said, "It's like this man, he's older than me, but I think he is me, he's cutting away at the weeds, they are trying to overtake him, bring him down. Once those weeds succeed, I wonder what will happen to him? Should he just let them? Let the plant infect his soul until it is over? Until it runs out of food and dies? Or should he keep fighting? What if that makes it worse? What if they never go away? Have I ever talked to you about this before?"

"I'm pretty confused right now, so I don't think so," She said. Cheshire had passed me a pure molly about an hour earlier, I hadn't realized it was hitting me till now. No wonder I was going to the dark places.

"That's funny, I'm getting better about talking about it," I said, "but I forget sometimes." He had told me the pill had triple the normal dosage. If zero fucks have ever been given about telling someone the most intimate aspects of your life, that zero fuck time was now. "It's funny, what I normally feel with light and music is what I am feeling right now with words, it's really funny, it's like touch, like when someone you love hugs you, but with words, every word is like love rolling off my tongue. I just want to keep talking. I have never told you about this before?"

"Yeah, I don't know what you are talking about, you're really confusing me" Raygun said as she continued to play with her toy.

"I'm talking about when I threw away 13 years of my life. I think maybe I have been making up for it. It was only about a year ago that I was engaged. And now I am single." I said.

"Are you talking about your ex?" Raygun asked.

"No, that's nothing, I'm glad I had that girl, I wish I

would have dated her when I was 23, I wouldn't be so behind now." I said.

"Behind? How are you behind? You are one of the most successful people I know."

"I'm getting better about talking about it. it's funny, right now I want to talk about it." I said. "It's very funny, I don't talk to my family about it. I feel like I need to have this conversation. He was just a dumb kid who liked a girl."

"Who?" Raygun asked.

"That person. He was thirteen. He was a pussy. He never asked her out. He didn't even know how. So he just let it sit there. He stayed depressed for a month, then two, then a year, then 13 years. He threw away thirteen years. He was so good at hiding it. He still doesn't know how to show it. He would want to die, and laugh about it, and people thought he was joking. But he wanted to die."

"Holy shit," she said. She understood enough.

"Yea it's funny, this feels really interesting, the way these words pulsate my lips, it's like they are sweet tarts rolling on my tongue. I think I am about to go into a bad down, I haven't had one in awhile. I think I am going into one. I feel like I am fighting it off. I'm really worried it's going to be really big. I don't ever want to go there again. I don't think I could survive this one."

Cheshire came up next to us, he was totally sober, still learning his lesson from EDC. "What's going on guys." But his cadence was weirder than normal, he probably did take some Adderall.

"We're talking really personal things that I am sure I would not be talking about if I was not rolling," I told him. "This stuff you gave me is really funny Cheshire."

"It's good?" He asked.

"It's funny, it's really funny."

"What are you guys talking about?"

"My struggle with depression." I said.

He wasn't taken off guard by this answer, but his voice became more understanding. "Do you still struggle with this?"

"Yea, of course, it's part of who I am, but I know how to manage it now." I said.

"Is this like undiagnosed depression?" he asked, "or is it diagnosed?"

"Oh no, if you are familiar with it, I have something called Type Two." I replied.

Cheshire's face dropped, he knew exactly what I was talking about. He didn't have it, he had something, People like us it's a given. "That's tough," he said.

"What does "that's tough" mean?" Raygun asked.

"It's the type of depression with the highest percentage of suicide, it's like getting dealt the worst card." Cheshire told her.

"What no!" Raygun screamed as she hugged her furry bear thing.

"I'm sorry," I said. "One out of seven, isn't that insane? One out of seven people with Type-Two kill themselves."

"One out of seven?!" Raygun started to tear up and then I realized how much I was hurting her.

"I'm still here, I'm still fighting." I said.

"What do you take?" Cheshire asked.

"I don't take meds?" I told him.

"Why not?"

"Well at first, it was because I didn't want anyone to know. But now, when I see my friends take them, they lose their edge. I'm not a hero though, I hate when people say that."

"But they help, you'll be happier."

"When that's all that matters, then I'll give up."

"I don't get it," Cheshire said.

"No one does, but I do, and it's important to me." I changed my voice, acted happy, tried to make them know it was alright, "look, I am very functional, I went from being suicidal for maybe 9 months a year, to being severely depressed for at most 3 months a year."

"That's still a lot!" Raygun said.

"Yea, but it's a fight. like I'm always fighting, I have to be very aware of it. People try to cure me and it pisses me off."

"Most people don't feel like they have to fight to be happy." Cheshire said.

"I don't really understand what that means, I don't know any different."

"You have a good life," Cheshire said.

"You know, people always say what doesn't kill you

makes you stronger. I think they're wrong, I think it might maim you for life," I said.

"Seriously dude, you have a really good life," he said it again.

"What have I ever done?"

"People light up when they are around you," he said.

"I've succeeded at shit," I said.

"You know I created my first game at sixteen," Cheshire said. "It was a blockbuster, millions and millions of people played it, it became one of the most successful sharewares in history. So what? You and me are here doing the same exact shit. You've done so much."

"You created something, I've done nothing." I said.

"What are you talking about? You made movies, you've put on shows, you have helped artists get jobs. You're everywhere."

"Nothing that was all that successful."

"So what? Creators create, that's what we do. Successful or not, whether we get paid, whether people steal it from us. Whether people love it or hate it. Doesn't matter, we keep on creating because we don't know how to do any different. Maybe we're idiots. You build. You keep creating. You keep giving, maybe you get rich, maybe you cut off your ear and go insane while people get rich off you. But you sit down, and you have to get up because you have to build. What else are you going to do? Sit here and mope. That's not you, you can't help yourself, we can't help ourselves. It's just what we do." And then he said it again.

"You have a good life."

I don't know if I felt better or worse. The molly was making me think about stuff I never knew was there. None of it made sense. "You know what?" I said, "We have been out here a really long time and it's cold, and we're all rolling on molly, except for you Cheshire, but I think you are high on Adderall. I can hear the DJ inside and he is doing that wood bouncy sound that makes me want to move my feet and shake my hands in the air as if it was the most amazing thing a human being has ever created, and actually, I think it probably is the most amazing thing a human being has ever created, and we're just ignoring it, we're out here, instead of in there."

I got up and walked towards the door, "You have a good life," Cheshire said. I turned around and looked at him, those caring eyes of his. "Dude, you have a really good life." He said it one last time

Day One - Tuolumne Meadows

Whenever I am feeling worthless, I tell myself "I am feeling worthless because I am worthless."

This brings me to motorcycles, to turn right on a motorcycle you have to turn left. To someone who doesn't ride, everything about this seems absurd. How can pushing the opposite direction turn you in the right way? Here's the truth. You have no control of the 500-pound bike at 50 mph, there is no way you could ever turn it. By moving those handle bars in the opposite direction, you are looking the bike in the eye and saying, "I know I can't beat you." Your body pushes against the bars, causing your hips to shift. It pushes the bike down causing it to lean into the very direction you want to go.

By accepting a negative feeling, by saying " Hey friend, thanks for visiting me today." You are putting it in a place you can understand. Enemies make us defensive, make us stupid, friends make us comfortable.

When I am feeling worthless, I tell myself, "I am feeling worthless, because I am worthless." And that leads to, "so what can I do not to feel worthless?" By treating a negative feeling as a friend, you are not accepting it. You are understanding it.

I WAS SOMEWHERE on the edge of Mulholland drive when I decided to go on this trip. People who have never lived in Los Angeles think of the city as Hollywood, the beach, and Malibu. But if you have been here long, you know she is defined by her mountains. The Angeles Crest which keeps the marine layer from dissolving into the desert, giving us that Mediterranean climate. The smaller mountains which divide this city into two, and The Hills, that reincarnation of Mount Olympus. People come to Los Angeles and move to the Valley's in hopes of achieving their fantasies, always knowing those hills are watching them. The lucky few will attain their dreams and become the Gods who live on the mountains. We can feel them looking down on us, looking down on the world they now control. This strange city only exists because of those who manifested their mental absurdities. It's no wonder it attracts a certain type.

I jumped on my motorbike and headed towards the Sierra's, I was going to meet up with a few backcountry hikers in Yosemite. I would start here, then off to a Burner party in the middle of the desert, up the coast to some hippie retreat, all the way to Whidbey Island on the Puget Sound, where I would try to be still and quiet, away from booze and drugs and music and costumes.

"You have a really good life," continued to ring in my ear.

WE SANG ALONG with Ranger Eric as we sat around one of those half circle bench things made from old tree trunks. I was now at the Tuolumne Meadows campground in the backcountry of this great national park. Ranger Eric had walked up to each camper he saw, and invited them to this great circle of fire for stories and song. Much like EDC was the most American thing in the middle of Las Vegas, this is the most American thing inside of Yosemite. People from all over the world, singing campfire songs about our great wilderness. I look at a Japanese family and wonder what they are thinking, this all must seem so foreign and weird to them. The funhouse mirror version of what Americans feel like when they go to a tea ceremony in Kyoto.

The ranger told us the story of the Clark's Nutcracker, a bird that has changed the very landscape of Yosemite. These birds always hide their seeds in groups of threes and fives. They often lose track of where their seeds are, causing groups of trees to pop up throughout the forest in these odd numbers. The Clark's Nutcracker species also hides seeds in higher elevation than most other birds, burying them above the tree line, among the granite slabs, where they normally would not root. This gives protection to the animals who reside high on top of these cliffs. This is mother nature and evolution at work. Animals changing their surroundings to fit their needs.

Then his tone turned harsh and ominous, as he began to talk about man's introduction of fish into the alpine lakes and how we were destroying the natural ecology of the park. I looked around at everyone nodding in agreement, at the blight humans are to our planet, and I couldn't help but wonder why they weren't pissed off at the stupid Nutcracker bird.

What birds do is natural, what humans do is not natural? Human's are either special, or we are not. If we are special, then we are unnatural and everything he says, might be true. But if we are not special, if we are just another animal on this planet, then anything we do is natural. We are either part of nature, or we are not. I think maybe we are just another animal, and the only thing that makes us special, is feeling we are not.

I READ ONCE that the human mind can only comprehend 150 other people on this planet. We can only have 150 personal relationships. We can only imagine that 150 other people have the same goals, needs, wants, and emotions, as we do. The reason being, for most of human history, people could not survive in groups larger than 150. Then we invented farming, and that forced us to create sewage, and electricity, and central air. But there's something else about this, something I never hear discussed. Within a group of 150 people, you are important. Whether you succeed or you fail, you are important. Your failure may bring the entire tribe down, your success could be the one thing that saves everyone you know. It is impossible to be worthless within that world.

Here, in this camp, there is no Internet, there isn't even a phone, it's just you, nature and your fellow travellers. This is the entire world. I do a quick head count. Probably 150 people. Every person here matters.

Day Two - Lunch on Devil's Dance Floor

Our small group of adventurers already did eleven miles on the day, aided by our three hundred dollar Gore-Tex hiking boots and synthetic down jackets. This world could not exist without those on the outside. It makes me wonder what the purpose of this trip is. To clear my mind? Appreciate society more? How much more exciting would it be if we were in search of a new hunting ground? Or a passage to the sea? We are not built to live in this world we made, but we were made to build this world.

We took our lunch on the Devil's Dance Floor, a slab of rock on the southern edge of the canyon. There was a round piece of iron plunged into the granite below our feet. It was a geological survey marker placed here when the first map of the area was scouted. This old chunk of iron had defaced our sacred ground, yet everyone here found it to be beautiful. We touched it, took pictures of it, and thought of the people who pounded it into the rock nearly a hundred years ago, back before anyone knew a safe passage to the southern rim existed.

I think a lot of people assume that if you are an environmentalist, you hate humankind, when we just hate crap. We hate plastic knickknacks that clutter our world. We love actual human creations that are meaningful. We love this slab of metal, because we know what it stood for, just as much as we love rocket ships and innovative engineering.

We believe humans have a responsibility to live up to the examples of this earth. We have a responsibility that when we destroy nature, we make something great out of it. We love the environment because we know humankind would be worthless without it. It's not that different from the world the festivals are trying to create. Happiness first, meaning last. Always living in the now, not focusing on past or future. Think of that organic coffee shop that just opened in your neighborhood. The one that respects their workers and supports its local community. The one that has art on the walls created by people in your city, and whose employees look like they actually want to be there. This culture created that. This is the festival ethos. It's changing the world.

Day Two Night- Sometimes life does not change at the margins

One moment you are looking over the top of Yosemite falls, down a 2000-foot granite cliff, water droplets splashing against your skin. The next moment you are looking death in the face, laughing about the way you are going to die.

I had summited El Capitan earlier in the day, also the lesser known, but more beautiful Eagle Mountain. I looked at Yosemite Valley from its highest perch and It brought me to tears.

I ended the day at the top of Yosemite falls. We were to make the trek home in the morning. The ground was granite, there were only three trees at our campsite, they had no right being here, up above the tree line. I set up my hammock, I laid down in it, I looked up at the blue sky, I wanted to fall asleep, but I knew I still had to make dinner, force calories into my starving body.

Then the hammock began to stretch. I could feel my back touching the shrubs just above the rocky ground. My whole body landed softly. I heard a sound, it was a vicious and loud sound, the sound of atoms ripping apart. I knew that sound. When I was a kid, I took a blowtorch to a ball bearing, I wanted the marbles inside of it, steelies we called them. The iron turned a deep red, almost translucent, it looked like candy. I doused it in ice water, and the metal broke apart, it was the sound I was now hearing. It was the tree. The tree was ripping apart. The tree is coming towards me, I had seen it since the beginning, but my brain could not process a 30-foot tree that weighed thousands of pounds breaking in half just from the weight of my body. The straps that held my hammock up were pulling it right towards my face. I had maybe 2 seconds, a lot of time I thought.

I swung my shoulders so that I would roll right, roll away from the tree that would kill me, but I could not move. I am in a hammock, the hammock has wrapped around me. I am tied up in my hammock, and this tree is headed right towards me. I will die.

"This is how I am going to die?" I thought, "A tree? Of all the dumbass, crazy shit I have done in my life, this fucking tree is going to kill me?" And as that tree came down towards my face, I had four distinct thoughts, the last four thoughts of my life. The first was just that.

"This fucking tree, this is how I am going to die?"

About an hour earlier we came to our camp. I saw those three trees. They were shaped like an L. My friend had set up her hammock on two of the trees, and because of the shape I could set up my hammock, using one of her trees and the tree that had yet to be touched. After she set up, she realized that her hammock was too taught, she asked me if I had any extra carabiners, I did, I had two. And these were not normal carabiners, these were top of the line, 5000-pound carabiners. The best carabiners money could buy, not the cheapo ones people usually set hammocks up with.

She readjusted her bed for the night, it seemed fine. She decided not to test it out. She thanked me, then asked. "Why do you have two extra carabiners?"

The second thought I had was regret, not the type of regret you hear about in movies and bad daytime television. I didn't wish that I spent more time with my family, I didn't think I should have been a better man, or lived a fuller life. No my regret was sharp and specific. I wished I had created more. I wished I had worked harder. I wished I had left more behind for my fellow man.

"I am more than I have become, and soon I will be forgotten."

A month prior to this excursion, I was at an outdoor store. I was on my way to my ballet class. Lightning in a Bottle was that weekend and I needed to buy a new tent and hammock. While I stood in line, waiting to pay, it occurred to me that the hammock probably came with those cheapo plastic carabiners. Something about having this crap be part of my gear bothered me. There was no need for better carabiners, good carabiners are expensive, but plastic carabiners seemed improper.

I asked the checkout person where they sold carabiners and he pointed me towards the climbing section. I looked down the rack and found them, carabiners ranked for 5000 pounds. The best money could buy. I reached over the desk to grab two, and just as I did, I was yelled at.

"Sir! I will be with you in a second."

"I just need these," I answered back.

"Sir, give me one minute."

The carabiners were technically behind the counter, but they were right there, and the employee was talking to another customer. I was already cutting my class close, I shouldn't have even come to this store. The class was five minutes away and it was about to start, I hate being late, I can't stand being late. I felt my anxiety rise, I lost my cool, I grabbed for the carabiners again.

"Sir, please!" He raised his voice. I wanted to punch him.

I listened to their conversation. It was the stupidest conversation I had ever heard in my entire life. The lady was asking about climbing gear, she had no clue what she was talking about, she wasn't a hiker, she was not going to buy anything, I could tell this in two seconds, yet the conversation went on and on. I looked at my clock, it had been 10 minutes, it had been ten fucking minutes.

The third thought was complete and utter acceptance of death. I was at peace. I was now going to die.

"The other side will be interesting, or not interesting at all."

Finally, the attendant came up to me. "Can I help you." I think he hated me as much as I hated him.

"Yes, can I get two carabiners?" He grabbed two carabiners, and can you believe it? Two of the same color. I know I am not alone in this, I like all my carabiners to be different colors. "Actually, I know this is weird," I said, "but could I get two different colored ones."

He pulled the carabiners back, grabbed a five pack and handed them to me. "Here, these are all different colors."

I didn't need five carabiners, I needed two. Carabiners are expensive. A box of five carabiners was 80 dollars. 80 dollars! I was late for class, I hated this guy, I didn't want to spend 80 dollars, but I did, I think for no other reason than that I didn't want to see his face any longer. Because of that asshole I had three extra carabiners, three carabiners ranked for the best climbers in the world. Three useless carabiners, two of which, my friend borrowed to make her hammock more comfortable for sleeping.

I was trapped, I could not move, that giant tree coming towards my face, I had accepted death. Then, at the very last moment, it veered right. It veered to the very place I had tried to roll just one second earlier. My friend's Hammock had saved me, each side had two carabiners, one of hers, one of mine, each of hers had snapped instantly, my two carabiners were not even damaged. The smallest corner of one hers held to the corner of my hammock strap like a baby might grab onto its mother's thumb. Those heavy-duty carabiners had saved my life.

I went into shock, I was shaking, someone held me. I got up, I pushed the tree, it would not budge, it was thousands and thousands of pounds. It was now as permanent as the rock. I should have been dead, except for that asshole who sold me the extra carabiners.

I told everyone my fourth thought, "You will never know what joy is, until you see a tree veer away from your face at the last second." We laughed, we ate. It was a complete lie.

Fuck this earth and mother nature, human life is special. I don't care what anyone thinks or says. What we do, does matter. It's not just about running around and having fun. There is something more, God knows I have no clue what it is, but there has to be. My dead body had to have meant something. A fucking hammock, I was killed by a hammock. Life can go in a blink. It has to mean something.

My fourth thought, just as I realized I was going to live, just as I saw that tree veer away from my face. Utter disappointment. It was the worst heartbreak I had ever experienced, the biggest defeat I had ever known. I had lost the state championship, my college application was rejected, my wife told me she no longer loved me. I am not proud of my forth thought. I don't know if it is the thought you would have. I hope not. It was not a good feeling. I had just come to terms with death, only to have it torn away from me, like that tree was torn apart.

"I accept my fate, but my fate does not accept me."

Chapter Twenty-Four:

Day Five - I have my pants on

"Only Guests are Welcome!"

It's funny the things we notice and the reason we notice them. I saw a path across the desert brush, a building that looked like an old horse stable. A sign read that only guests were welcome. I should have been ecstatic about that sign, instead I felt like I was trespassing, that I was going to get in trouble. I turned back and tried to find my way home.

I DON'T KNOW why I was headed to this party in the middle of the desert. This whole trip was about taking a break from the life. Maybe that's why my bike broke down, the Universe was trying to tell me something. Telling me this was a mistake. I guess the Universe doesn't know me very well.

I was riding up a dirt road in the middle of the Central Valley, about to make a blind turn when I lost all power. I was nearly killed just four days ago by that stupid tree and now here I was in the middle of nowhere, just me and the stars and my dead motorcycle. Maybe the Universe did know me.

I had been working on the bike for over an hour when my shadow reached out from the ground and grew in size.

A vehicle was approaching from behind me, its headlights taking the mystery out of the darkness.

I stood and looked into the passenger's window as it rolled down. Three young women were inside. "I don't suppose you guys are part of the pantless thing?" I asked.

"I don't think so," the girl driving said as she smiled.

"Sorry, I don't know how else to ask." I said. The only thing I knew about this party out in the middle of the desert was that no pants were allowed, the invite said it was a good icebreaker.

"I am curious," she smiled again, "Can we help you? You need a ride?"

I was stuck at the worst possible place to be on this road, if I left my bike here, someone would crash into it, it was nearly invisible from the opposite direction. But I was also ten miles from civilization deep into the night, if I didn't take this ride, I'd be out here for a long time.

"I don't want to leave my bike, I'll figure something out." I said. They hesitated, but finally left me alone, giving me their number, in case I needed anything. Not that there was any reception here.

It had been about forty minutes since the girls had left me. I decided to try and back my bike down the steep hill, and into a small gulch where it would be safe. Ten grueling minutes of wrestling with my bike while trying not to drop it finally led to success. I wiped my hand against my scalp and felt the dust scrape against that sticky wet stuff that is human sweat. It always feels like a job well done. I walked through the desert brush, looking for a place I could set up camp. I'd be spending the night here, might as well be comfortable.

Car lights appeared behind the turn. They blinded me as I blocked my face with my hand. The truck pulled up, windows rolled down, the girls were back. "I'm sorry," the driver said, "we can't leave you here. Get the fuck in." I did the math. They had driven twenty minutes discussing my plight, then turned around to save my ass. These were good people. I grabbed my gear and jumped into the back of the truck. It was the only good decision I would make over the next 48 hours.

YOU HAD TO give it to the Burners, even here, in a crappy campground, they threw a killer party. They erected a full kitchen and bar, yoga tent, cuddle puddle, DJ booth, and a raging fire that everyone was dancing around. For a second I wondered how they learned to make a place like this, then I remember, Burning Man was a blank canvass in the desert as well.

I spotted Little Heart, she ran up to me and gave me a hug. "Take off your pants!" She yelled.

"I'm sorry," I said as I unbuckled my jeans, "I just got here." The two of us stood there and stared at each other, then realized we had nothing to talk about. For the place she held in my heart, we couldn't seem to communicate. Maybe we didn't have anything in common, some friendships are just like that. Or maybe it was because she was cute, and I was afraid of falling in love with her.

There was a sexual energy in the air. A couple of girls gave me hungry eyes, but they all seemed to have boyfriends, and I have never learned the proper way to ask whether someone was in an open relationship without looking creepy. Then again, I had a strict policy of no in-group dating unless I knew it was going to be serious. I like group dynamics, and realized at a young age, you get one or the other. It's the reason why all my pickup artist friends find themselves constantly alone or only friends with other pickup artists.

I sat down next to a girl by the fire. We smiled and watched everyone dance. The dancers began dry humping each other as they mimicked a clothed orgy. I thought about how much fun my old high school friends had before they discovered alcohol. Then how they couldn't have fun without it. Drugs were like that. Sex was too.

"What's everyone on?" I asked the girl.

"Oh, I don't think anyone did drugs today," she said, "We just passed around a little acid." If this answer confuses you, imagine someone asking you if you drank today, only to reply, "No, I just had a beer."

"Is there any left?" I asked the girl.

"We're a bunch of Burners, what do you think?" She reached into her purse and passed me a tab.

DUN CHIKKA DUN dun. Dun chikka dun dun. Dun chikka dun dun dun.

The drums were beating. They weren't coming from anywhere. They were just there. I guess my life now had a soundtrack. Dun chikka dun dun. Dun chikka dun dun. Dun chikka dun dun dun.

So I am lying in a hammock. The laser lights are shining on the distant trees. The wind is blowing their branches. I notice how each branch moves with the wind, both separately and together. I can see the wind. I can see the entire structure at work. I've always had an engineering brain, but now it is very clear, how this entire ecosystem came about. How the wind forced the trees to grow their branches in certain places to get the most sun.

The wind blowing against me, the hammock moving side to side, that soothing rocking feeling. I think I'd rather be in the South Pacific right now, no not now, in the 1950's. So I am, because why not? I swing back and forth, listen to crashing waves, smell the sea salt and think I would rather be high up on the cliff, not on the edge, but a few feet down on the side of the cliff. So now I am on the side of the cliff a mile above the ocean, swinging back and forth in the hammock. Because why not?

It is very comfortable here, so high up, if I roll off, I will fall and die. Heights have always calmed me. Being on the precipice of life has always made sense to me.

I feel a pen in my pocket. I wonder how long it has been there. I pull it out, look at it and wonder what a writer feels like. So I make myself a writer, some sort of famous poet who lived in the South Pacific. I now know how this feels, how to be this. Because why not?

The brain has some tricks. I now control these tricks. You dress the part, you became what you wear. We carry a moleskin notebook so we can feel like a writer. Wear hiking boots to feel like an adventurer. It's all a facade to trick the brain, but the whole world is a facade anyway, so why not control it?

I look down at the trees. I see a treeman peek out from the forest. He waves at me, so I wave back. He then does the most obnoxious dance I have ever seen. I give him a thumbs up, he waves good-bye, and walks back into the shadows. He was awesome. I had never seen a treeman give less fucks, but then again, I had never seen a treeman before.

Little Heart leaned up against my hammock, "We're going to meditate in the tent, wanna join?" I was back at the Burner party. I looked back to the trees, they were dancing to the music.

"Sure, where?" I think this is what I said. The one thing I had no control of was my speech. I could not talk or think in words. I could only think in music and pictures. I remember this experiment once, these scientist wanted to prove that senses did not exist, the brain just allocated information in different ways. They proved this by making a guy see out of his tongue. Which is kinda weird. But I could feel my brain doing this now. It was crossing the circuits, sound was confused with sight.

We were in the tent, Little Heart was looking super

cute, but mostly I was staring at the topless mermaid swimming behind her. The tent was underwater, and the canvas was made of glass. We meditated and I never lost focus, even though the mermaid did everything in her power to make me do so. Then it ended.

"How was your experience?" Little Heart asked me.

"Can we talk about the fucking mermaid?" I wanted to say, but instead just replied, "it was fun."

The tent was about to manifest itself in Tibet, and I didn't want to go there, so I walked through the door, and was now at the Burner party again. I knew about this. When you walk through a door, your brain resets itself. That's all this was, it was just more apparent now. Here, I can manifest my own reality, but it was just firing synapses and chemicals in my brain. Everything was malleable. No wonder this made people more spiritual. It was like a bunch of rich kids believing in Divine Right. They just changed the term to manifestation.

I looked over to a painting that Little Heart had been working on. I had seen this type of psychedelic art before but never really had seen it. I guess paintings now moved, and they were thick, they had layers, each layer was its own individual plane of existence. She created a portal into her soul.

Two trees waved at me in the distance. I decided to walk towards them. I passed a bush, and three purple ladies were hiding within it, or maybe they were the bush. They were very pretty, they had purple skin and hair made of leaves.

The world was now 2-d, it was very sad. The stars were no longer far, I could take scissors and rip through the universe. I was all there was. It was very sad. We are all on our own journey, we are not in this together. It was very sad. Evolution depends on us being together, and we no longer are. It was very sad. But shouldn't that mean that both evolution and happiness are connected. That happiness must cause our species to spread? Almost all animals have gone extinct, maybe we were going extinct ourselves. Why do humans hate themselves so much? Why do they think they are the blight?

I thought about alien worlds in the movies, they always lived one with their environment. Their cities looked like they had grown out of the ground. But wouldn't they think the same of us? Would our skyscrapers look that much different from our trees? Is suburban sprawl that different from a forest? Is an anthill or beaver damn natural, while freeways are blight? Maybe we are too far removed from the outcome to understand the process.

I was living completely and totally in the now, my past did not matter, my future had not yet been created. It was pathetic and useless. I live on the shoulders of giants. Everything I was doing, only existed because of those who had come before.

The effects of the drug were evening out. I walked down a small path that led to a hot spring. It was about a two-mile walk, exactly what I needed. I had an air of confidence within me. I don't know why, but I started to have a feeling that everything would be okay, that I was close to finding my answer... An answer I didn't even know I was looking for.

IT WAS HARD to remember if your eyes were open or closed. You know when you start to dream? It was like that. I closed my eyes and stared at the back of their lids. Nothing, no pictures, no hallucinations. I guess the effects were now gone. I had been looking at the stars for hours. They were playing me a movie, then a sort of photo presentation like back in grade school, but now they were just stars again.

The sun was coming up. It would be hot soon, and I was wearing a down jacket. I had to get back to camp. It had been an interesting week, molly followed by the greatest therapy session I had ever had with two dear friends, followed by the beauty of Yosemite and cheating death. And now I was here, in the middle of the desert. I had to figure out how to get my bike fixed.

I started my hike back to camp, I looked at my phone to time the mileage, you always time mileage, it's one of the best methods to know where you are going. In these conditions, I was a 20-minute per mile hiker, 40 minutes tops back to camp. But my phone was dead, so it didn't matter.

As I hiked towards camp, Everything looked different, I cursed myself for not doing my normal turnarounds on the way down so as to look for markers. But no worries, it was an easy hike, and I would run into the camp soon enough.

After what felt like half an hour, I hit a small summit on a hill, This allowed me to see at least a mile in front of me, the trail seemed to go on forever. I should be able to see the camp by now, I thought. So I turned around and looked where I had come from. That's when I saw it. The trail I was on was traversed by dozens of other trails. They all looked exactly the same, I could be on any of these, I could be completely and totally off course and would never even know it.

I did not panic. Panic leads to being dumb, I had to keep my smarts. It's easy to get lost in a place like this. There are stories of people being lost for days just a mile from the highway. I scanned the horizon and looked for the highest hill I could find. I worked my way up to it, and saw a small road just a football fields distance away. I crossed the brush and came to an old wooden structure that looked like a horse stable. There was a sign there which read:

"Only Guests are Welcome!"

I stared at that sign. I felt like I would get in trouble for entering. Maybe the people who lived there were asleep and I would wake them, they would see some stranger walking through their yard, I'd probably get shot. And it wasn't like I was lost anyway, I'm an experienced hiker, I'm not stupid. I wasn't lost. I would find my way back on my own, not with anyone's help. So I crossed back over the brush, and continued my journey home.

I was walking back and forth from trail to trail, making the same mistakes over and over again. It was getting hot fast so I wrapped my jacket around my head hoping to protect myself from sunburn. My sweat stuck to that plasticy down lining and rubbed against my skin, it felt gross and awful. Everything looked the same, every hill, every new dirt road. I could wander around here for hours and never make any progress. There was only one smart choice, head down. The hills fell into a small valley where the hot springs must be located. I would hit a stream down there and be able to find my way back on the proper trail. I was sick of the unknown, so I hedged my bets and headed for the known, I headed down the ravine.

It wasn't long before I heard the stream. I was tired, and knowing that my journey was almost over brought me a new strength. I had been such a dumbass. I should be back at camp by now, figuring out what the fuck to do with my bike.

I reached the water but did not drink, water in places like this was infected with bacteria that could make someone incredibly sick, even hospitalize them. I would have to do the final two miles without any new hydration.

I looked up to the mountains which were now on both sides of me. There was a trail that crossed the water, connected by a giant rainbow-colored bridge. This made absolutely no sense. The trail on my side of the hill was going away from me, on the other side, it was going the way I had come. There was no way I could have crossed a giant ravine.

I knew I was near the Pacific Crest Trail, the 2,663-mile trail that may be the most famous hiking route in the world. This giant bridge had to be a major crossing. It had to be the PCT, and the PCT must cross the springs. It would make sense to build the trail that way. So I stayed on my side of the hill, knowing I would run into something soon enough.

The sun kept getting higher, the trail stayed flat, I went miles and it stayed flat, this wasn't right, so I turned around until I hit the bridge again. I looked around. I was making bad choices, and I knew it. What was the smart choice? What would bring me home?

I jumped into the stream and started hiking up it. This water had to be coming from somewhere, it had to hit the hot springs. It was slow going, but I knew I would hit the source, I would hear voices, see someone. I continued on for hours, and then my progress was stopped. In front of me was an impassable waterfall.

Where the hell was I? How did I even get myself into this position, why did I come to this party? What the fuck had I been doing for the past few months of my life? The past few years? Forever!

I wiped my forehead expecting to feel that sticky, moist, sweat, but it was dry. I felt nothing except for the sand on the back of my hand. I had stopped sweating. Holy fuck, I was dehydrating myself. My body had stopped working. I fell to the ground. No sand stuck to my skin. I freaked out and began to scream. "HELP!!!!!" Can anyone hear me!"

I had read stories about people like me. experienced hikers who got lost. I was that idiot who died on an easy trail only to be found months later, torn apart by the coyotes. "Is anyone there!" I yelled again. I contemplated death over yelling. My pride was literally trying to kill me. "Help!!! Can anyone hear me!" I yelled and yelled and yelled. There were no replies, there was no one here to help me.

I sat there breathing, mouth dry, body dizzy. I had to make a decision. I had to do something drastic or this was my life, and then I would die. The hardest thing to do when you are lost is to admit you are lost. Really, truly, admit it. This was no longer about getting home, this was about not dying. I had to be brutally honest with myself.

"Your gear is back at the campground" I said it out loud, "it will probably get stolen." I thought about this, was my life more valuable than my gear? "Your motorcycle is on the side of a dirt road in the middle of the desert. I have no clue how you are going to get it back, it may get wrecked, you may never see it again." My life was worth more than my bike. "You are going to die very soon without water." My life was more important than getting sick from that stream. "This is no longer about anything other than survival," I said, "No, this is about living. If you want to live, you have to make a major change. You got to quit being stupid. You're letting your gear, your bike, your pride, your trip to Seattle hold you back. Fuckling quit it. Quit making excuses, start living for yourself."

I walked over to the stream and filled up my bottle, I gulped down three liters of water. Then I thought about the smart thing to do. There really was only one full proof plan. I knew what direction the closest city was. It was twenty to thirty miles away. I could do that hike. It was a dramatic move. It was scary, but it would assure my life. It would take me days, but I could do it. I would live and have a hell of a story.

I sat there, I thought about it, weighed the alternatives and made the decision. I didn't know if it was the best decision, but I made it with conviction. I would push ahead and walk to the city, who knows where it would lead me.

"MOMMY STOP SPRAYING me!" I heard the voice of a child echoing off the canyon walls. A family playing in the water. I walked down to the stream, and there they were. Five of them. Husband and wife, three kids. Americana and a picnic. I wasn't excited, I did not pick up my pace, there was no sense of relief. I had made my choice hours ago, and I was at peace with it. Maybe I had just turned left to go right.

"Excuse me!" I yelled down to them.

"Hi! How are you?" The mother yelled back.

"I'm trying to find the hot spring, you know where they are?"

"There aren't any hot springs around here," she said.

"What about the ranch?"

"The ranch?" she stopped playing with her kids, "wait, are you talking about the hot springs where all the hippies go naked?"

That sounded like a place Burners would go, "yeah, that's got to be it," I said.

"You came from the ranch? How did you do that, you passed that a long time ago," she said.

"Is this the right trail?" I asked.

"Well sort of, this is the PCT, it crosses the springs, you're on the wrong side of the mountain."

I tried to make sense of this answer, but I couldn't. "Is it past the rainbow bridge?" I asked.

"Yea, way past, just go back that way, about a days hike."

"Do I cross the bridge?" I asked.

"Yea, absolutely, that's the PCT, after that, it's about another four or five miles to the intersection that leads to the springs."

Four or Five miles? I thought. That meant I was at least seven miles off course. I hadn't crossed the ravine, I had gone so far that the entire landscape had changed. I thought about how far seven miles was from my home in Silverlake. This is why the skilled get killed. Only someone who was so sure of himself could be so stupid.

I took a short nap by the water and made the trek back to camp. Five hours later, I was leaving the campground on foot, thumb in the air looking for a ride. As I walked through the gates, it occurred to me, I had never seen what the entrance into the place looked like. I was in the back of the truck, in the middle of the night, when I had arrived, I never even looked up.

So I turned around. Things look a lot different going forward than they do looking back. This place didn't look anything like a campground. It looked like an old horse stable. There was a large sign that read:

"Only Guests Are Welcome!"

You don't dance with the devil, the devil dances with you.

Day Six - Inside a Cheap Motel

It took four hours to guide the tow truck to my motorcycle and another three hundred and fifty dollars to get it towed back to Los Angeles. As soon as I entered my house, I grabbed my keys and jumped into my car. I didn’t even repack my bags. I knew if I didn't leave now, my journey would be over. I drove as far as I could before I fell asleep at some cheap motel on the side of the road. Up until this point, everything had been telling me to stop. How could so much go wrong so fast? There had to be something waiting for me up there in Seattle. There had to be, right?

Chapter Twenty-Five:

Day Seven: The Edge of the World

I sat on a grassy expanse that overlooked the Pacific Ocean with two others guys, a techie and a Transformational. The beginning of a bad joke. We were at some sort of rich person commune near San Francisco. I had planned on spending a few days here, but after everything that happened, I could only stay for a few hours.

The techie pulled out a sewing kit from his bag and began to stitch together a leather holster, it's a common item at the festivals.

"You're into leather making?" The transformational said.

"Been into it since I was a little kid," the techie answered.

"What got you into it?" the transformational asked.

"I don't know, just felt like doing something tactile." Most of the techies I know like to build things with their hands, probably has something to do with writing ones and zeroes all day that disappear into thin air.

"How did you give it that texture?"

"A laser cutter," the techie answered.

"You own a laser cutter?"

"Yeah."

"You live in Berkeley?" The Transformational asked.

"Yeah."

"Can I try it out sometime?"

"Sure, anytime" the techie said, then he smiled, "just tell me how you managed to get two girlfriends."

It's no wonder these two cultures are merging, they compliment each other in every way. The three of us met a couple hours earlier over a conversation about open relationships. The Transformational was in one, and the techie and I wanted to know how he made it work.

"It's easy, you just have to be honest," he said.

"You must know different girls than I hang out with." I said.

"Humans weren't meant to be monogamous," he explained, "you just have to be honest about that with your partners. I am accepting the reality that most marriages end in divorce, we pre-empt that by allowing each other to have multiple partners."

"Are we just talking about sex here? Like freebies?" I asked.

"No, that's a given, I have two different girlfriends, number one and number two, I love them both, they love me."

"There's this quote I like," I said, "love is the condition in which the happiness of another person is essential to your own."

"I don't like it," the techie said.

"Me neither, that's codependence," said the Transformational. "You can't allow someone else to bring you happiness."

"Well no, but sometimes you have to push down on the pedals of your bike, to go up hill. You should not be reliant on someone for your happiness, but you can allow it. One is co-dependent, one is a choice. Parents live for their kids, this is not a bad thing, having someone's back and they having yours is also not a bad thing."

"You can't ignore people's sexual needs," he then said.

"No, but that to is a choice, it's what separates us from the animals. You can turn it off." I said. "When I am single, I go into a bar on the prowl, when I am with someone, I do not go into a bar on the prowl. If you give me the option, I would stay on the prowl, my priorities would stay sexual, instead of trying to build something meaningful."

"Isn't happiness more important?" The Transformational asked.

"There are different types of happiness. Someone digging a ditch may not be happy, but if he is doing it to support his family, he has meaning. The institution of family created our modern world, let our species survive. The family unit is stronger than anything else, even church and government."

"You're right," the transformational said, "that's why you need an entire village to take care of your family. Multiple lovers make life easier, not harder."

"How can that really work? I'm asking. I mean unless you plan on staying in the same city, same neighborhood, keeping similar jobs and lifestyles. You have this huge family. It's hard enough to get a husband and wife to agree on something." I said.

"That's why we have places like this? We are creating a commune." He replied and then added, "Let me ask you something. Is duty more important to you then your happiness?"

I had no reply.

THE TRANSFORMATIONAL WALKED me to my car. I looked over the Pacific and remembered we were at the edge of the world. "What about the other person?" I said.

"You mean the wife?" He asked.

"No, the person who the husband or wife is going after." I said. "The person you are trying to fuck?"

"I don't understand?"

"If I hit on a girl at a bar, she has the general understanding that I am single, that something may come from this, aren't you deceiving that person?"

"We're all adults," he said, "if it comes up, I would never lie, but we all have different morals. Her morals are affecting me just as much as my morals are affecting her."

"We don't live on an island," I said, "our choices, our actions, affect those around us."

"Now you sound like the spiritual one." He said.

"You can't really have any of these conversations without bringing up the God question huh?" I said.

"I call it The Universe," he said.

"Of course you do," I smiled. "I'm just saying, if you make sex meaningless, it will become meaningless."

"Maybe it is meaningless, but in that moment, why would you hold back on that connection you have?"

"You know everyone I know who is in a good relationship, would disagree with everything you say."

"Of course they would, they are in good relationships, most people aren't. Times are changing, something's going on, we all know it, and none of us have answers." He said.

"I agree, I don't know what to do."

"At least you're doing something." He then hugged me, "I love your spirit," he said, "I wish you loved it as well."

"Thank you." I jumped in my car and turned on the engine. I couldn't help but think, Techies use the word "disruption," Transformationals say "transformation," they mean the same thing, utter and complete destruction of our way of life, with no regard to what will be left in its wake. War doesn't come from poverty, it comes from modernization, even if that modernization is in the right direction. I think I would be happy in the world the Transformationals created, but I would also hate it.

Day Ten: Tech Rich on the Side of a Cliff

"You give good directions," Goat said as he walked up the hill towards me, his wife right behind him.

"We missed you at Mount Saint Helens," She said as she ran up to give me a hug.

"Yea sorry, I didn't want to tell you I'd be there and not know if I could make it."

"You would have liked it," Goat said.

"I've been before," I said.

"You know, I used to live down the street from here," Goat's wife remarked, as she stared at the headstone. We were in a large cemetery in the Capitol Hill district of Seattle, standing over the gravesite of Brandon and Bruce Lee.

"I try to make it once a year, I'm gonna hit up Jimi Hendrix's grave on the way back," I said.

"Why do you like him so much?" Goat asked.

"He changed the way we looked at each other," I said.

"The key to immortality is first to live a life worth remembering," his wife read from the text that was etched into the cement bench in front of the graves. "Would you rather be immortal and die at age thirty two or live a long life?"

"I don't think he cares, he's dead," Goat replied.

"You're no fun." She said. It was fun to watch their relationship.

"Read Brandon's," I told her.

She looked at his grave, "God, I can't believe he died at twenty-eight... Because we don't know when we will die, we get to think of life as an inexhaustible well. Yet everything happens a certain number of times, and a very small number, really. How many more times will you remember a certain afternoon of your childhood, some afternoon that's so deeply a part of your being that you can't even conceive of your life without it? Perhaps four or five times more. Perhaps not even that. How many times will you watch the full moon rise? Perhaps twenty. And yet it all seems limitless."

I looked down the hill and saw a few young Asian kids waiting for us to leave. They wanted a chance to pay respects to their hero. "We should go, we're hogging the gravesite," I said, "How far away are we?"

Goat took one last look at the chiseled black and red granite. "It's about a thirty minute drive, I'll text you an address."

"YOU'RE HARD TO travel with," Goat told me as we crossed the Puget Sound by ferry.

"What are you talking about?" I replied, "I'm the most self sufficient traveller in the world." We had been friends since fifth grade so tact was not necessary.

"That's the problem, you suck with plans, we can never plan anything." He said.

"You don't have to worry, I'll take care of myself."

"It doesn't work that way,"

"Plans trap me, I don't know what I will be doing, and then I have to be somewhere." I remarked.

"So you're irresponsible."

"No, if I made plans and broke them, that would be irresponsible. I'm saying you do whatever you want, I'll join or I won't, you don't have to worry."

"Life doesn't work that way ever. We think about you. You don't think there is part of us that hopes you'll show up? We really missed you at St. Helens. You can't just take yourself out of society."

We were headed towards Whidbey Island to visit Goat's in laws. I could see its large cliffs rising out of the ocean in the distance, giant alpine trees jutting out from in between the beautiful, oceanfront houses, teetering over the sea. Human beings are amazing. We can thrive anywhere.

"I know you aren't hurting anyone, you're just not making it easy. It's shitty to the people who care about you to not lay down roots."

"I'm sorry." I said.

"Nothing to be sorry about, you live how ever you want, we'll always love you. I'm just letting you know."

A crackling voice blared through the intercom, "Please return to your cars, we will be docking in five minutes."

"We'll wait for you right past the landing," He gave me a bro hug and walked away.

I looked up to the intercom. It was caked in 40 layers of white paint, protecting it from that salty sea air. That smell, we don't have that smell in Los Angeles even though we are on the ocean as well. Life was so different up here.

WE HAD A family dinner then everyone went to sleep, everyone except for me. I sat outside looking at the giant freighters push through the channel to enter the Puget Sound. I could feel the creation of man all around me.

The desert is defined by its smell, the ocean by its music. The buoys' clanking against their chains, deep foghorns in the distance. Everything is muffled yet sharp. The combination of senses makes something new.

The in-laws won life's lottery. Tech rich Gods living on their mountain while looking down on the ocean and the men who toil to survive. Yet everything about them was so damn normal. They have a bigger house, eat fancier meals, go on more exotic vacations. That's it. Life is not dramatic, we just wish it were. We envy the outcome, but not how they got here. We envy their money, but not what they do with it.

I'm reminded of a young girl who walks up to the greatest violinist who has ever lived, she tells him, "I'd give up my life to play like you."

He replies, "I did."

Maybe I thirst for tribalism, small communities and festivals, because I know, deep in my heart. I wasn't good enough to make it in this modern world.

Day Twelve: On the Side of the Road, Just North of Los Angeles

I was in that all too familiar Mexican standoff with the girl behind the window of the generic fast-food restaurant. She would not hand over my drink, until I gave her the money. I wonder if people not paying for their drinks before they drove off was a real problem?

The tradeoff was complete, so she passed me my change in a paper taco of inconvenience. Receipt folded over the dollar bills, which contained the coins. A balancing act I had performed a thousand times before. I dumped the quarters into my hand, while I placed the bills into my wallet, separating them from the receipt, which I tossed onto the ground to join the rest of the fast food trash that accumulated on my journey. Twenty seconds later, I had my two bean burritos and three regular tacos which I consumed as I drove down the coastal highway looking at the moon rise above the Pacific Ocean.

There was a time that this was the edge of the world, back when only Pangaea existed. The cliffs to my right were on the outer most edges of the giant continent. I was at the most foreign place on this planet, and I felt like an alien.

It was not a good trip. I couldn't last more than one day on that beautiful island with two of my best friends. I left, making them feel uncomfortable. I was running away. Perhaps it was the comedown from the drugs or maybe the near-death experiences. I felt hollow and pointless. Nothing impressed me. Nothing made sense.

I usually travel by highway, but decided to take the interstates, so I could get home faster. It felt like taking a guided tour of Europe, you see everything but experience nothing. Not much different than life in the modern world. We pack our days full of stuff, but never sink our teeth into anything. We want to say we had a lot of experiences, forgetting that value comes from creation.

I drive through the Central Valley, people here work with their hands, growing food, raising animals, never claiming it is anything other than work. Living the dream festival goers claim to care about. But their culture could not be more different. They believe in the institutions of family, of government, and God.

San Francisco is a few hours away. The art and music of Haight Ashbury is still with us, but could only exist because the people on these farms fed the artists. They fed them with money by consuming their records, and the food, grown by their hands. In return, the musicians fed the intellect of the farmers by entertaining them with some of the greatest songs ever created. Songs that came from the experiences of LSD and the other so-called hard drugs.

I am reliant upon people I despise for my way of life. I cannot see a society standing that does not accept this. Yet instead, we boycott companies because they do not align with our political beliefs. We refuse to buy a musician's album because of who they vote for. Vilify a comedian because they say something offensive. We are all isolating ourselves into our little islands. Trying to change the world, not realizing that by changing it, we will destroy it. These two cultures could not exist without each other, yet they both hate what the other stands for. Maybe we don't need to transform each other, maybe we just need to respect and love one another… Fuck, I am a hippie.

"I HAVE TO tell you something, this is crazy," Kane said. I was only a couple of hours away from Los Angeles when my old friend called me. "You remember Scott Sith?"

"Yeah, of course." Scott was Kane's favorite photographer, he always hoped to apprentice under him.

"So I'm at the bank last week, actually inside the bank. I can't remember the last time I had been inside a bank waiting for a teller. The ATM wouldn't read my fucking check. But right in front of me is Scott. So I introduce myself and I pull up some of my pics, and he loves them. It turns out, he rides motorcycles, and always wanted to own a Harley Springer, so we traded bikes for the day, and have been riding all over Malibu. I'm helping him out on a shoot tomorrow."

Kane's parents named him after the Sheriff in the movie High Noon. It was a fitting name for the person he had become. He was one of the most successful people I had ever known. You could drop him in a foreign country, not knowing anything, and three months later he would be dating the prettiest girl in the village, while running an illegal casino. He was fearless and smart. I envied the fuck out of him.

"Look, I know you don't believe this shit, but you know that whole, throw it out to the universe talk? The perception is reality people? I think they're right. I mean, who the fuck does this happen to? But it happens to me all the time. And that's just it, it might take years, but I throw that shit into the universe and it always comes flying back at me. What if the fucking dumbass hippies are right?"

"Et tu Kane? Et tu?" I said.

"What?"

"Sorry, it's Shakespeare."

"Ha, like I would know Shakespeare," he said.

"It's pretty famous," I replied. I couldn't believe he was the one who was preaching this hippie shit to me. No place felt at home. No one felt like my friend. Nothing felt right.

I watched the dark freeway unwind before me. Those yellow stripes gliding past my car. That dark black tar rolling underneath my tires. That soothing white sound. Life was more fun when I thought success was always around the corner. But it made it hurt even more when I turned that corner to find nothing.

I thought about the sheriff from High Noon. At the end of the movie, he threw his badge into the ground and left the town he had just saved. Every American Western is the same movie. A man goes into the wilderness and civilizes it, then hates the place he created. The end of The Searchers finds John Wayne standing at the front door, looking at the family he had just reunited. But he can't find the will to cross the threshold, he turns around, and walks away. I feel like that a lot lately, and I don't think I am alone.

Maybe I didn't fit in this modern world, maybe it was time I turned around and walked away. It was time for my journey to come to an end. I didn't have the time or money, I didn't know how to get there, I didn't have a ticket and It was only two weeks away. But I had to go. It would be a fitting end to whatever it was that I was doing. I was going to Burning Man.

Part VI

Burning Man

WE WERE DRIVING down a creepy highway somewhere in Nevada. Every town we passed seemed to be abandoned, not ghost towns, it was like everyone had just disappeared. Didn't they used to do nuclear tests up here?

"Let's go over the ten principles of Burning Man." Quicksilver said. I had only met this guy two days ago, and now he was trying to preach the ways of The Burn to me? 'How bout we just listen to some fucking music?' I wanted to reply.

"Principle number one," he read from the Burning Man instruction manual, "radical inclusion." Poncho was sitting in the backseat, I had just met him as well, he was a Burning Man virgin like me. "What this means is to be open minded about everyone. Be a friend to everyone. Literally love every human being you see."

We were slowly making our way to that ancient lakebed that the Burners call home. Cheshire and Puppy were two-car lengths ahead of us, and the Russian Mafia was a hundred miles back.

"Number two, gifting. There is no exchange of money at Burning Man, everything is a gift, you don't barter, you give without any expectation of return. Number three, decommodification. This is basically anti-consumerism, we are looking for an experience on The Playa, not material possessions." No, we would be bringing all of our material possessions with us. I must have had two thousand dollars of gear in the car.

"Number four, radical self reliance. Don't be

someone else's problem. Bring water and food and clothes. Know your limits." What a conservative thought for a bunch of hippies.

"Number five, radical self expression. Express yourself in anyway you feel fit as long as you don't harm others. Number six, communal effort. So basically, you must have radical self-reliance while also realizing you live within a community. Take part in activities, take part in art, show respect."

"That's a lot rules for a place that's supposed to be so free," Poncho said what I was thinking.

"It's a state of mind, that's it. Just trust the process for a week," Quicksilver said as he continued, "number seven, civic responsibility, If you build something, make it safe."

"Is there a code book? Who can I sue if I get hurt?" I asked.

"You guys are horrible!" Quicksilver said.

"I'm sorry, it's ridiculous," I said, "rules?"

"No, it's not rules, don't think of them as rules. Number eight, leave no trace. There aren't even trash cans at Black Rock City, what you bring in, you take out."

"Okay, so this is stupid," I said, "You know what would be a better idea? Having fucking trash cans."

"It's so you can actually see the trash you are creating."

"And people abide by this?" I said.

"Yes, very strongly," he said.

"There's no litter at Burning Man?" I said.

"You'll get yelled at for moop," He said

"What is moop?" I asked.

"Matter out of place."

"What the fuck is that?"

"Anything that you bring in and leave is moop. People go on moop patrol, it's more than litter, it's about respecting your home. Even cigarettes, you ash in a tin, you don't ash on the ground, would you ash inside your house? These aren't rules, these are principles. The word moop is a game changer. It is a different way to think. It's not about littering, it's about asking yourself if this matter has a place here. It's about getting rid of all that crap and shit we buy. Asking what actually makes your life, and the world better… These aren't rules."

"Go on," I said.

"Number nine, radical participation, push yourself to try new things. Number ten, immediacy. We spend enough time worrying about the past and future, Burning Man is about living in the experience, being present, not worrying about anything except what you are doing at that very moment." Then he said one last thing. "I wouldn't be here if it weren't for you. I am eternally grateful. I'm so lucky to be going home."

Chapter Twenty-Six:

The Playa Will Provide

This is our time, this is our world. It really feels like that, in this venue, maybe a thousand people, fifty to a hundred dollars a pop, fifteen dollar beers, but most people are drinking five dollar waters - I'll let you determine the reason. A giant chandelier hangs over our heads as we dance to the primal sounds of the electronic dance music, manipulating our emotions as they mix with the booze and drugs in our system.

I stand at the balcony looking down, my dear friend Cheshire hitting on a hot young girl behind me. The audience is mostly Asian, some Persians, a few Indians. These were kids who worked their assess off, had stress and responsibility since age six, now they get to let go. This is their time.

I raise my hands into the air, I can feel the adrenaline that comes from a good DJ set. We jump and dance and scream and laugh as we manifest happiness into the universe. Trust us, we're making a real difference in the world.

It was midnight, I was bored, I had a big festival to go to in the morning, but it didn't start until noon and I needed some debauchery. Cheshire was at a swanky club in Hollywood at a show put on by Insomniac. I figured I could find someone in line with an extra ticket.

The security guards patted me down, and I couldn't help but think of how lawyers had ruined everything. I also still had no explanation for why light gloves were banned everywhere.

I drink a large overpriced beer while I wait for Cheshire's text. He gives me perfect directions to his location. Something he had a knack for.

We meet on the upper balcony. We flirt with young Asian girls. Both of us love meeting new people, it's probably not healthy, always needing that stimulation of new friends. First conversations are easy, it's keeping a conversation going that is hard.

This life is addicting, but when I think about it for too long, I find it pathetic. I don't want to get married, but I don't want to be that creepy sixty-year-old uncle who never had a family. Then a hot young girl begins to kiss me, and I forget whatever I was thinking about.

"Oh shit, I need to figure out how the hell I am getting to Burning Man," I said as I pushed her away.

Cheshire turned to me, "You're going to Burning Man?!"

"Oh shit, yeah," how did I forget to tell him? "I just decided yesterday on the way back from Seattle. How do I get tickets?"

"How was the trip?" He asked.

"It sucked," I said.

"I'll take care of you," he then grabbed me by the hand and pulled me into the middle of the dance floor as if he was in love with me. The bass stopped as the electronic taps became louder. Cheshire looked up into the sky then yelled, "I can't believe you are going to fucking Burning Man!!"

THE CLUB CLOSED, so we drove to an illegal Korean Noribang. I drank myself into a stupor, knowing I would regret it in the morning. Cheshire told me everything I would need to know for The Playa. A few hours later, we found ourselves at Hard Fest, somewhere east of Los Angeles.

It was a forgettable experience except for that moment when a bro pushed me aside from the water line, cutting in front of 20 people so that he could fill up 10 water bottles for he and all his fellow bros. He turned back to all of us, and with a shit eating grin said, "peace, love, unity, respect."

It's because of him, that people with guns, stand on tall wall, to protect our right to party, and dance, and pop pills.

I WAS WALKING around an empty warehouse, assuming I was in the wrong place. It was load day for the Esoteric Outsiders, my new Burning Man camp. We were a large theme camp that planned on building a five-story tree house somewhere in Black Rock City. Fuck if it made any sense to me.

I passive aggressively texted Cheshire, "You helping

out with the load day?" Hoping his response would let me know if I were at the right place.

"Yea, I'll be there in a few hours," he texted back. Damnit!

I had to give it to Cheshire, in only three days, he had managed to get me a ticket to Burning Man and an invite into a major camp.

I slowly paced around this large space, not sure what I should do, when the head of a short cute girl popped it's way through the entrance. "This the Esoterics?" She asked.

"I have no clue," I said.

"Well I can't imagine two of us would have gone to the wrong place," She said as the rest of her body entered the building. She looked like she had stole her outfit from Charlie Chaplin's corpse. "I'm Firestarter."

"I guess we're the idiots for thinking a bunch of Burner's would be on time." I replied, then wondered if I would get to see her naked at the festival.

Over the next few hours, people trickled in, until there were about forty of us. The entire production was about twenty tons, three cube trucks and two steak beds. I watched as a few of the larger men passed the scaffolding to even larger men standing on the stakebed. I watched as another group ratcheted down the main stage into another truck, while yet another group daisy chained the smaller stuff into a cube truck.

This was a more elaborate setup than most Los Angeles clubs, and we weren't even considered a large camp. The logistics that went into this, were as complex as any movie I had ever worked on, and these people were volunteers who had no clue what they were doing.

A mid-sized camp, setting up a 20-ton production, in the middle of the desert. There were about 140 people in my camp. Burning Man had somewhere around 60 thousand in attendance. What was about to happen in the desert? What had I gotten myself into? Everything at Burning Man was made by the campers. How many millions of dollars in services and structures and food and drink and dance and music would be created in Black Rock City? Ten million dollars? One hundred million dollars? More?

The wealthiest members, of the wealthiest country in the world were creating an alternative universe in the shitiest place on the planet. The dry prehistoric lakebed of the Black Rock Desert. If anything sums up the absurdity of humanity in the 21st. century, I was looking at it right here.

"WE'RE PICKING UP supplies, do you need any shrooms or E?" I was caught off guard by the question, I had just gotten back from the hardware store, and supplies meant something terribly different to me. Plus, I had never even met this man.

"No I'm good," I said.

"Thanks again! Just let me know if you need anything at all." Cheshire called me earlier in the day asking if I had room in my vehicle for a friend of his. I didn't, but figured I could make some. Then the friend called and asked if I had room for a friend of his as well. I absolutely did not, but I said yes anyway. I could have never made it this far without the help of strangers, so maybe it was time I helped a stranger myself.

"I'm sorry, tell me your name again," I asked.

"It's Quicksilver, my friend is Poncho."

"See you guys tomorrow." I said.

The logistical nightmare that was setting up the Esoteric Outsiders camp was almost equaled by the logistical nightmare of figuring out what I needed for my first burn. I would be spending seven days in the middle of a place that was always to kill me. One hundred degree afternoons, followed by forty-degree nights. Dust storms of Alkaline silt, made up of million-year-old dead fish and algae that would clog your pores and irritates your throat. No food or water except for that which you brought in. The only thing I was absolutely sure of, was that I would need a lot of costumes.

Chapter Twenty-Seven:

Travelling to the Promised Land

When I was a kid, my parents brought me to this big Broadway play. It was about a French guy who stole a loaf of bread and spent five years in jail for his crime. Actually, I don't remember how long he was in jail, but it was a long time, and I think he had to do hard labor.

When he got out of jail, he couldn't find work, so he ripped off a church, only to get caught again. But this time, a priest had mercy on him, and gave him two silver candlestick holders or something. The thief was so humbled by this act, that he decided to live the rest of his life living up to his potential. Soon, he adopted an orphan and was on the run again for doing something stupid, like not showing his ID to get into a club. A police officer overreacted and chased him all around France. But the now wanted man, made himself a mission. He would give that orphan the life he never had.

Everytime they would enter a new city, the curtains would close in the large amphitheater, and the name of the city was projected onto a typical white screen. Cannes followed by Bastogne, followed by whatever other cities are in France.

Then we had our intermission. I begged my dad to get me a soda and some candy. I got bored so I returned to my seat. Music was playing, the most dramatic music I had ever heard, more dramatic than any DJ set. The curtains were wide open revealing the cityscape. The name of the city was being projected directly on to those buildings. It was hard to read, but that made it that much more powerful. The man and his adopted daughter had come all this way, they had traveled across the country, they had learned, and overcome a lifetime of lessons. Their journey of redemption would end here, in Paris.

That's kinda what going to Burning Man for the first time feels like.

"THE ONLY TIME I ever did mushrooms was at Burning Man." Cheshire said as we loaded up on calories. "I'm with the Spaghetti camp, they tell me to jump on a bike, and I can't, biking was not possible, but they said I could do it, and I don't believe them, but they keep commanding me, and I figure they must know what they are talking about, I mean they are a bunch of drug addicts. So I jump on that bike, and sure enough I have the ability to ride a bike, and I'm like, wow, I can ride a bike."

My meal is 2573 calories. I know this because of the new menu rules that make all restaurants place the exact calorie count on each meal. Pancakes covered in strawberries and whipped cream, doused in butter. It's delicious, I never eat like this, no wonder everyone is so fat.

"So, I am riding around The Playa, just trying to avoid different colors and shapes that I assume are other bikes and human beings. I lose everyone or something. Who the hell knows because I'm on mushrooms, and I am straight edge, so I don't even know what the fuck I am doing when I am drinking beer. But I am all alone in Black Rock City, high as fuck, on shrooms."

Cheshire was at ease. I had never seen him like this, he almost seemed happy. "So I'm starting to come down, or settle in, or whatever they call it. I walk into this tent and It's dark, I see a bike in the middle of it, it's dark but my brain just knows it is a bike. So I jump on it, and begin to pedal. The pedaling lights up the room, it's hooked up to a generator, and it turns on this creepy light. The walls are covered in newspaper articles, you know like a crazy man would have in his apartment. There is this one headline that just touches me, so I keep peddling and stare at it."

"What did it say?" I ask.

"Fuck if I know, but in that moment, it was important." He said.

We are eating at a diner that is inside a casino, which is inside a truck stop. I felt like I was dating the red-headed stepchild of Las Vegas. Sadly, this would be the last semblance of civilization I would have for at least the next week.

Cheshire bit into his fried pancake ball covered in gelatinized sugar as he continued his story. "And as I am peddling people begin walking in, they start talking to me, asking me about my art project, thinking I created this place. But I don't answer, because I can't talk, because, I guess sometimes when you are on shrooms you just can't talk. So I make a facial expression that tries to show them I have no ability to talk in this moment, then continue to peddle. More and more people enter the tent and they are all thanking me for my contribution to The Burn, so I don't know what to do, because I am not allowed to talk. So I just get off the bike and give like a welcoming hand signal."

Cheshire stood up from the table and showed us the signal. The universal two arm movement that says, "Would you like to give it a try?"

"But no one gets on the bike, so I don't know what to do, and now it's dark. So I just get right back on that bike and continue to peddle. Then everyone starts apologizing to me for offending me about my art piece, they are like, "we're sorry, we didn't mean to offend you, we really like your artwork, we are so sorry." And then everyone leaves, and I am there all alone. So I just keep pedaling while I stare at the newspaper article."

We were three hours from Black Rock City. Cheshire and Puppy were going to stay in a hotel for the night, then head into the festival in the morning. But Quicksilver, Poncho and I decided to make a go for it now. I felt like we were crossing into West Berlin under the eye of the secret police. This may be the last time I saw Cheshire and Puppy ever again. He gave me a hug as Puppy waved from the passenger seat.

"See you at home," he said.

I WAS SITTING on the curb while Quicksilver and Poncho rode their bikes around the gas station. They were throwing a Frisbee back and forth. It felt like back when my parents made me head home when the streetlights turned on. I was allowed to play in my front yard, but never more than one house over.

I'd sit on the curb and talk to friends as they rode around in circles in front of me, we'd usually toss a football back and forth. Now I was doing this again, not because I wanted to, not because we were trying to relive some childhood fantasy. No, we were trapped in this parking lot, killing time, wasting time, in the most natural way humans know how to. Play.

We had planned on leaving for The Playa as soon as Cheshire and Puppy left us, but a text from the Russian Mafia told me they were only an hour behind. They had a 31-foot RV, and I thought it would be a good idea to caravan up with them. I knew the line into Black Rock City could be four hours long, and having a place to put our feet up would make the experience a lot more tolerable.

"Welcome Home!!" a passerby yelled as they waved to us. We all waved back.

I could tell Quicksilver and Poncho wished I hadn't made the executive decision, even I wanted to be on the road, but if I had learned anything in the past five months, it was to never take friendship for granted.

"Welcome home!" A young couple ran up and hugged me.

"It's not my home yet," I said.

Then they hugged me even stronger. "A virgin!!!!" They yelled.

"Welcome home," I said. I didn't understand the home thing, I wasn't sure if people were joking or not. They didn't seem to be joking, but to call a place home was so over the top, it felt wrong, like using the lord's name in vain or not respecting your elders. You just don't do that.

I looked at the bicycles strapped to the back of the cars in the parking lot. We were all here for the same reason, we were all in this together.

"How's it looking?" Quicksilver yelled to me.

"Haven't heard from them," I yelled back. Then, like magic, a giant RV pulled off the highway and into the parking lot, heads and hands sticking out the windows. Dimitri jumped before it even stopped, running up to me and hugging me. "We're going home!!!" he said.

As soon as the vehicle came to a complete stop, everyone else joined him, They all hugged me while they jumped in the air.

"This is Quicksilver and Poncho," I said as I signaled them to join us.

"Welcome home!" Nabes yelled to them, followed by one last group hug. Then we went to Burning Man.

WE DROVE DOWN the desert highway at twenty-five miles an hour. We were not even abiding by the proper speed limit plus one rule. We didn't want to give the police any excuse to pull us over. Cops were everywhere, and they knew there were drugs in each vehicle. They would look for any excuse to bring the dogs out. The only crime was getting caught. Why should I be spared? Because I hid my drugs better? Is that the society we want to live in? To the cunning go the spoils, to the dumb jail time and a rap sheet that will stick with you for the rest of your life? Give the man power and he gets to choose who he shall have mercy upon. The prisons must be full of idiots who broke the speed limit.

The fear of the authorities was much greater here than at any other festival I had gone to. I knew by now that almost all the rumors of the cops were untrue. I had never seen anything but kindness from any officer I encountered. As long as you didn't make a scene, or do anything blatantly illegal in front of them, you would be okay. But this was Nevada, the greatest contradiction of a state in all of America. And getting arrested here, didn't mean you would just lose out on a great festival, it would make you miss Burning Man, something you had been looking forward to for at least the past year.

Quicksilver was now driving my car, following the Russian mafia's RV. We turned a corner as the elevation began to rise, making a sort of S shape that allowed us to look back to the road we had just traveled from. That's when we saw it, we were leading a caravan of hundreds upon hundreds of vehicles, as far as the eye could see, headlights shining down onto that dark highway. Thousands of the most law-abiding citizens that have ever driven on any stretch of road anywhere in this country. Hands at ten and two, four-car lengths distance between each, all driving the exact speed limit.

I had hid my stash in a series of beer bottles that I weighed and recapped so as to look like they had never been opened. I thought I was being paranoid, until I learned the Russian Mafia had placed theirs in a sort of anchor they had created out of thick PVC pipe, which they then encased in cement. It would be impossible to ever get to their drugs without the high-powered industrial drill they had stashed in a friend's vehicle, keeping the incriminating evidence away from the only way to find it. You can tell a lot about how much somebody has to lose, by how well they hide their drugs.

I turned to Quicksilver and asked where his stash was. "It's in my shoe at the bottom of my luggage," he said with pride.

Fuck.

I HAVE NO clue where I am, I have no clue where I am going. In this moment, everything is a mystery. The smells are new. The sounds are new. The experience is new. Time moves slowly, the way God intended it to. I am here, surrounded by friends, none of which I knew even five months ago. I am in a car, with two people, I did not know last week. Cheshire was no longer with me. He was at the hotel, probably getting one last clean fuck in with Puppy before they would have to deal with the sexual realities of playa dust. I can hear myself breathing, my heart beating. I notice every sound, every sight, every feeling, and it is all beautiful. I am very happy.

I watched as truck after truck passed us on the other side of the road. Giant cube trucks and stake beds, semi's and vans. All empty. They were coming from The Playa. They had done their duty, providing their services and now would be parked somewhere near Reno.

I started counting as I often do. 1, 2, 3… They continued to drive by, 12, 13, 14… They never ended… 33, 34, 35… How many were there? 79, 80, 81. In Hollywood, we measure productions by the amount of trucks they use. A mega blockbuster would be a forty or fifty truck production. What was Burning Man? A thousand-truck production? A ten-thousand-truck production?

The thought gave me chills. Right now, we were headed to the largest production ever put on in the history of Mankind. The most powerful civilizations in the world could not pull this off, but we were. This was bigger than anything, anyone, had done... ever.

Chapter Twenty-Eight:

Full Circle

It's funny how freedom can make you miserable. We left the highway asphalt and turned onto a vast expanse of dirt. Orange cones were placed to create twelve separate lanes. We had just entered The Playa. I was now on the holy ground for the Transformationals. I could feel the vehicle sink about an inch into that ancient silt. Giant speed limit signs informed us not to go more than ten miles per hour. Quicksilver turned on the radio, and we began listening to a station created just for Black Rock City.

"The current wait time on gate road is four hours," the voice was monotone, eerie, very appropriate. We were driving with dozens of other cars. The silt flung up into the air creating a sort of mist. The smell had a faint aroma of alkaline batteries, the taste was that of metal. For a second, I thought I smelled Creosote, it was my favorite smell in the world. The plant sweats a sort of oily wax, that when wet, was the most beautiful fragrance I could ever imagine. If you have ever been in the desert when it rains, you are familiar with the smell.

I was exhausted. I could feel myself going in and out of sleep. But I was calm, I had no choice. I used to go on road trips with my dad, we would drive through the night, I was powerless yet I felt protected. I would stare out the window, watching the mile markers go by. Falling in and out of sleep. Listening to the sounds of the road beneath me.

We came to a stop. We turned off our car. We were surrounded by vehicles. "They do bulk movements, "I heard Quicksilver tell Poncho, "It's so we can all turn off our cars, the line moves every ten minutes."

I shut my eyes, later I heard the radio on. "Place your car pass on the bottom left of your windshield, if you do this, you win Burning Man."

My dreams were vivid and short. I wasn't even sure if they were dreams anymore. I felt the passenger seat recline, Poncho was now sleeping.

The car started up, we moved twenty feet forward. I looked outside as the entire playa took on a sheen of red, all the brake lights changing the very essence of the place.

I had dreams, many dreams, but they all disappeared. I remember having joy in them, but nothing beyond that. I looked to the right, I saw porta potties. The car turned off again.

I awoke, looked around. To my right were the same set of porta potties, We had been here for a while. I looked at the clock, it was an hour later. We hadn't moved in an hour. This wasn't right. In the distance, a lightning strike, then another. That smell, the feel, I knew this feel, I knew this smell.

"We gotta go," I said, "we have to go."

Poncho didn't move, so I shook him. "What?" He said.

"We have to go now." I said.

"What why?" He was confused, I would be too.

"We got to get out of here." I said.

"I'm good."

"C'mon." I jumped out of the vehicle and opened his door. I pulled him out of the passenger seat and we ran up to the Russian's RV, the door was locked, so I knocked. Dimitri saw me and let us in.

It was a party in here, I was immediately offered blow and booze, "Shhhh," I said. It worked. Even a group of Burners, high on Yay, about to head to the biggest party in the world, shut up when they were shushed.

I listened... Blop, blop, blop.

I knew that sound. The blops became louder and faster until the rain began to pour down. It was a desert rainstorm. Within minutes, the ancient lakebed became alive again. A phoenix arising out of its ashes. The structure of the vehicle shifted, as it sank to the new base level of silt. Had we left five minutes later, we would have been stuck in that car for the night.

"Holy shit," Dos said as he squeezed his face against the window, "this doesn't happen." Everyone was looking outside, seeing the water rise, watching the lightning reflect off its surface.

"What the hell is this?" Dimitir said.

"I grew up in the desert," I said, "this feels like home to me."

You can't manifest your realities, but you can manifest your attitude. It's like that friend of yours who complains about the wait time at an American airport, then talks about the superiority of the slow pace of living, in some third world country. We live the reality we want to live.

Here we were, stuck on gate road, just outside Burning Man with no way to get in. This could be a horrible situation, or this could be an adventure. The choice was up to me.

"Fuck" I said, "We should have stayed at the hotel with Cheshire." I drank myself to sleep.

I WAS PASSED out on the floor. I don't know how long the sun had been up. I could hear voices outside, the porta potty doors slamming shut, beer cans opening, laughter.

I moved to the front passenger seat and saw the destruction. Cars caked in mud, giant footsteps through The Playa. A random Burner was walking towards me. He had plastic bags on his shoes. I remember back when my parents made me wear plastic bags on my shoes so I wouldn't destroy them in the rain.

He signaled for me to roll down my window. "Have you heard?" He asked.

"I don't think so," I said.

"Black Rock City is completely closed, cars are stuck on gate road, the city is a wreck. They're turning people away at The Playa entrance and making them drive back to Reno. If you are in line, you are stuck here, they're not letting anyone in today and you are not allowed to turn back. They don't even think we'll be able to get in tomorrow."

You would think my heart would drop, in two weeks I had gone from not going to Burning Man, to getting a ticket at the last minute. I went from having no clue who I would go with, to having two strangers in my car. I went from having no place to camp, to being invited to one of the most amazing camps on The Playa. It should have been bad news, instead I felt free. I felt free because of my lack of freedom. Freedom had been making me a slave. This was now my Burning Man, whatever this was. This was my festival.

Right then and there I made a decision. Whatever happened, for the next seven days, I would be the single best human being I was capable of. For the next seven days, I would be the kindest person I had ever known, the most confident I had ever been, the most giving, the hardest working, the most adventurous, the most open minded, the most loyal, the most duty-bound person I could possibly be. For seven days, I could be the best reflection of myself. Trapped in this mud, in this line, we would make this the greatest festival Burning Man had ever seen. Fuck Burning Man. This was Waiting Man 2014.

"TIME TO TURN our perception into reality," the DJ told me as he handed over a large worn out speaker. We were unloading his school bus. He had already set up a computer and turntable on the roof, and was now looking for the last of his gear. We weren't the only ones, camps were springing up all along gate road. This place was becoming one giant party.

"Those head south," the DJ pointed to the dark clouds in the distance, "then we are okay. But if they head east, this is our Burning Man."

We had been watching the clouds all morning, listening to their thunder, they were getting closer every hour. The Bureau of Land Management had shut down gate road. They were monitoring the storm minute by minute, not letting anyone into BRC until they were sure the storm would not hit us.

The DJ plugged in his speakers, and they became alive with a loud hum. The cracking ground that was slowly turning back into playa dust began to dance with the vibrations.

"Welcome to Waiting Man 2014," I told him.

He smiled, yelled into the microphone. "Everyone! Listen up! This is Waiting Man Two Thousand and Fourteen!" The crowd erupted, music began to play, they began to dance.

The Playa isn't loved because she is great, she is great because she is loved.

"DON'T YOU FEEL sorry for all those people stuck on the other side of the gate?" I said to a group of bros had set up a barbeque out of their van and were serving free burgers to anyone who sat with them. It took a second for them to get the joke, but as soon as they did, they erupted into laughter.

"I love you!" One of them said, "Who are you?

"They call me the White Suit," I said. I was walking to will call to pick up my tickets, making friends along the way.

"It's totally true, all those assholes in Black Rock have no clue what they are missing in Waiting Man," a bikini clad girl told me as she poured herself a mimosa.

I bowed and continued my journey, spreading the good news that was Waiting Man 2014. This long line of cars stuck in the mud was the greatest thing going on in the world. Sit with that for a moment.

After six hours at Will Call, I finally had my ticket. The sun was setting and Quicksilver and I decided to take a stroll through the desert. We walked half a mile out into that flat expanse of land. It was a strange thing to be able to see so far, it may have been the first time I ever really knew what flat was.

Four or five miles away, was The Man. He looked like a toothpick statue, his hands reaching above his triangular head. Far behind us was the entrance to The Playa, it was now closed, but I could make out the place where the black road turned into playa silt. To my left were those dark clouds, they were hovering above the mountains, making their decision whether to head south, or to fuck our burn. Then we looked to the right, miles and miles of cars stuck on gate road. To my right was everything we would know for the next week, our equipment, our water, our friends.

"It's really beautiful," I said.

"This is a special place, I'm glad to be back home." Quicksilver replied.

We sat down in the sand and talked to anyone who walked by. People joined us, we laughed and sang, we all had an instant connection. I wish people always loved one another this much. "I don't get the home thing," I asked, "is it tongue and cheek?"

"No, what do you mean?" Quicksilver said.

"Why do people call it home?"

"Because it is home," he said.

A slight breeze began to roll over the desert, but it wasn't any type of breeze I had ever felt before. It was a force of energy. I looked towards the road and people were running. Everyone could sense it, this was something different, in the past 60 seconds, something dramatic had changed.

Quicksilver and I looked at each other, stood up, and began to run towards the small plastic fence that separated the desert from the road. Far, in the distance, maybe three miles away, headlights were turning on. This was not a breeze, it was the rumble of thousands and thousands of cars starting their engines. Cars were moving. The cars that had been stuck at Will Call were moving.

"Gate road is open!!!" It was not a lone voice, it was not a yell, it was the sound of hundreds of people saying the same thing, feeling the same thing, laughing and crying together.

We were in that line for twenty-four hours. Waiting Man 2014 was now ending. Burning Man was about to begin.

Chapter Twenty-Nine:

Black Rock City

"Remember, the speed limit is five miles per hour, this is still public land, if you are going one mile over the speed limit, they will pull out the sniffing dogs," we were at the gate. The Black Rock City ranger checked our tickets as his assistant shined a light into our car looking for stowaways. "Don't give them any reason, don't fuck your burn on the first day."

This amount of honesty was overwhelming. There were no pat downs, there was no plausible deniability. They commanded you to obey the law, because they knew exactly why you were here. To do a bunch of illegal shit.

He waved us through the gate and we were now on the long expanse of road that separated the ticket window from the entrance to Black Rock City. We were moving at five miles per hour. Do you have any conception of how slow five miles per hour is? We were going this speed on a long expanse of flat desert at the same place where they test the land speed records. This road was made for accelerations, and I had to hold back every urge within me not to go faster than idle.

To my left were cops sitting in their SUV's. Their flashing lights were like beacon posts of places you did not want to be. Their dogs at the ready, looking for a reason. We did not play music. We did not wave. We definitely did not drink or do drugs. We were all in this together, me and the hundred or so other cars on this road. The mission was simple, make it to the greeter gate without fucking our burn.

A police SUV sped across the road in front of us, picking off an old shitty truck to our right. We watched as the dogs gave a signal allowing the cops to pull the passengers out of their car, and search their possessions. It was like they were culling the weakest of the herd. Only the strong to survive. It reminded me to drive up with my lawyer next year.

The bright white lights of the greeters gate grew larger, I hadn't realized just how far away it was. It was an entire complex. I could feel the anxiety release within me, only to realize my foot was pushing down on the accelerator. I quickly caught myself and slowly pulled into one of the station.

An old lady walked up to us, a smile across her face, it was pure and completely genuine. She looked at me, the way my grandmother would. She looked at me the way all human beings of this planet earth should look at each other. Be kind, we are all fighting a hard battle I thought.

"Welcome home!!!" She said as I rolled down the window, "Do you boys know where you are headed?"

"They do, I have no clue," I said.

"Well you must be the virgin, normally we do our whole thing, but with all the commotion, they are telling us to just pass people through. You should come back, do the ritual tomorrow." I had absolutely no clue what she was talking about.

"Welcome to Black Rock City, welcome home." She reached through my window and gave me a hug, then waved us through into the city.

I was not excited. I was still scared. This place was huge and foreign. I felt like a stranger in someone else's house. It was a hell of a forty-eight hours and I just wanted to calm down.

We pulled into the city's outermost ring. Quicksilver explained the design to me. East/West streets were named after time. Ten o'clock being the most eastern road, and two o'clock being the most western. They are broken into thirty-minute sections. North/south roads are named alphabetically, except for the most inner road, which is very confusingly called the Esplanade. So they go E, A, B, C, D. The entire shape of Black Rock city was that of a giant half clock. We were driving down Lapis street, the L street, the outermost street, which meant it was the longest due to the clock design.

He pointed for me to take a right down Eight O'Clock, and as soon as I did, I instantly recognized that every single thing I knew about Burning Man had been completely wrong. Glowing aliens were walking down their streets.

I say "ALIENS", because I had never seen anything like them. Their costumes lit up in an array of colors. I had seen el-wire before, I knew what led tape was, but this was different. These people created their clothing with nighttime conditions in mind. The lighting was there for safety, and being a necessity, it was no longer a novelty. People used lighting to create actual styles within their clothes, in the same way you would use denim, or silk for different practical situations and conditions.

I say walking down "THEIR" streets, because these were their streets. They were like kids trick or treating within their own neighborhood. They had a sort of ease and style in their walk. They were not guests, they were home.

And I say "STREETS" because these were real streets. These were not fake streets placed here just because the festival planners thought it was a good idea. They were as real as any real street in San Francisco or New York City. This was not a festival. This was a city. Not a faux city, this was a real and vibrant city that was created organically. It was not constructed, it was alive. There were major avenues and arteries throughout Black Rock. The people who organized Burning Man did not plan it this way. It just became. People set up their bars and restaurants, their installations and lounges on certain streets, in certain areas, because that is what made sense. They set up their personal quarters and living spaces behind these streets, because that is also what made sense. Alleys popped up between camps, because you need alleys in a city like this.

I saw the artifacts of every city I ever visited or lived in right here. We try to force our urban planning, but you can never conquer an organic movement. This place existed this way, because this place was dominated by a culture of building and exploration. People here wanted to walk, wanted to bike, wanted to socialize. Drop them on this blank canvas and this is the city that would spring up around them. The people of Burning Man were not a herd, they were a pack.

I DIDN'T KNOW where I could park to unload my gear. Quicksilver assured me it would be no big deal, but I was out of my element and afraid of breaking some non-existent rule. I'm not good with rules in general, and I often do something wrong without even knowing it. I didn't want to piss off my camp, or sixty thousands Burners on my first night.

We parked the car in the middle of 4:30 and Basra. There must have been ten parties within eyesight. I would have to dodge more than one large glowing car and dozens of small shining bicycles in order to make it to my camp.

"Are you sure I can park here." I asked.

"You're fine." We crossed the street to my strangely quiet camp. The Esoteric Outsiders sent an alpha team out a week early so they could build the giant tree house that was now standing in front of me. Five stories, a zipline, rope ladders, rope bridges, two DJ booths, a dance floor, a lounge, a bar, and that was just the public space. I knew we were loading up something big, but I couldn't help but wonder how the hell they pulled this thing off out here.

I walked through the structure and pushed through a pair of curtains, which separated the public area from the private area. I was hoping to see anyone I knew, I wished to death Cheshire had come with us.

A naked girl ran up to me. I went to hug her, knowing it was the proper way to greet a Burner, but quickly pulled back. "Am I allowed to hug you when you are naked?" I asked.

"You must be a virgin!" She said as she hugged me tightly, then grabbed my butt. "You always hug, no exceptions!"

It's funny, I'm not a very touchy feely person, but ever since I started hanging with Burners, it has become second nature to me. I can't even imagine why people don't hug when they greet each other. It's nice to hug.

After a few more minutes, one of the leaders of the camp saw me and showed me where I could set up my tent. Quicksilver unloaded my car and I handed him my keys. - There was no parking at my camp, so I thought it was best to leave the vehicle with him.

"Thanks for everything," I said as I gave him a hug.

"Don't worry, we'll see each other soon," he told me.

I wasn't so sure, I wasn't sure about anything anymore. I could feel all my old insecurities bubbling up. Not understanding the innate ways of the Burn, wanting to be liked, feeling like I was disappointing people, feeling like no one wanted me here.

I sat with these emotions as I set up my tent, remembering that lesson the King of Israel taught me a lifetime ago. Spending a few hours now, would ensure that I would have a comfortable place to live for the rest of the week.

Maybe it was all a game. It took me this long to learn these skills, level up, acquire all this gear, and the potions of course, to finally complete this mission. Kill the final boss. Everything had lead up to this last level. I placed my fur vest on for old time's sake, then added the cowboy hat and American Flag shirt just to complete the circle. I had started at Desert Hearts. I had been to Lightning in a Bottle. I experienced EDC. I had been to every festival in-between. I spent the last few months at warehouse parties and transformational workshops. It's time to see what this culture is really made of, what it can really offer us. Here, at the holy of holy places for the Transformations. Burning Man.

I JUMPED ON my bike and rode towards The Man. The city was too much for me, so I headed towards the desert, where that giant statue lifted his hands above us all. I stopped as I reached the Esplanade, the de facto main street of Black Rock City, the oldest, most established camps were built here, at least that is what it looked like. I biked down that avenue and was greeted by a giant Tesla coil and bumper car races, fighting arenas, bars and restaurants. It was about the greatest thing I had ever seen, but a little overwhelming for a virgin Burner who was all alone. So I continued into the desert.

Riding through The Playa desert for the first time is basically like being dropped off onto the interstate between

Earth and Mars in the year 4037. You find yourself dodging different spaceships while you try to determine who has the right of way. Giant freighters move slowly through the void, while multiple smaller vessels hover along their sides. In the future, all spaceships glow, most blast electronic dance music, and the largest of the ships always have dancers on top of them. Also, I guess there is a unicorn design option when you pick your vehicle from the dealership.

I parked my bike near The Man and looked over the city. The Man was about a mile from the Esplanade. The sounds of all the camps floated over the desert silt to create a mashup of harmony that became something new. Looking over that city reminded me of looking at Los Angeles from the hills. The scope was unreal. I have to imagine this is what someone from a small town feels like when they end up in New York City for the first time. I didn't know whether to stay and be still, or to keep on exploring.

I continued on to the deep playa. I wasn't sure how far I was allowed to go. I rode past a temple that was still under construction and multiple other art projects that were being built right before my eyes. I don't know if this was normal, or if the rain had just screwed everyone up. I couldn't believe how big this thing was. No matter how far I went, I came across more Burners and bikers, as well as the occasional asshole who laid out in the middle of the desert with no lights on to blend in with The Playa.

The strangeness of it all was comforting. Like being in a foreign land that speaks a foreign tongue. You can't help but find yourself being present. It's a weird form of meditation.

A few hours after the sun rose, I decided to head back to the camp. I didn't want to exhaust myself out on the first night. As I walked through the sleeping quarters of the Esoteric Outsiders, I saw a new tent popped up next to mine. A whiteboard on the entrance read: Cheshire and Puppy. I AM ASLEEP!!!!"

I fell onto my bed and closed my eyes. You could never really escape Burning Man in a tent. I could hear the music and fellow campers all around me. There is no such thing as alone time here. I would have to fully accept this place, or go insane.

Chapter Thirty:

The First Day at Black Rock City

My camp was abuzz with energy, it was topless, bottomless mimosa day. Meaning that if you showed up to our bar topless, you were given as much champagne and orange juice you could consume. I was standing outside the dining area with a couple of female campmates.

"So you're really are a virgin?" The prettiest of the two asked me.

"Well, I was a virgin yesterday, now I am just awkward." I replied.

The girls laughed at my silly jokes and ease of conversation, little did they know I was dying inside, afraid that no one here liked me. What the fuck was my problem?

"You don't seem that awkward to me," the second girl said.

"No I am, I'm just good at hiding it," I said, "but maybe you two can make me feel more comfortable."

"We'd love to," the girl replied as she smiled to her friend. Insecurities aside, it was going to be a fun week.

I grabbed my bike and began to ride into The Playa. Burning Man of the day was completely different from Burning Man of the night. It didn't feel like a drug infused festival, it was more like spring break. The high of choice was booze, and the clothing of choice was none.

I had been told again and again that seeing so many

topless girls would desexualize them, yet this didn't seem to be the case, and I was having the sneaking suspicion that guys were just saying this in front of the opposite sex in hopes of getting laid more. There is something innately beautiful about the female body. It's no wonder festivals are so effeminate. The female body, mind and soul, are put on display as the pinnacle of humankind. The nurturing mother, feminine strength, the empathetic listener. Amazing traits that are vital to society, yet I do not see the same respect giving to masculinity. In fact, masculinity is redefined to be more feminine here. The sensitive man is the real man among the Transformations.

There is a certain entitlement to this belief. We live on the shoulders of men who sacrificed themselves so that women could be safe while they raised their children, while they raised us. Times have changed, and these defined roles are not as important as they used to be, but we ignore them at our peril. Just as a healthy society needs both artists and engineer, it also needs the innate gender differences that are man and woman. Both sexes are important, and ignoring half the spectrum will lead to a feeling of worthlessness among today's males. We cannot change biology.

I look around and wonder how many of the men here espoused this feminine ethos, just so they can skirt their responsibilities to society? Would these men let women and children go first? No wonder we live in a world of boys.

Maybe we also live on the shoulders of those who have yet to come. This peaceful scene in front of me, may just assure that our children will once again have to fight for the way of life we take for granted.

I BIKED INTO the deep playa, where two giant figures were holding each other. Theirs was an ancient love, and the desert had grown up around them, burying everything below their waists in playa silt. As lovers do, they became the center of the universe they created. They were happy, yet selfish.

The upper bodies of the two souls rose over seven stories into the air, and seeing them from a distance, made you realize that you were in a very special place. They would only exist for a few more days, set to be burned in a morning ceremony. All that would remain were the ashes they left behind and the memories they gave us.

I don't know why art like this does not exist in the default world. In just one day, I saw the best of human creation. "The Embrace," stood above them all. A giant wooden structure depicting the artist's visual representation of love. The inside was hollowed out so that you could climb into their bodies and look through their eyes. I had never seen anything like it before and I didn't know why.

We are so stuck in our ways that we can't conceive of anything better. Why do skyscrapers have to look like skyscrapers? Why can't they look like this? Why do towers, and pieces of city art all seem to look back for inspiration, when they should be looking forward? I can think of no other reason, except that most people don't care. People just don't give a shit about what they are doing. Giving a shit seems to be the rarest commodity left in our world of abundance and wealth.

I was joined by hundreds of other Burners as we explored the different works of creation. A sense of awe and wonderment was everywhere. Humans should create amazing things. When something is built, we should look up to it as an inspiration for what we are capable of. We have a special place on this planet, and we need to act like it.

Most of the world's problems would be solved, if instead of throwing money at them, we threw people at them. Solutions come from people who give a shit, solutions are not a commodity. Capitalism has created the highest standard of living in the world, but we may be on the verge of something new, something better.

AFTER SPENDING SOME time on The Playa, I finally explored the city. I had a map of where each of my friends were camped, and wanted to see as many as possible. It was one of the things that continued to irk me about these festivals. People never went out of their way to find their friends. I seemed to be the one exception. As I rode from camp to camp saying hello to any friends I could find, the scope of the place continued to amaze me. I couldn't help but think of how different my experience would be depending upon where I camped. There were thousands of separate stories and adventures going on all around me. I could never experience them all.

The sun would soon set, and my first day at Burning Man would come to an end. I headed back to my tent, so I could get dressed for the night. It was the night I had been waiting for since this whole journey began.

Chapter Thirty-One:

The White Suit Returns Home

"People never dress for the occasion anymore," I bowed to the cute passersby and tipped my white hat.

"Oh my God! I want to take a picture of you but my phone is dead." She said with the energy of an annoying teenage girl.

"It's okay, we're in a no photozone anyway," I pointed to a large group of naked men and women standing in buckets while they gave each other sponge baths. It was a game created by a polyamory camp to test your comfort zone.

"You sure know how to dress for the white party, everyone else is just wearing cheap undershirts!" She gave me a deep hug and kissed me on the cheek, then went off to wherever she was going.

I had come full circle, this is where it all started. The Abundant Sanctuary was throwing the White Party, the party, I had helped fund so long ago with my attendance. The White Suit was finally going home.

I entered the Russian Mafia's RV to the sounds of a NOS tank filling up balloons, Dimitri was mid inhale as he saw The White Suit for the first time. He began shaking and laughing as his now very not lucid brain tried to determine if I was a hallucination being created by the nitrous.

"The White Suit!" Nabes ran up and hugged me. "I

remember from lightning!"

"I didn't think you remembered me," I said."

"Oh, no, I don't know," only a cute girl with a Spanish accent could get away with such a non-answer.

"Holy fucking shit, that is so pimp," Rash said as he grabbed a balloon.

"I love it, cause you look amazing even though it is absurd," Dimitri said, finally coming down from the high. Everyone watched the effects of the gas hit Rash, and we all burst out laughing.

Dos walked out of the master bedroom, carrying a couple of fire spinning rods, he gave me that confident smile of his, "you should teach The White Suit G," he said.

"G scares me," I said.

"You sound like a broken record," he replied as he grabbed a can of kerosene and packed it into his bag.

"It's actually one of the safest, easiest drugs you can do, as long as you know how to do it," Dimitri said.

"It can kill you if you do it wrong," Rash explained.

"Yea, that sounds incredibly safe," I said.

"Dude, as long as you don't drink liquor, and do an exact dosage, you will be totally fine," he replied.

"He's really serious, you can't drink at all," Nabes looked at me, "you don't want to fuck your burn."

"I'm gonna pass, thanks."

We all exited the RV and began to mount our bikes, Dos looked towards me, "let me know if you want any G, I have extra."

"Thanks." Something was wrong, I could feel it. Everyone was hesitating. No one made eye contact with me, but they also would not get on their bikes. Whatever it was, it was directed at me. I started to list the reasons in my head, what could I have done this time?

Nabes finally spoke up, "we have to tell you something," she said.

"Yea?" I was afraid I was about to lose another group of friends.

"We all remember you from Lightning in the Bottle," she said.

"Excuse me?" I wasn't sure what was coming next.

"We all remember you, we didn't know you, and we didn't know what to think. You wear this white suit and talk to all of us like you knew us. We just thought you were some creepy guy, and we have all felt really bad about it for months."

"Yea, we all just wanted to say sorry," Dos said.

How many times had I been wrong over the past few months? Who the hell shows up to festivals not knowing anyone? Who decides to take on a new life at my age? Jump into a world they don't know or understand? "I'd probably have felt the same way," I said, then I laughed. "Seriously, you guys mean the world to me. I wouldn't be here without any of you. Thank you."

Dimitri pulled a card out of his wallet, "I have something for you," he handed it over. It was a normal business card, but instead of having any personal information on it, it just read: "You sir, are fucking awesome."

We all smiled. I hid my tears.

AS WE WALKED towards the Abundant Sanctuary, I wondered what Walt Disney would think of this display. A spectacle of lights and magic created by a bunch counterculture hippies. The happiest place on Earth was nothing compared to the Esplanade right before The White Party was about to begin. The music for the night included, Diplo, Skrillex, Infected Mushroom and half a dozen other top DJs. In Los Angeles, this show would have cost hundreds of dollars, here it was free.

Nabes and I had fallen behind the Russian Mafia. The three of them had attached giant glowing tails to their bikes, and could be seen from almost a quarter a mile away. Those tails were swinging back in forth a great distance ahead of us.

"Can I tell you a secret?" Nabes said as we slowly walked our bikes through the crowd of people.

"What is it?" I asked, worried she might say something too honest.

"I was like you at LiB," she said, "I love Dos very much, but everything here is so new. I have no friends. I'm really glad we are all here together. I haven't known these people much longer than you. And I want you to know, you can come over or call anytime you want."

"That means a lot to me," I said.

"I'm very serious," she said. "I come to this country I know nothing, this is my reality, I don't much, but I don't think this is reality for everyone in The States."

"Oh no, this is no different than Witchita." I said.

"I think you are kidding with me."

"I guess you'll have to go to Wichita to find out." A giant sardine can filled with dancers rolled past us, we both paused to take in the moment. "You having fun?" I asked.

"America is weird," she said, "but yes, very fun."

We walked to the back corner of Black Rock City where the sound camps were located, just as The King of Israel had told me back before I knew anything about this culture. By now, I wasn't even slightly taken aback by the sight that this stage, in the middle of the desert, funded by donations, was one of the best stages I had ever seen in my life. Fire shot up from the DJs as they blasted deep bass. Giant white totems danced with the audience as seven-story high art cars hovered above the spectacle.

We looked over to the bleachers behind the dance floor, and saw a dozen of people waving our way, smiles on their faces, happy to see Nabes and I. It was The Mafia with Cheshire and Puppy, along with a bunch of their tech friends. Here I was, at a festival of sixty thousand people, attending the hottest show of the night, and I was immediately waved down by friends who were happy to see me. I'd come far in five short months.

Within half an hour, our group had grown to thirty strong. I hate to be the type, but everyone here wished they were us. Some of us danced. Others stayed back. I enjoyed the show, but felt The Playa calling me. There was just so much to see, and wasting time on yet another EDM performance seemed silly. I'd rather spend the hundreds of dollars in LA to watch these acts, than spend the hours of my life here, and miss what was free for all on The Playa. I ducked under my group and climbed beneath the metal stands to get away from the concert.

A little ways past the stage I saw a group of fire spinners, they had a small audience and looked quite talented. It would be the perfect way to decompress from the dubstep that was Skrillex.

One of the spinners kept catching my eye. She had a sense of joy in what she was doing. It's infectious to see one doing something they love. She was short and sexy, wearing a small bikini bottom and nothing but pasties over her nipples. I couldn't keep my eyes off of her. Then I realized, I knew her. How did I know her? Was it Firestarter from my camp? Firestarter was cute, but not like this girl. I had to talk to her. I walked up closer to the area where all the fire spinners dip their poles into their kerosene. It had to be her. She seemed so in her element.

The show went on for another twenties minutes, then I saw her move over to her gear and begin to pack. It was the first opportunity I had to talk to her without breaking her off from her co-performers.

"Firestarter?" I asked in the form of a question, being afraid that I was wrong.

She looked up and immediately hugged me, "I'm so glad you saw us!" She was like a different person from the one I had met before, full of energy and life.

"That was amazing, that was so amazing, I know you told me you spun, but that was amazing." I couldn't think of anything good to say, so I was that dumfounded idiot who kept repeating "amazing."

She smiled then hugged me again, feeling her body against mine felt good. Not in a normal way, not in the way a female body usually feels good against mine. This was something different. It had been a long time since I felt this way. My ex made me feel this way.

We only talked for a few minutes, she had to return her gear and meet up with her fire group. I grabbed her hands and held them together, then pulled one to my mouth and kissed it. I wanted to talk to her all night. She pulled a shirt over her breasts, then placed a bright white, furry hoodie over her head. She turned it on, and now was a glow in the entire spectrum of the rainbow. She jumped on her LED decorated bike, and became her own moving light parade. As she began to peddle down the Esplanade, she turned back to me and smiled. I bowed and tipped my white hat.

It was a moment that has happened a million times outside of every high school in this country. That moment when two people start to have feelings for each other. You would recognize it in every way. You have even experienced it yourself. Only here, it was at Burning Man, with a half-naked glowing girl who just spun fire while a man dressed in white, high on drugs, watched her perform. We are not all one, but we aren't all that different.

I stood and watched her until I could no longer make out the lights from her bike. I felt a hand on my shoulder, I turned to see that it was Rash.

"You okay dog?" He said.

"Yeah. I just met a fucking awesome girl."

"You should give her the fucking awesome card."

"Follow me," I pulled Rash towards a small gate that separated the road from the Playa. We looked at the hundreds of art cars rolling through the desert, heard the sounds of the top musical acts behind us, felt the silt underneath our feet, watched a giant metal octopus shooting flames from it's arms drive past us.

"Can you believe this?" He said.

"This fucking exists." I said.

"This fucking exists."

"ALL ABOARD!!" THE captain of the ship yelled as we climbed onto the vessel. It only seemed appropriate that after the elegance that was The White Party, we would want to take a nice leisurely cruise through The Playa at night.

"We're all full," the security guard said to Nabes as she tried to board.

"It's okay, they're with me," one of the passenger's told him. It took me a second to realize it was the lead singer from Tale of the Sprinting Fox. We looked at each other, smiled.

Our ship was Willard the Unicorn, a three story, pink moving stage that blew fire from its horn. We were about to depart from her homeport of The Hollywood Roll, a cluster of camps on the outside edge of the Esplanade. The Russian Mafia, Cheshire as well as The Tale of the Sprinting Fox, Little Heart and her crew, had all met at these camp years ago, and were now all here again. It was a sort of class reunion. This was the way nights were supposed to end, a moving party with friends off into the desert to watch the sun rise over the distant mountains.

"Excuse me!," I yelled to a random person walking down the Esplanade, "You are fucking awesome!" She stopped, looked at me and pointed to herself, "yes you!" I said, "you have made Burning Man more amazing with your presence! Thank you so much for making the Burn so awesome by coming here!" She smiled and walked away, looking a little taller.

"You think you can hang with the Spaghetti dog?" Rash put his arm around me as I braced myself with one of the stripper poles located on the dance floor. We hung over the side of the ship while we waved good-bye to those who stayed behind.

The Hollywood Roll was made up of multiple smaller camps all based out of Los Angeles, the most infamous of which was The Succulent Spaghetti, known as the hardest partiers at all of Burning Man, their intake of drugs and lack of sleep was that of legend.

"If I can't hang with the Spaghetti, then who can I hang with!" I said back. The Spaghettis were formed out of one of the top universities in California. They were made up of Scientists and engineers and future politicians. Here on this giant moving ship, were the future leaders of America.

We slowly pushed out into The Playa. Black Rock City became smaller and smaller until its lights were distant dots on the horizon. Soon we were joined by dozens of people on bicycles riding along side us, like dolphins would out at sea. They all moved back and forth in formation to the music that was playing out of the sides of this giant unicorn. Dimitri, Rash and I looked at each other with an unsaid understanding that this was fucking awesome. Dimitri then pulled a rag out of his pocket,

"Want some Ether?" He said.

"I'm good," I replied.

Then another arm reached around me, it was Quicksilver, "Hey," he said, "I'm peaking."

"With what?" I asked.

"Crystal Molly," he said.

"That'll do it."

"I think I'm in love," his head tilted into the direction of a very attractive Armenian girl. She gave him hungry eyes.

"You sure it's not the molly?" I asked.

"This is real love, I can tell."

"Go get her." I said.

"Just wanted you to know." He then walked over to

the girl and began dancing with her.

I had thought I understood the size of Burning Man by now, but as we rode out past The Man, past the temple, to the point where I could no longer even see the lights of Black Rock City in the distance, I realized this was it's own world. The ink black night was disrupted by hundreds of other art cars in the dark void, other ships at sea. Some sailed alone, others sailed in groups. Many converged into circles, to create their own mini festivals, all throughout the deep playa.

I hung off the side of the ship and looked to the top floor, the floor reserved for people who had helped build Willard. I saw Little Heart dancing over the edge. She saw me and smiled. She had helped build this vehicle that was bringing so much joy to all of us. Burning Man is not a festival, it is a celebration, it is a celebration of the actual building of Burning Man. It was like the glass of whiskey at the end of a hard day of work, except that hard day of work was picking the wheat, aging the mash and distilling the final concoction that you were now drinking.

"LAND, LAND HO!!!" One of the passengers yelled as the trash fence came into view, a small four foot high orange plastic divider that protected the the desert from any moop that might blow past the boundary of Burning Man. We veered right and began to sail along this fence. The sun began to show its head out in the distance. The stars disappeared, and the black ocean changed into brown playa silt. A small, two-story wooden shed came into view and our good ship Willard pulled alongside it. Everyone jumped off and ran inside. The drugs had all worn off from the trip, and people were looking for a safe place to do uppers for the morning. It is one of the strange contradictions of Burning Man, for all the talk of illegal substances, you will never actually see any done in public, there are police and rangers all over the festival and no one wants to get caught.

I walked up to the dinky plastic divider and looked over the desert. I was joined by hundreds of other Burners in a human chain that stretched miles. Quicksilver stood beside me. He looked sad.

"You okay?" I asked.

"I'm good," he said. I looked back to Willard and saw his true love making out with a random guy. "Owwwwwwwwwwwwwlllllll!" He then began to howl at the sun. I thought this was sort of a strange reaction, until I heard the sounds of other howls. Like coyote's to the moon, Burners howled to the oncoming day.

Quicksilver dropped to the ground indian style and collapsed his head into his hands. "I really thought she was the one," he said.

IT WAS GETTING hot. I was wearing a full suit and jacket in the middle of the desert. The very reason everyone was so impressed by The White Suit was now going to be the death of me. I took a sip from my camelbak and realized I was almost out of water. I sat on the ground and turned my head to the sky, trying to determine the time by the position of the sun. We had been here for hours.

I looked towards the wooden shed and saw campers from the Succulent Spaghetti snorting blow and taking spoonfuls of G. Willard was blasting music, the DJ pounding her fists into the air as two of her scantily-clad minions danced on the stripper poles beside her. This party wasn't ending, this party was just about to begin. I should have known better, I would never be able to hang with the Succulent Spaghetti. No one can out party the Spaghetti.

I started to wonder why I even jumped on that giant pink unicorn to watch the sun rise at the trash fence. I could be asleep right now, in my comfy cold tent instead of being stuck here among this debauchery of drugs and sex. Fuck my life.

I started thinking of the vow I made on that muddy road just a few days ago. I had a duty to uphold it. I had to remain positive. I had to be the best reflection of myself. I knew I would be miserable if I stayed here, so I would leave, I would make that long walk back to my bike, back to my camp. I couldn't even see Black Rock City in the distance, but it had to be there somewhere. Didn't I walk twenty some miles just a few weeks ago? That was an adventure, and this would be too.

"I'm leaving," I told the Mafia.

"You were meant for that mission," Dimitri told me.

"Godspeed," said Rash.

I hugged them, and began my new quest. As I walked towards the city, I couldn't help but think that I am my past experiences, my current self is a stranger. I was doing this trek across The Playa because I knew it would make my future-self happy. It would mean he would be well rested for the next day of partying. I looked to my past-self to know this was true, I do not function well on lack of sleep, It is the one thing that remains stable in my incredibly not stable life. The only person I was not caring for, was the person I was right now.

An hour later, I was nearing the Esplanade, when I heard loud music coming from behind me. I turned around to see Willard The Unicorn driving back to the Hollywood Roll camp. As it passed by, everyone waved at me.

"Live in the now!" Quicksilver yelled as a new girl hung on his arm. I watched them drive by, smiled, and continued my journey home.

Chapter Thirty-Two:

There is No Magic in a World of Logic

It was an uneventful day. The walk home from Willard had exhausted me, so I had spent most of the afternoon in my tent. However, today would be the most important day in the life of The VP, she was to be married just outside the now finished temple. I would not miss this occasion.

I was biking towards the event, when I saw a haboob rolling over The Playa. I always hated that word, haboob. When I was a kid in the deserts of Arizona, we just called them dust storms. They were about the most ominous looking thing you would ever see, a giant rolling ball of sand that looked like death. However, the insides of which, were usually quite pleasant.

I braced for that moving blob of playa dust to overtake me when. Whack! It was like that kid who threw sand in your eyes during recess. It came out of nowhere, even though I saw it coming. I was knocked off my bike and into the ground, I grabbed for my goggles and swept them over my eyes as I quickly pulled my scarf against my mouth and nose. The entire landscape became dark, but not dark like the night, dark as if the universe was submerged in a deep orange clay. I lost all sense of direction, praying that the arts cars were smart enough to stop in these storms. God, please don't let those driver's be drunk and high. They would think this was some acid induced hallucination.

I needed to find protection, but I had no clue where to go. I looked at my bike, the front wheel should still be pointing towards the temple road. I grabbed it and began to walk forward, swinging my arms in front of me, hoping to hit something. The blindness was bad enough, but the sound, the roar of the wind was worse. I could hear nothing.

My hand felt a large round object, splinters in the wood. It was a pole, one of the light poles that led to that holy of holy places. I left my bike, and like a monkey swinging from vines, I moved from pole to pole, doing my best not to lose my way. Soon, I reached the outer wall of the temple grounds. I hugged that wall until I found the entrance, a few steps further in was the temple. I shoved my way inside that sanctuary and pulled my scarf off, getting my first good breath of air since that monster overtook me.

Inside, were hundreds of people, sitting indian style, hands pointed towards the sky. I could see in their faces lies. Some were here to escape the storm, but most were here to worship. I pulled my goggles down and took my red cowboy hat off. It didn't seem appropriate to wear them in this sacred place.

We were the last of humanity, who could have survived whatever that was on the outside. The walls strained with the sounds of a submarine diving to the depth of the ocean. I wondered how long they could win the battle against The Playa wind and dust.

I looked around this place. The temple was strewn with pictures and artifacts. The wooden walls were covered in graffiti and notes.

"I used to beat up Jeremy in high school because I knew he was gay, I hope he forgives me." "I cheated on my wife and made her feel like she was the bad guy." "Please God, just give me an answer."

I kneeled down into the silt and grabbed at the pieces of paper, pictures, and letters. Why were we here? What were we trying to figure out?

I pushed my hands against my scarf and coughed as much of that sand out of my lungs as I could. I imagined The Playa dust was now part of my body. I sat there, hoping the storm would end. I looked at this great structure, built on a computer, cut to pieces by lasers, then constructed here. Human beings are beautiful.

The VP was probably dead now with the rest of the world. I hadn't seen her since she left me in that restaurant, but I still loved her. Some friends are like that, you need time apart, but they are always there.

I looked up and saw a familiar face. It was the portrait of an American actor. He killed himself just a few weeks earlier. I felt like he was staring at me, telling me something. "If I can't make it, who can?" He had given so much, and now he was dead.

I put my hands on my knees, pointed my palms towards the sky. I knew it was all a lie, but I was sick of the logic. I wanted the fairy tale to be true.

IT TURNS OUT, the world had not been destroyed. In fact, people were just walking around as if our species hadn't just escaped extinction.

The wedding took place on the outside edges of the temple. The sky was blue, and the temperature was a blazing ninety-five degrees. A few hundred of us watched as the ceremony ended with a rap song, lots of nudity, and a kiss. Typical wedding stuff. The VP and Lego were now husband and wife.

"Would anyone like to speak?" Lego asked the audience.

A few people did, I don't remember what they said, it was the basic love and unity and peace bullshit that you hear at every wedding.

I needed to say something, so I walked up to the front of the ceremony and looked into the audience, I did not look at the VP, because I knew I would cry.

"Let it out brother," Lego told me.

"You don't know me well," I said.

"He's a crier, something good's about to happen," the VP told him.

"I think I might be the VP's best friend," I told the audience, "But I don't want to talk about the VP today." Friendship is a funny thing, I guess it's not that different from characters in a book. We choose our friends for different reasons. Sometimes I couldn't stand the VP, sometimes I wanted her out of my life, but when I needed her, she was always there, and I think she always will be. The

VP was a beautiful person, a beautiful handful, that's what I needed to say. "I want to talk about Lego," I said. "When you are friends with someone, you don't have to talk about them. However, seeing someone treat the VP the way Lego does, means I will always love that man. You see, Lego was the first person that the VP has ever dated, who I knew would understand the absolutely beautiful handful she is." I was afraid to say the last line, but it was honest and true. Aren't we all beautiful handfuls?

The VP hugged me and cried, "thank you for always being there," she whispered in my ear. I walked back through the crowd, feeling a bit ashamed that I had been cynical about this temple, cynical about this place, cynical about this ceremony. The Playa was not only a rebirth of life for me. It was a rebirth of old friendship.

The wedding ended so I walked back to the courtyard of the temple. Elache was sitting alone on one of the wooden benches. She was staring into the ground. I loved that girl. If it weren't for her tiny act of bravery, I doubt I would be here. She had no clue, and probably never would. "Elache? Little Heart? Are you okay?" I asked.

She looked up to me and nodded, "I'm good."

I didn't believe her.

EVERYTHING BECAME VERY interesting. It had been a few hours since the VP done got hitched, and now I was staring out into that vast expanse that was the gate road. The road between the greeters and gate to be more specific. The headlights of a single car was coming towards me, very, slowly, coming, towards, me. A few days ago, I had driven this same road with hundreds of other vehicles, but now, near the end of the burn, the cars were sparse. They were very interesting.

The dust hovered through the air, giving everything a dream-like state, or at least the forced dream like state they create when they are creating dream-like states in movies. I kept thinking, that over there, on the other side of the greeters, the cars were in one world. But over here, we were in another world. A real, tangible line in the sand was created. It was our choice to cross over, and it was very interesting.

I watched Cheshire dancing, my whole camp was here, they were wearing onesies, you know those children's pajamas that look like costumes. I think Cheshire was a dinosaur. He kept waving at me, trying to get me to join in. But I found him to interesting to walk over. I was more interested in analyzing his dance. My camp greeted anyone who crossed this invisible border, they would hug them, welcome them home, and then make them yell and ring a loud bell if they were a virgin. I watched all of this taking place in front of me. It made more sense than I could have imagined. Plus, It was very interesting.

I turned around and saw a little girl pedaling my way. She was like a grade schooler coming home from a long day of class to play with friends. I could recognize that girl anywhere. It was Cheshire's Puppy.

As soon as she saw me she dropped her bike and ran my way, "Oh my gosh!" She said, "I have so much to tell you!"

"I miss my Nickel," I said.

"What's Nickel?" She asked.

"From another life," I said.

"I had so much fun today! I have to tell you everything," she said. "First, where's Cheshire."

"I'll take you to him, but we have to walk baby steps," I said.

"Why?" She asked.

"I don't know, but it's important."

"Are you on acid?" She asked.

"No," I said.

"Are you sure?"

"I think I'd know."

We walked at 4 inches per step, still faster than five miles per hour I'm sure. "Okay, so let me just tell you about everything," she said. "I biked all over while Cheshire was here, I went into bars and lounges and I drank and every guy wanted to talk to me." How different life must be for a hot Asian chick, I thought.

"That's super interesting," I said.

"Then I learned Lira, which is this hula hoop thing, it's awesome! And then they threw silks up, you know Cheshire does silks right?"

"Yes I do, I've never seen him perform though." I said.

"Do we still have to walk this way, I can see him?" She asked.

"I do, but you go ahead," I said.

"We need to hang more," she said as she walked towards Cheshire.

"Hey Puppy," she stopped and looked at me, "that story was really interesting," I said.

"Thanks." Then she went full on sprint and tackled Cheshire to the ground, they hugged and kissed and looked very happy. They stood up, dusted off the silt, talked among themselves, and ran towards me.

"Very interesting," I said to myself.

Puppy grabbed my hand, "sorry, no more baby steps," she said as the two of them started dragging me towards the center of the greeter's gate.

"Everyone!" Cheshire yelled, "We have a virgin here!" The camp surrounded me. Cheshire looked at me, that smile of his, those eyes, "I want you to lay down in The Playa dust." I did and he kneeled next to me. "Roll around," he said. So I did, he waited till I was good and dirty, then put his hand on my shoulder. "This dust is now your friend, it will get into every crevasse of your body, learn to love it, or live a miserable existence here in Black Rock City." He paused, waiting for an answer.

"I love the Playa dust!" I yelled.

"Good," he and Puppy then lifted me to my feet.

Puppy handed me a large mallet, "you are no longer a virgin," she said.

I knew exactly what to do, I swung that hammer against the virgin bell and yelled out, "I am no longer a virgin!" The bell rang and echoed across our land. This world we call The Playa.

THE THREE OF us looked upon the giant robot standing in the middle of The Playa. I was no longer a virgin, so I might as well experience my first burn. Cheshire pulled off his scarf and set it on the ground for Puppy to sit on, it was quite cute. We looked up to that massive piece of machinery. Why he had come to this desert? The Burners broke into two camps, one believing he was here to destroy the world, the other, believing he wanted to save mankind. There had been protests all week by both sides, but the robot just stood there, watching. He never spoke. He never moved.

The situation was getting dire, and we all feared war was upon us. Military vehicles had been converging near the giant machine all day. We weren't sure if they were here to protect him, or us. Now on the fourth day of The Burn, I wondered if anyone even remembered what started this fight in the first place.

The robot had done no wrong, but he also looked like he would. He was obviously a giant war machine, what would happen if he decided to attack? Could mankind fight him off? But what if he was here to save us? Teach us how to survive in this world we no longer understood?

None of it mattered anymore. The Burners had dug

in, caring more about being right than being kind, arguing instead of listening. Maybe the outcome was assured from the beginning.

The tanks rolled up, but the machine just stood there, and for a second, I thought it smiled. It was the protesters who fired the first blow, attacking the army that they were sure was here to destroy their savior. The tanks fired back. An all-out war was happening right in front of my eyes.

I don't know who won this war, but I know who lost. I do not know who fired the killing shot, but the robot began to burn. The flames spread through his body until he crumbled to the ground. Humanity was either saved or destroyed.

Burners create their perfect utopia here on this blank canvass, then destroy it, only to rebuild it a year later. Burning Man is not reality, but for one week, we get to be exactly what we want to be and do exactly what we want to do.

We built this place, not because we wanted to, but because we have to. We are the fools. We are the engineers and the artists. People will step on us and take what we have made, condemning us when we ask for anything in return. And we will keep building. It is who we are. It is in our nature.

This place, this city in the middle of the desert. This is not reality, it is not the way things are supposed to be, but is not a forgery either. It is a place to experiment and learn, see what works and see what does not. Then bring those things back to the default world. This imperfect fantasyland, makes the non-fantasyland more perfect. This is not reality, but it can create a new normal. I think what America is to the world, might just be what Black Rock City is to America.

"YOU'RE BEING A third wheel," Cheshire said. It wasn't a mean thing to say, Cheshire just didn't know the right way to say things like this. He didn't know the right way to tell me that I needed to leave him and Puppy alone, so they could do molly, and fuck all night. "Tonight's the night," he said, "we haven't been fighting, and she is looking particularly hot."

"Have fun," I said, then smiled, trying to mimic that sly smile he always gave me, that half grin that is both naughty and nice at the same time. I did not succeed.

I had an hour to kill so I climbed up to the top of the Esoteric Outsiders treehouse so I could see the vista of Black Rock City. It was beautiful. Then, as if she came out of nowhere, Firestarter was standing right next to me. We looked at each other and smiled, "how have you been?" I asked.

"That's the most boring thing you have ever said," she replied.

"I think we're past pickup lines." I said.

"You're too sure of yourself."

"I'm actually a scared little kid, it's just no one believes me." I then grabbed her hand, and we began to dance. "I can't wait to see you in Los Angeles." I said.

"Why not here?"

"Love never lasts on The Playa."

"I think it does," she said.

We stared into each other's eyes, and then she left. I watched her climb down the tree house and walk into the sleeping quarters of my camp. She did not enter her tent, she went to another guy. The Playa is a brutal mistress.

I WAS BIKING figure eights out front of the Russian Mafia's RV. I wanted to go play, and I wanted to go play now! An energy was overtaking my very being. I felt like I should run a marathon, or sprint a marathon. Perhaps it was the chemical reaction in my brain from Firestarter's earlier rejection, or maybe it was the G flowing through my veins. Whatever the case, my greatest fear was that my friends would be couched for the night, and I would have to explore The Playa all alone.

"One more hit, I swear," Dimitri said as he peaked his head out of the door. Why they would ever do that downer of a drug in a funland such as this, I just didn't understand.

I burst inside the RV, "Couch patrol," I yelled, "I am the authority of making sure you do not get couched on this night."

"Want a balloon?" Rash asked.

Damnit, not only were they passing around the bong but also the balloons. It would take the entire force of the couch patrol to fight off this blight that was getting couched by downer drugs.

"I'm good, no balloons for me tonight. Let's play."

Dimitri burst out laughing as Rash sucked down his balloon to escape reality for a few seconds.

"I swear, just one more hit," Dimitri said again. We would never leave this RV. Couch patrol would be a failure.

An hour later, we found ourselves biking through Black Rock City. I had not succeeded in my mission, but a group of females who wanted to hang out with us did. I was riding next to an extremely beautiful Thai chick. She smiled at every move I made, it was one of those moments where you could do no wrong in the eyes of a girl you were trying to court.

"We should play a game," I said.

"What game?" The extremely beautiful Thai chick replied.

"Let's stare in each other's eyes and see how long we can go without crashing," I said.

"That sounds like the worst game ever," she was right, it was the worst game ever.

"Okay, you pick the game," I said.

"I want to find a tea house."

"I like your game, I have only been to bars and restaurants at the burn."

She picked up speed and yelled, "Follow me!"

We got lost multiple times, but she finally got her bearings. We parked our bikes outside of an ornate tent and walked inside. As we crossed the threshold, we were teleported to some sort of caravan in India. The room was lit by nothing but candles. A server sat at a small coffee table surrounded by pillows. We kneeled around the man and waited for instructions.

"You have come at a good time," the man said as he poured some hot water into his tea kettle. "I have been waiting for this moment, I am going to share a tea that was given to me in Peru by a shaman of Ayahuasca."

"This isn't a special tea is it?" I asked.

"All tea is special," he said.

"The real question is, would I legally be able to drive after I drank it?"

"Yes, there is no strong medicine in this tea."

He passed around small cups that looked like little saucer pans. They were about the size of a silver dollar, holding three sips of tea at most. At first, I found this peculiar, until I realized it created a sort of fluid motion within the creation of the tea. We couldn't just take our drink and leave. It allowed the barista, or whatever the fuck they are called, to keep the tea fresh while we all conversed and got to know one another. It was one of the greatest icebreakers I had ever seen, and for a second I wondered how great a pantless tea party would be.

"This is incredible," I said.

"The Chinese know how to do it," our tea ceremony master guy replied.

"I didn't know this is how the Chinese did it."

"Yes, they would sit with small cups of tea and chat all night while music played."

"I'm imagining that," I said, "Chinese men coming home after a day of work. there's not many options. I'm thinking of the time around the Boxer Rebellion. So they can go home, get drunk, or drink tea. I live in LA, I wish we had a tea room."

"I live in Los Angeles as well, you are welcome at my house anytime friend."

"Thank you," I said.

"Change is the natural state of man," our tea master told the table, "yet we all seek out permanence. We move from places that have seasons to those that have good weather. We say we want adventure, but trap ourselves by stability. That is what the tea house is, it's a third way, it's a place of both change and stability."

"I have to give it to you Transformations," I said.

"What's a Transformational?" The hot Thai girl asked.

"It's just what I call people like this, people who believe in transformation."

"Why don't you let them name them-self?"

"I think I did," I said.

"You can just call me a human," our tea ceremony guy said.

"You have me there," I replied.

"I'm joking, I like Transformational, it's respectful," he said.

"I think you should let them name them-self." The Thai girl said again.

"Sorry," I had offended her somehow, she instantly

shut me off. "Would you like some more tea?" I asked.

"No," she turned her legs and shoulders towards the Mafia and the other girls.

I was all too used the cold shoulder by girls in the festival scene by now, so I returned my attention to the tea master. "I've been thinking, I lost my phone the other day somewhere on The Playa. I don't miss it. I don't miss the Internet at all. But things like this tent, tactile real experiences, I miss them everyday."

"And we call it progress," the tea master said.

"I think we're digging our own grave," I said.

"That's why we are trying to transform everything."

"I don't think you will succeed," I said, "I think the future is about choice, most people will choose to live the passive life, people like us will always fight to live the active life."

"I have more faith than you," he said.

"You've got that right. Do you ever serve at The Synagog?"

"No I go there, but I have never set up my table." The Synagog was an illegal Burner club near Venice.

"You should," I said.

Then the hot Thai girl turned back to me, "you go to the Synagog?" She asked me.

"Yea," I said.

"Do you own a furry vest?"

"Yes, I do."

"I knew it, I knew it was you!"

"What?" I said.

"I know you, we met at The Synagog, we talked for hours. We talked about your vest, you were talking about being new to festivals, that you worked in film but now worked in Tech."

I tried to place the events. I did remember this girl, she was right. We had talked for hours, she was amazing and I really liked her. "You were there alone right?" I asked.

"Yes," she was pushing her words, trying to show me she was angry when she was not. She was hurt, or had been hurt, I couldn't tell. "Funny, I still have your number in my phone," she said. "I texted you."

"I'm sorry, you caught me at this weird time, I'm really sorry I didn't text back."

"You know, I liked you, I talked to a guy friend of mine, asking him why you didn't text back. I didn't understand why you didn't text back. We had so much fun."

"I'm really sorry, I really liked you too, if you give me your number, I promise I will call you and text you. You're really awesome," I said.

She looked at me, gave a fake, hard smile. "You had your chance. You fucked up."

Dimitri, and Rash watched the entire encounter, holding back their smiles, hoping we soon would be alone so they could rub the salt into my wound.

"I'm sorry I really am." I said.

"Your loss," she told me.

I looked around the tent, to my friends, to the tea man. "I need some air, I'll meet you guys later." Then left without saying anything else.

I grabbed my bike and began walking it down the street. There was a dim blue light in the distance which marked the place where porta potties were located. I parked my bike and entered one of the empty stalls, then sat down on the closed toilet lid. Porta potties are often the only place you can get away from it all at the festivals. They are the one place you know you will never be bothered. I sat there, thinking about the Thai girl.

I had met her just a after Lightning in a Bottle. I was having a hard time, going into a down of depression. The real kind of depression. All my energy went into trying to fight off those vines. I had low self-esteem and It was hard to think past an hour. I didn't return her text because I couldn't help but have anxiety about what I would do next. What would I say? Should I ask her out? Where would we go? What if she figured out I was a complete fraud?

This beautiful girl was there for the taking, and I ran. Had I dated her, I would have felt better. The right choice was right in front of me and I just didn't do it. How many opportunities had I wasted in my life?

I sat there for a while and then left. I grabbed my bike and started to head back to camp, but my introspection was interrupted by a voice coming from the distance.

"Oh my gosh!!!" The female voice yelled at me, I couldn't figure out where it was coming from. "I see you!!!"

"Puppy!" I yelled back. I saw a small figure waving at me.

"Yes!!!" She yelled back. I jumped on my bike and peddled towards her, she ran up to me and hugged me, "I can't believe I just found you! What are you doing here?" She said.

"I'm not feeling good, I need to get a beer." I said.

"Oh, this is Joe, he's my new friend," there was a confused man standing next to Puppy, I hadn't realized they were together.

"Hi," he said.

"Joe wants to come with us," Puppy told me.

This was a bad idea, Joe was a shell of a human being. "How are you Joe?" I asked. He looked down and away. It was the best he could give me.

"He's super high on Acid," Puppy said. "Anyway, Cheshire is rolling and just decided to go to sleep, he does that sometimes, so I have been on an adventure. Want to go on an adventure with me?"

"As long as it involves alcohol my stomach is killing me and I need something to calm it down."

"Are you an alcoholic?" Puppy asked.

"I didn't think so until I just said that," I replied.

"Anyways, I'm rolling balls on the good stuff Cheshire gave me and it's no fun to be alone when you are rolling balls. Everything is interesting though, get it? huh?!" Puppy punched me in the arm then said. "Joe you coming with us?"

Joe stared at Puppy. We watched him as he tried to sound out the answer. "Yeee aaaa sssss."

"Where should we go?" Puppy asked me.

"Let's drop our bikes at camp and walk somewhere," I said.

"Joe doesn't have a bike, it may take awhile to get there."

"Okay," I said, "I'll take care of Joe." I turned to him and connected with his eyes, "Joe," I said very slowly, "When we get to wherever we are going, I will tell the universe where we are." Joe's eyes lit up in a spark of understanding. He then sat down in the middle of the road indian style.

"I will be waiting for the sign," he said.

"Amazing!" Puppy smiled and grabbed her bike, "Let's go!" We biked down the Esplanade and headed for the Esoteric camp, then Puppy said one more thing, "I had no clue you knew how to talk to the Universe!"

"I can do a lot of things," I said, "let's go play."

BLACK ROCK CITY is a completely different place on foot. Burners stand outside of their tents, waving us to come in, for free food and services. Understand this, they are functioning in the exact opposite way that vendors work in the default world. They are begging to give, with no expectation of anything in return, and they are happy.

"Would you like to join us for tacos, beer and a massage?" a pretty girl asked us.

"No, I think we're good, but thank you." I said.

"Please come back tomorrow! We have plenty of food for all."

Puppy turned to me, "I'd like a private lounge. You in the mood for anything?"

"I'd kinda like a Moscow Mule," I said, "I think the ginger would be good on my stomach."

"Oh, I know a place!" Puppy grabbed my hand and we began to skip down four o'clock street. It was amazing how much of the city I had missed on the back of a bike. She pulled me into an open lounge and dragged me towards the bartender, "you guys still have Moscow Mules?" She asked.

"Yes we do," the female bartender said.

"That is so awesome!" Puppy screamed, she then pulled out her cup and reached for mine, "we'll have two of those then! This is so great isn't it! We wanted Moscow Mules and they have Moscow Mules!"

We got our drinks and sat down on one of the many large couches that made up the walls of the bar. Soon, another man joined us. He was tripping on acid as well. Puppy attracted these types.

"Don't mind me," he said, "I will help you find your way." We ignored him.

Puppy turned to me and began to talk, "I am so glad Cheshire has you as a friend." molly released the inner child of Puppy, and she was an absolute joy to be with. "I don't know how I feel about his other friends."

"Cheshire and I have a special bond, I'm not really sure why. We didn't know it at the time, but when we met, we both had just gone through something really similar."

"I know, he told me about your ex, you guys are so similar, it blows my mind, like I think you think the same, no one thinks like Cheshire. You hide it better though."

"We are very, very different, but our brains are really similar in a lot of ways," I said.

"I just wish he would understand what he has, I wish he could be happy with what he has done." Puppy said.

"You have to understand, he was with a girl for 14 years, he was ready to have kids, have a family. Then everything changed. You don't come back from that, when life is going one way and everything turns out to be different, you don't come back. You change and adapt, but you will never be the same."

"But you see, he changed then." Puppy said.

"And it took something that big, change comes at the margins, or by having your life turned upside down." I said.

"You don't want to get married anymore?"

"I wanted kids, I wanted a family, I really wanted that, now I can't even conceive it. I just want to fuck around and meet people and do whatever the fuck I want. Like, I had everything I wanted and I didn't like it. And now, even though people look at me and think I am a total fuckup, I have never felt more like myself."

"I don't think anyone looks at you like a fuckup, and I

really believe people can change, I think Cheshire will change, I just don't know how to help him."

"You can't help him, people can only help themselves."

"I can help him!" She sounded like a teenager.

The man tripping on acid had been listening to us the entire time, his head bobbing back and forth as we talked. He placed his hand on Puppy's shoulder, and grabbed my side. "I want you two to listen to me now, I can hear your inner spirit talking to me." He looked up to the sky and took a deep breath. He then came incredibly close to Puppy's face and looked into her eyes, "you already know the answer, you don't need to ask."

"Thank you for that amazing wisdom," I said.

"There is no need to thank me, someday you will understand like I now do."

Puppy looked at him, it was the most angry I had ever seen her, "Okay you can go now," she said.

He stood up, looked to the two of us and said, "my work is now done," then he left the lounge.

"Puppy, let me tell you a story about a girl I dated."

"Your ex?" She asked.

"No, no, this one only lasted a month. We fell hard, you know how sometimes you just know. She told me she had never felt this way about anyone before, I decided to make it a go, I went all in, all fucking in. I did everything to make it work. Then she became distant, she said she was depressed. And I know depression. So I did whatever I could. She told me she was too tired to see me, that she was being introverted. She would apologize. I just told her I was always a phone call away. I was worried sick about her, worried fucking sick. I was home alone, sleeping alone, eating alone, the whole time thinking she was all alone too. This went on for a couple weeks, then I got suspicious and found out the truth."

"What happened?" Puppy asked.

"That whole time, she had been going over to another guys house and fucking him. I don't even think she liked him."

"Why would she do that? That doesn't make any sense." There was an innocence in Puppy's eyes. "Why would she do that? Why?"

"I don't know, people do dumb things, I've done dumb things before, people are self destructive."

"But that makes no sense, she was making sure she would stay miserable."

"Puppy, that's not even the point, I would have forgiven her." I took the last sip of my Moscow Mule as Puppy stared deeply into my eyes, looking for answers where there were none. "I confronted her, and she was completely honest, she told me everything. But she cried and cried, she kept telling me she had never felt this way about anyone, that she didn't like the guy. I finally kicked her out, and she just kept telling me that she would fix it, that she would fix this, she didn't know how, but she would make it up to me. I wish she had."

"What did she do?" Puppy asked.

"She went right back to the other guy, she hung out with him the next day." I said.

"I don't get it," I looked at Puppy, and felt bad for her.

"Puppy, because people do not change. She did not change, she doesn't know how to fight for happiness, all she knew how to do was survive. Cheshire will not change. I will not change."

"I just don't believe it," Puppy said, "I really believe people will always change for the better."

"I want to tell you something, this is important, sometimes it's not about you."

"I know that, I want to help Cheshire," she said.

"You don't understand. I'm not talking about Cheshire, I'm talking about myself," I said.

"What do you mean?" She asked.

"Sometimes it doesn't matter how much you love somebody. Sometimes it is just about respect."

"Respect?" She asked.

"It's disrespectful to the people who treat you well, to chase after someone who treats you like crap."

Chapter Thirty-Three:

Tonight The Man Will Burn

I was biking down L street with Brock, a Tech Bro who lived somewhere up north. We had just left the turnkey camp where he was staying. Basically, he payed a shit ton of money to have a campsite built for him. It would put most motels to shame.

"Doesn't that kinda defeat the spirit of Burning Man?" I yelled as I tried to keep up.

"Oh, please, it's always been about money, I mean ever since it became this shit. Think about it, what kind of person can afford a three hundred dollar ticket to take 10 days off work and live out in the middle of the desert?" Brock shouted back.

"Rich people and hippies?" I yelled.

"Exactly, We build the shit, give the artists money, and in return, the hippies have sex with us. It's pretty much that simple."

Brock took a sharp right, I imagined he did BMX racing or something, the guy knew how to ride. "See it's all bullshit, but only people like us seem to get it. Everyone says that Burning Man is the way the world should be, if only everything worked like it did at Burning Man. All this place proves is that if you take a bunch of rich white people and put them out in the middle of the desert, they can get along for a few days. Let's see how long these people last in the hood. Oh that's right, they gentrified all the hoods then complain about how shitty it must be for the people they displaced." It's hard not to like a guy who doesn't give a shit about what he says.

"You know what it reminds me of?" He said. "All those people in the default world that think the rich pay taxes to help the poor. We pay taxes to keep the poor from revolution. We give them just enough so they become dependent on us and won't burn down our houses. We control the poor with handouts." We were headed to the Distrikt, a giant day party in the city.

"You don't think the principles make you a better person?" I said.

"Please, you mean the radical everything? Radical Inclusive? Radical giving, whatever the fuck? It's 80 20 all over the place." Brock yelled.

"I know 80 20, this doesn't seem like 80 20." I said. 80 20 is the theory that 80% of everything you have, comes from 20% of everything you do. 80% of your money comes from 20% of your effort, 80% of your stress comes from 20% of your clients. The goal is to cut out and expand on these twenty percents.

"How many people in your camp?" He asked me.

"I think a hundred forty?" I answered.

"How many actually helped, hell how many will stay for breakdown?" I quickly did the math in my head, probably thirty people, about 20% of my camp. "20% right?" He said.

"Yea." I answered.

"20 percent of the people make this thing happen, the other 80% just pretend to. And here's the thing, that 80%, they don't want to admit they are in the 80%. Losers can never accept that they are losers. That's why they always give advice. So that 80%, they have to put meaning behind it. So they call it spiritual. Makes it feel like they are doing something. They'll say they are manifesting this place with good vibes or some shit, probably not vibes, I don't think anyone uses that word anymore."

"I think they just say love now," I said.

"Yea exactly, love. Only a fucking loser would say that" He stopped his bike, I pulled up next to him. "Its right around here." We began to walk. "You know what it reminds me of? I'm like you, I was born Christian. Our church always thought we were building up to something, some sort of revival, and it never came. People kept believing, yet they did shit. I guess that's where the hippies are right, fuck the future, live in the now."

We turned the corner and were rewarded by basically the greatest day party I had ever seen. I guess I was a broken record. Hundreds of naked and near naked Burners danced in front of the massive stage as they got fruit based alcoholic drinks from the open bar. Just when I thought I could no longer be amazed, Black Rock City has once again proven me wrong.

"C'mon," Brock turned to me, "I want to discuss astrology with some hippie chicks."

"You're into astrology?" I asked.

"Of course I'm not into astrology, 90% of men are not into astrology, but 90% of women are. You can lie, or stay a virgin." This was strangely profound.

After a few minutes of pushing through the audience, Brock found his mark, a topless girl with a giant tribal tattoo on her back. He walked up next to her as she swayed to the deep house beat.

"Excuse me!" He interrupted her, "hey this is gonna sound kinda weird, but I think you might be the right person to ask. So I know what signs are, but I guess there are like sub signs and rising signs or something."

"Yes, there are lots of derivatives of the signs," she didn't even look at him.

"This makes so much sense, see I'm a Pisces, but I have never related with that sign, I feel like there is something wrong with me."

"There's nothing wrong with you, I love your honesty," he was in, she was smiling.

Fuck, I envied him.

BROCK ENTICED A couple of Burner chicks to go back to his camp with the promise of a hot shower. In this world of playa silt, sweat, and sex, nothing was more valuable than soap, and clean warm water.

I had biked past the Russian's RV but they were not there, so I decided to look for Avalon and Wolfgang's camp. The Burn was coming to an end, and I had barely spent anytime with my old friends. As I walked down the alley trying to determine which small camp was theirs, a giant godlike figure came out of no where and pounced on me. It felt almost sexual as he lifted me into the sky. It was The Pacman.

I had met The Pacman a few times before, I first noticed him at Lightning in a Bottle. He was impossible not to notice. He towered above anyone he met, at over six foot five in height. He had played college basketball and was the only Transformational I had ever met who had experience in sports. This made me instantly respect what he had to say. I trust people who have played team sports.

"Look who I found!" He yelled to his camp, "This is perfect timing! I'm about to teach my class."

He dropped me to the ground and led me around the corner to show me Wolfgang and Avalon's camp. A dozen people were waiting for his gift to The Playa, a course in speaking from your soul through the art of divine rhyme.

He walked to the front of the audience and spoke. "They call me The Pacman. Today I will teach each of you how to speak from your soul through the power of freestyle rap." Anywhere else, this would have gotten a laugh, here, it was one of the more sane things I had heard. "We are going to break down your filters through a series of exercises, and then you will do one of the scariest things a human being can do. You will stand up on this small stage, and speak from your heart, you will perform, while we all watch."

The Pacman had a confidence in his voice, it made you listen to him even if everything he said was bullshit. Confidence was funny like that. As he talked, I looked at him and thought, there was probably a scared lonely boy underneath all that power and strength. "It is my hope, that you find your honest voice, and learn something about yourself."

I was a trained public speaker, but as he taught his lesson, I decided to do the thing I hated most, I would show weakness. The trick to public speaking is being so prepared that you cannot fail. The preparation makes your speech look like a magic trick as the words flow off your tongue as if was the first time you were saying them. I decided right then. I would go in blind.

"I want you all to know, you are all courageous for being here. And courage is the most important of the human traits. It is the trait that all others stem from," he finished.

We began the class by doing a series of exercises, they were similar to the Romney exercises but with no agenda. It is amazing how much agendas matter. The Pacman was not getting paid, the people here did not come for a reason. It was just fun. There were nothing but good intentions in all our hearts.

Then, one by one, we got up on stage and began to speak. People were surprisingly good. Wolfgang was there, he blew away the crowd with his style and humor. Avalon also spoke, the audience fell in love with her genuine approach. Person after person did better than they could have expected.

Pacman saw that I was uncomfortable, so he made sure not to call on me until the very end, allowing me to sit in this emotion. I stood in front of that audience, and I was silent. My mind went blank. I had nothing to say. So I just started talking, I started saying whatever my brain was telling me. "I have nothing to say." I said to the laugher of the audience. "No really, there is nothing here. I am scared and unprepared, my mind usually cannot shut off, and now that I ask it to talk, I can't even walk. I just made up that rhyme so I would fit the class, wishing I was in church listening to mass." People continued to laugh, knowing exactly what I was doing.

I looked up to the blue playa sky. I stared at the clouds floating over head. I took in a breath and smelled the prehistoric dust in the air. "I look to the sky, wondering where you are. Are you near? Are you far? I believed in you, I trusted what you said. And now I think you must be dead. I tried so hard, but I am always beat, my only reward is a bitter defeat, yet I keep on going, reaching for that sky, but still I do, I wonder why! Why the fuck, I've been good I say, and you just tell me to go out and play! I took on this mission, and now I am lost, my friend, my life all my beliefs were the cost. Where are you, what should I do? I'd feel so much better, if I only knew. Why I try? I never know why. Until I die, I still will try..."

I sat down as our host thanked everyone who came. I

then walked away, my head staring at the ground, I was ashamed for some reason. Not doing my best I guess. The Pacman grabbed me, and looked me in the eyes. "That was incredible." He said.

"I think it was pretty awful," I remarked.

"That wasn't the point of any of this, when you looked to the sky and yelled at God, that was the most honest thing I have ever seen in my life."

"That is my life, it defines me, I wish it didn't."

"It's a mission, it's a quest, you are on a lifelong journey."

"I wish I wasn't."

"They all wish they were." I couldn't tell if he was being honest or cute.

"I think I'd just like to be happy." I told him.

"No you don't. If you wanted that, you would be. People do what they want to do." He was right. "You're courageous, you're a hero, people follow you," I didn't always agree with the Pacman, but I did respect him.

"Pacman, I love you. But the hero is a fool. He runs into battle and dies. All these people, these people walking around the streets of Black Rock. Contributing nothing, going to the theme camps, taking your workshop, giving nothing in return. They are the smart ones. They do nothing, and gain everything. The hero is a fool."

He looked at me, one of those piercing looks, at first I thought it was pity, but then his eyes lit up, and a giant smile came across his face. "A wise man would have fun being the hero."

He patted me on the shoulder, letting me take it in. It was one of those moments, the perfect answer, he knew it. It's not often my entire philosophy on life is destroyed by a single sentence, I could feel my heart drop to the floor. In one sentence, he answered everything, everything I had been trying to figure out during that day, during that seminar, during my god-awful freestyle rap.

"You have an obligation to yourself to enjoy this one life. Whatever that means. Whether it be happiness, or meaning, or searching." He became stern. "You are being disrespectful to this one life God has given you. Don't you understand that? You talk of duty and respect and loyalty. When I see you, all I see is disrespect. And I mean that from a place of kindness and love. You are insulting every other person who lives, has lived and will live on this planet by not taking full advantage of this one life you have. Here ends another day, you have two eyes, two ears, two hands, and the entire playa. What have you done with it? Just another day. Another day gone. It's not about you, it's about all of this. Quit fucking being disrespectful to this one life you have been given."

I'VE ALWAYS BEEN lucky to have friends who call me out on my bullshit. I rode out into the Playa, pissed off at being lectured. Chemicals in my brain, I thought. In a few minutes, they would subside, and I could really think about what The Pacman had told me.

I kept thinking about something an artist once said, "Does anyone ask a flower why it is beautiful?" Does art need a reason? Does life need a reason?

The God question didn't matter anymore, not if you had fun being the hero. This entire time I thought it was one or the other, live for the afterlife, or live for yourself. It could be both. The coward could game the system. He could get the money and the girl, he even may be remembered by history, but so what? Would he have fun? Would he be happy?

I imagined all the great men and women of the world wishing they were here with me in Black Rock City. With limitless power, money and prestige, where would I rather be?

Life is organic. You cannot reshape the trunk of the tree, only the branches. You can't get a tomato plant to grow apples, but you can have a lot of fun trying. It was possible to live a life without failure, by living a life where failure did not exist. If I painted a painting because I wanted to paint a painting, I could not fail. It didn't matter if other's loved the painting, it didn't matter if I made money from the painting. I just painted it because I felt like it. I built for the sake of building. I learned to enjoy the fight. It's always going to be a fight, so why not enjoy it? The challenge can be the dream.

THE MAN WAS set to burn in an hour, we all met at the RV. It was the Russian Mafia, Nabes, Puppy, and Cheshire.

Dimitri and Rash had been doing nitrous balloons while we waited for Dos and Nabes to get ready. This was the one drug I actually had extensive experience with. When I was a kid, I had an awful gag reflex, and the dentist had to put a nitrous mask over my face so I wouldn't get sick when he worked on me.

So much of my childhood seemed to revolve around this drug, it was a two-hour break from reality. Two hours where I didn't need to worry about my depression, about my suicidal thoughts, about feeling completely left out in this world.

Dimitri passed me the balloon, "Just breathe in and out, like hyperventilate," he told me.

I grabbed it and hesitated, something deep inside me said I should pass it back, but then fuck it. "I guess we're all gonna go the way of Universal Entropy." I said.

"What's that mean?" Dimitri asked.

"It's a smart way of saying nothing matters," Cheshire answered, "scientists believe that the big bang is expanding the Universe to a point that it will tear itself apart and lose all it's energy. Basically freezing us into tiny motionless neutrinos. Meaning everything we do is pointless."

Damn I loved Cheshire, he always knew what I was trying to say. I took in a huge puff, and nothing happened, so I did it again, and again nothing. I swallowed heavier and heavier and began to wonder if I was doing it right. So I took the largest breath that I was capable of. I looked to Rash and Dimitri as they became fuzzy and started moving backwards, everything was moving backwards, pushing away from my reality. I knew this sensation. I had seen this before. Where had I seen this before? It was television, when you turned off an old television set, the picture became smaller and smaller, like it was zapping out of existence. I could not move, but I could see their faces. They looked scared. Puppy's mouth was open, like she wanted to say something. Cheshire reaction was different. He was afraid, but not stunned. He ran towards me. He held my head, my hand. I didn't have to look at him, I could see him, I could see Rash and Dimitri and Puppy, I shouldn't be able to see them? They were all in my field of vision, down that tunnel that was getting further and further away.

I could feel Cheshire's hands, but that too was slipping away. It wasn't just the visuals that were leaving, it was touch, and thought, and smell, it was everything that was human. I was traveling through a tunnel, backwards... Through a tunnel?

Televisions did that when they turned off... the TV was off? My brain was shutting off? Holy fuck my brain was turning off! Cheshire was trying to save me, but he didn't know how, so he just stood there and held my hand. I remember thinking I wanted to do that once, didn't I tell people I wanted to do that once? Everything that had happened to me, my 36 years on this planet, the five months that had just passed, everything I had learned at Burning Man began to fade away as I left my body and my friends.

... And then I was back. Like one of those mini power outages, for one second you think your whole day will be ruined, and then snap, everything turns back on, like nothing ever happened.

I looked to Cheshire. He was scared, but he was there, after all this time, he was the one person who was still there. He held my hand, I couldn't tell if he wanted to hug me or punch me. I said the only thing that came to mind. "You remember the Red and Black game?"

He looked down, the hints of a smile at the edges of his lips, "We beat the shit out of that game." It had been six months since Romney, six fucking months. How could I have changed so much in such a short time? "You know, I block anyone who calls me about Romney now." He said, still smiling.

"It's funny, because it wasn't bad, it's just people took it too serious. " I said.

We didn't hug, we didn't kiss, the moment did not last long. Cheshire wasn't an asshole, he was one of the best people I had ever met in my life. It's just easier to be an asshole sometimes.

Tonight The Man would burn, and it was no time to be sentimental. It was time to party and have fun. So I turned to everyone, a smile on my face, excitement in my voice, and said, "You wanna hear what happened?" I thought they were going to cheer.

"Fuck yea that was tight!" Rash yelled.

"It's called fishing out, I have never seen it before,"

Dimitri explained, "Your brain loses too much oxygen and it is filled up by the nitrous, that was fucking insane."

Cheshire looked at me, touched my cheek like you would a girl you liked, he then purred and licked me on the face. Cheshire was the perfect example of how a genius could never be normal. He was one of the most impressive human beings I had ever met, created some of the most amazing things I had ever seen, but had no clue how to create a life. If you are really good at one thing, it probably means you forgot how to learn some of the basics.

We all jumped on our bikes. It was Dos, and Rash, and Dimitri, that Russian Mafia. It was Nabes, the Argentinian sweetheart. I hoped I would get to meet a girl like her someday. It was Cheshire and Puppy. Where would I be without Cheshire? And it was me. It was me. I felt loved and respected. I felt like I belonged here. For the first time in my life, I actually fit in.

We headed out to the middle of The Playa, and watched The Man burn. It filled with flame and fell to the ground. It was the least impressive thing I had seen all week.

Chapter Thirty-Four:

The End

I woke up early and depressed. It was 8AM, and we had a long day ahead of us. We had to start breaking down the camp, and the five-story structure we had built. Burning Man was now over for me.

After an amazing week, after everything I saw, the climax was a disappointment. Everything led up to The Man burning, and it ended up being just another party. Funny how we judge our adventures by how they end. Everything about this week had been beyond extraordinary, and now I didn't even want to return next year.

I was functioning on two hours of sleep and would spend the rest of the day doing hard manual labor. I was hung over and miserable. Everyone in my camp was placed into a group and designated a task. I looked around, a large percentage of my fellow campers had taken off early. Eighty-twenty, I thought.

I was designated to the Distro group, a film term for the electrical team. Our camp was providing power for everyone who camped on our block. As I started rolling wire and unplugging breakers, I was onery. The lack of leadership pissed me off, no one seemed to take charge. I guess I could, but why? I just wanted to finish up this work and get home.

I've always liked to work with my hands. Gyms never

made sense to me. Why not just build a patio? I looked at my fellow campers, everyone was miserable. It's fun moving in, it sucks moving out. I was expecting so much more here, an electricity in the air. Instead, it felt like a New Year's Eve party, not the party you imagined, but what New Year's Eve always turns into. Just another day.

After I finished the distro work I climbed up the scaffolding. I was one of the only people here who knew how to break down stages, I had worked in production for fourteen years before I moved to tech. I started hammering out the railing, and pulling them down when I looked at my camp once more. It was over. The camp was becoming a shell of itself. Maybe it was just the coffee, maybe I was waking up. I stared at that camp for five minutes.

People who had never built anything in their lives, people who had no clue what a production was, had never torn down scaffolding, had never put together sound stages. I saw them doing their best to be part of our team. The one thing that was missing from all the festivals, from all the experiences I had been part of in the past five months. The team. The team was here. They were learning, it was like the first day of practice. They wanted to be part of something so bad but did not know how. They wanted to be part of something bigger than themselves. They wanted to create. They wanted to find worth. They wanted to change the world in some way and just had no fucking clue how to do it. So at some point, they decided to come to The Playa, come to Burning Man. They joined a large theme camp and helped build Black Rock City. Now they could be part of bringing joy to others and maybe find a little joy for themselves.

I watched them likes ants on the scaffolding. I watched them as they stood around having never done anything like this before, trying to look busy, trying to feel part of our team, my team.

The Man burning meant nothing, this was the climax, this was that special moment I had been hoping for. I could feel the camaraderie. I could feel everything I had been seeking for the past few months, past few years, maybe forever.

It was not perfect, it may not have even mattered, but it was honest. We were not the Lost Boys, we were the pirates trying to go back home. We had been lied to by everything we had believed in as children. We were lied to by our parents, by our religion, by our institutions. We had all been lied to by everyone and everything we trusted. So we made our own reality. Second star to the right, and straight on to morning.

BURNING MAN DOES not end with the Temple going down in flame, this is where it begins. Here we bury our past, let go of our memories, and move on to be reborn. This new life will continue for the next 364 days, until The Man burns again. Humans need second chances, we need to grow and learn from our mistakes. The Temple allows us to do this.

I don't know why I wrote this book. I just thought that maybe if you read my journey, you could have a journey of your own. I don't claim that everything here was true, but it was honest, and I have learned, honesty is harder than truth.

I watched the audience as the giant structure went up in flames. I wondered if this would be my last burn, last festival. This life has overtaken me, and I still have a lot I want to do in the default world. I listened to the moans of the Burners, feeling the death and rebirth that comes with this ceremony. I felt their prayers, as they hoped this year might be better than the last.

Most of these people will stay in this world. They will talk about being enlightened and transformed, but they will only be able to use their skills in this strange land they have created. Life doesn't work that way. It shouldn't work that way. You must be able to leave The Playa and take what you have learned with you. Here, you can Be, but to get here, you had to Do. It is the Do that leads to Being. The Be is important, but it is a matter of how the Be became.

Even the Have, in the end is part of the equation, but the Have is in a constant state of flux. Sometimes it is abundance, sometimes it is poverty. But whatever state it is, remember, you are lucky, because even that you get to experience. Tech, Drugs, Sex, Spirituality, and The Facilitators.

The Tech Industry.

Tech is simple. It gives you the choice to live an active or passive life. Most will choose the passive, and see the world from their computer. But the lucky few will choose the active, and use tech to find new experiences; as well as bettering the experience they are currently having. Most of tech is noise, don't fight it, ignore it.

The Drugs.

I don't doubt that drugs have helped create this spiritual recrudescence. Drugs have many benefits, from killing the bacteria of an infection, to helping the depressed have a normal life. But slowly, we are becoming reliant on these substances. Not just festival goers, all of us. Is this human? What is human?

I cannot imagine lying on my deathbed after a life full of festivals and drugs, and thinking 'job well done.' I can't imagine anyone looking back and being happy about the percentage of their lives they spent in that ethereal mist that is the joy and fun of drugs. I like to get my buzz on as much as the next guy, but I want it to push reality forward, not create a new reality. The greatest times throughout my life have always involved doing real things with real people. Drugs, and these festivals, have been a blast but drugs should never be more than the gravy of life. They are for celebration and introspection and should never be a replacement for living.

The Sex.

I see broken relationship after broken relationship. This is true, whether they are open, or not. Relationships are hard in the modern world, and much about them will change. I do not know if I can be in a long-lasting relationship, and I do not know if humans were designed for such a construct. But I know this, building a family is something real, and it is respected. I respect no one more than my parents. I respect no one more, than those who have created a family. I respect no one more, than two people who have stood by each other, through thick and thin, good times and bad. Yet I, and many of my generation run from this. I do not think we are headed in the right direction, and I do not believe anyone has an answer. All I know, is that we are forcing our own extinction if we do not figure this out. Human's are not the blight.

The Spirituality.

I am not spiritual, nothing I have seen, or experienced in the past year has changed this. However, I respect spirituality. I have seen nothing but kindness among the Transformationals. They can be annoying when it comes to pushing their beliefs on me, but so can Christians and Mormons.

I do not understand why people hate them so much. Is it our old tribalistic traits of hating those who are different from us? Or is it the envy of watching them play while we toil and work? I love the Transformationals. I love the festival goers. I love these people. They will always have a place in my heart. The last few months of my life have been more important to me than maybe anytime before. I may not always agree with them, but I respect and love them. I would not be the person I am today without them.

Spirituality is about finding hope. Hope leads to power, and power leads to action. I would rather believe in a false hope than a real universal entropy. You have to have hope, without hope, there is nothing. I may not believe in the power of prayer, but I do believe in its effectiveness. For most of our existence, praying for a disease to go away was healthier than going to the doctor. If you have a virus today, this is still true. Quite often, doing the logical thing is the least logical thing to do.

Prayer is our way of saying we are humble. We do not understand, so we will throw it out into the universe. It's about remembering that with all the great things we have accomplished, we are still human.

The Facilitators.

The fraud economy could destroy our way of life. Maybe it already has. The stronger it becomes, the more it will proliferate through the fabric of society. I have seen it impair the younger generation with student debt, and my generation with delusions of grandeur. The world is very cruel, and is also very beautiful. Ignore this at your peril.

This new economy is the natural outcome for a rich society that is taken care of. It's not much different than the rich kid who doesn't think rules apply to him, they don't, he's rich. They don't apply to those who live in the industrialized modern world either. We don't have to live in reality, so we choose to live in the fantasyland of our dreams, always knowing there will be someone there to take care of us if we should fall.

This blight will increase the income disparity in this world so greatly, that it is the one thing I really fear. It has affected every aspect of business, from environmentalists, to tech. It is so easy to take advantage of our fellow man. Honestly, we want to be taken advantage of.

If there is any place in this world that needs heroes, it is within the facilitator economy. These heroes will earn less than their fraudulent peers, and will not get as large of a following. But they will remain human and be able to look themselves in the eye. You must learn to have fun being the hero. You must have humility in your beliefs, and share your wealth with anyone who joins you. As a society, we must figure out a way to reward our heroes. The only things I have ever kept in life are the things I have given away. They may get fame and wealth, but you will have dignity and happiness. Remember to enjoy the fight.

The Perpetual Hope Machine.

Together, this is the merging of the tech industry, spirituality, drugs and the facilitator economy. This is the future. This is the perpetual hope machine.

Chapter Thirty-Five:

Welcome Home

And now I was all alone. The Russian Mafia returned to Los Angeles. I hadn't seen the VP since she married Lego, Cheshire and Puppy's tent was gone, and Firestarter was fast asleep. I never expected to be here this long, and I still wanted to stay.

My camp was nearly cleared. The last of its members were breaking into couples and close friends. I looked around for a bike that was still in working condition and began to ride down the Esplanade. The streets were empty, but the city still existed. It reminded me of Los Angeles on a Thanksgiving night. This giant city built just for me. It made you feel both alone and alive at the same time.

I went to the outer ring of Black Rock City and watched as the giant EDM stages were torn down. I rode to center camp, only to find it was the last place that still had life to it. I walked into any bar that was welcoming, meeting the last of the Burners. Then I biked out into the middle of The Playa.

The Man was gone, the temple destroyed. All the major landmarks had disappeared. It was now easy to get lost in this vast, flat desert. I made a mission for myself. Firestarter had been working on an art project in the deep playa. I set out to find it, a near-impossible task under such conditions. But I learned long ago, any journey is worth taking on, adventure begets adventure, it gives you a reason to push forward.

Before I knew it, I was turned around and had no clue where the hell I was. I looked for any negative space, reversing the normal function of my brain, trying to find shadows that blocked the city lights. I knew in one of these spaces was her art project. I looked for people congregating. I looked for art cars. I tried to find any clue that would help me achieve my mission.

Then, in the distance, I saw a string of floating lights, they must have gone for a mile, just a span of lights that had a life of their own. They didn't seem to be attached to anything, yet they didn't float away.

As I biked towards them, I saw the truth. It was not some mysterious throng of floating lights, it was a string of helium balloons reaching deep into the sky. A single LED light attached to each knot. A man was holding the string like a kite, moving the balloons side to side. He handed me the end and asked if I would like to try it out. The force of the helium pulled on me. The wind grabbed my feet and pushed me around. The vibrations pulsating through the plastic cord and into my soul. I felt like a child, wasn't this a child's dream? Every kid has thought about the power of helium balloons. Every child has wanted to be dragged around by the force of the balloons, and here I was, doing just this.

Sometimes the best art is that which reaches into our deepest regrets, the type of regret that you have no excuse against. You have always wanted to make a mile-long string of helium balloons. You now have the money and know how to do it. You are now an adult, no one can tell you to stop. But you never made that string of balloons. Why? Everyone has a helium balloon somewhere in their heart, some big, or little thing that gnaws at you, something you could fix right now. But you just don't do it.

Behind the man holding this long string of balloons was something even more powerful. It was another art exhibit, here in the middle of the desert, someone had tethered a hundred balloons to the ground. Each contained a light that pulsated with the sound of a human voice, a female's voice. She walked around these balloons singing, but her song was turned electronic and ethereal through a computerized filter. The balloons changed colors and vibrated to every sound she made. They were her dancers.

Another man walked around with her, quietly comforting those balloons, those glowing angels in the middle of this hellish place, this god-forsaken desert that was The Playa. As I watched, I began to tear up, then cry. I wanted to thank the angels. I had to thank the angels. I had to thank them for turning this blank slate into something beautiful.

The man walked near me and I grabbed his shoulder. He did not break character, he did not pull away. "Sorry," I said, "this is my first Burn and I just wanted to thank you for ending it in such a beautiful and perfect way."

My tears turned to sobs, I almost collapsed. He grabbed my hand. "Would you like to come in? " He asked.

I walked into the pixel forest with him. He pulled me to the center and sat me down among the glowing balloons. The glowing souls of every childhood fantasy you ever had, every excuse you have ever told yourself. The balloons were not angry, they were not sad, they were telling us to go ahead, build those things you wanted to build, sing those songs you wanted to sing, be that person you always wanted to be. They were not here to make you regret, they were here to tell you that everything was going to be okay.

I sat there, continuing to cry, harder and harder. The singer came to me, sat down with me. She sang to me, talked to me, her words turning to music through the technology that made the entire art piece possible. She then hugged me as I caressed the sides of her coat, thanking her over and over.

She covered up her microphone and asked, " What is your name? "

I answered and thanked her again. I touched her cheek and stared into her eyes. I wanted to kiss her. Not out of lust, but out of love. I saw the human being that she was, that we all are. Then she touched my cheek and told me one last thing.

"Welcome home."

I SAT ON The Playa silt and sobbed until nothing was left, until every emotion had been exhausted. I cried and cried. It had been the most profound week of my entire life. The Playa had changed everything for me. And now, it was over.

I am a Burner. I wear this name with pride. It means something. It means I am in some secret little club. I know the truth of The Playa. The festival life is now part of who I am, it runs through my veins and will forever change everything about me.

But I know you can never experience something for the first time twice. The last six months have changed my life, I experienced things I never could have imagined, I saw things that I did not think were possible. It was as if I had seen a new color for the first time. How can words do such things justice? How can I explain a flavor you have never tasted? How can I describe a feeling that you have never felt?

I have now witnessed the best and worst of man, the best and worst of this culture, of the festivals, of spirituality, of electronic dance music, of drugs and love. I have witnessed the imagination of grown men seeking to be childlike again. But my journey has now ended. Wherever it goes from here, the festivals will never be the same. I have gone from being a rookie to being a veteran. It pains me to my soul. But my life in the festivals is now over.

Epilogue

Football season had returned and I decided to watch the game at a friend's house. It wasn't the game I cared about, it was seeing my old friends. That's the thing about these festivals, about warehouse parties, EDM, drugs and the night. They take over your life. Normal people just don't live this way.

I hadn't been to a festival since Burning Man, I hadn't even been to a party. I had not done any drugs and even quit drinking. Life had been feeling pretty dull. It was boring and normal.

I was now building real things, a new company inspired by the experiences I had over the past few months. But nothing could compare to the excitement and adventure I had come from. I missed it all so much. But life cannot always be exciting, if it were, we wouldn't know what exciting was.

Life is an hourglass. You take, and then you give. Your experiences change you, then you use those experiences to change others. Maybe that's the trick to it all. Exploration leads to creating and creating to exploration.

Sometimes I think about the last seven months of my life. It had only been seven months since Desert Hearts. Seven months that had forever changed who I was. My kids and grandkids would talk about this, I would tell them stories. It was beautiful.

I pulled up to Miki and Elias's house. They lived in the

middle of the suburbs of the San Fernando Valley. They had recently moved here and I didn't know which house was theirs. I saw some kids playing basketball out front but I didn't recognize them.

"Excuse me, I'm looking for Miki's house?" I asked.

The tallest of the boys spoke up, "It's the one right there, good seeing you! Where have you been?!" I guess they recognized me.

This house was more modest than their old place. I had known they had some money problems. They never talked about it, but it's easy to tell when someone is struggling with money. The BMW's were no longer new and the large house in the hills became this suburban dwelling. But these two had a real marriage, and I envied it. They were partners in crime, they always had each other's backs. This was a typical, conservative, American family, even though they were both immigrants.

I couldn't help but think how money struggles pull so many families apart, yet it seemed to strengthen this one. They no longer had all the stuff, but they had each other. You could feel this was a home. Not just four walls, not like my house. It was a real home. It smelled like a home, felt like a home, kids playing basketball out front, friends over watching the game, like a home should be.

I walked up to the front door, not sure if I should knock or just open it. Miki spotted me through the kitchen window. Her face lit up, and she began to wave. She ran over and gave me a hug. "Where have you been?! We missed you!" She said.

I had been so nervous to see my old friends, I had felt like a loser, I felt like I wasn't pulling my "friend weight," and nothing in their eyes said anything but love. Real, true love. Real true friendship.

I walked into the house, a typical Americana Sunday night. Men watching the game while their wives and girlfriends cooked in the kitchen. Half of the house was for kids, the other half for adults. I grew up like this. Most of the people here were Filipino in origin. Some were born in The States, some born in the homeland. I always had this theory that the only true Americans are the first-generation Americans. They aren't so far removed from their country of origin, that they forget how special their culture is, while taking advantage of every benefit one gets from living in the most powerful nation in the history of Earth. They are humble and grateful and extraordinary.

Shaolin spotted me and gave me a hug. He had moved to Orange County, and seeing him once every seven months was the normal in our relationship. Miki had told me that he had just broken up with his fiancé. I had gone through something similar once, and wanted to talk to him. We chatted for hours.

It's hard to predict where life will take you, one minute you think you have everything figured out, then everything that you know collapses. You'll never be the same, maybe that is a good thing, maybe it's not. I think it just is. I wish everything happened for a reason, it doesn't, it just happens, you find the reason. Then you can stay where you are, or take a step forward and become something new. Maybe the Transformations were right.

I played poker and lost every hand. I am a good poker player, but I didn't care. I just wanted to feel what my life used to be like, surrounded by the friends I used to have. Old, good, amazing, loyal, friends. People who never lived in the now, people who were the opposite of radically self-reliant, people who relied so much on one another, they might as well be co-dependent.

These were people who didn't do drugs except for the occasional beer. Didn't need drugs in order to find meaning, hated EDM and free love, looked at religion as a series of important rituals. They created friendships and families that would last their entire lives. They created children, who assured the human race would continue to survive. They built for the future, measuring their time in years instead of sets and acid highs. They would never celebrate the burning of art, they would cry at its destruction. They were the shoulders our future generations would stand upon.

Miki began to play the piano. We gathered around her. They were familiar songs. We all began to sing together. We held each other, smiled and laughed. I was surrounded by people who unconditionally loved me. We talked about important things and unimportant things. Nothing about this night, nothing about this moment would look good on a photograph we posted to a social network.

There was nothing here to envy, there was nothing here to brag about, no one dreamed that they would grow up to be this. But this room, this family, this moment, was the dream, it was the human dream, it was what we all strive to have. They loved, and gave, for no other reason, then that is the way it is supposed to be.

As I looked at them, I felt out of place, like I did not belong here. I always feel on the outsides of my friend's lives. As soon as I get comfortable, I move on. As I stared at them, I just kept telling myself. This story has to have a happy ending.

The End.

Acknowledgments...

This book was dedicated to the people who made this adventure possible. They were the ones who made this book possible. The acknowledgments go to the people who helped me actually write this book.

First, Just A. Name, yes, he is so awesomely weird he had his legal name changed to Just A. Name. He read my mind, and called me out on my bullshit and agenda. Time and time again, he showed me places throughout the book that had no reason for being there. He helped me cut this book down by thousands and thousands of words, and was a guiding force through its final writing.

Jodi Scott Elliott was the first person to read any part of this book. At a time I was about to just toss it out and move on; she gave me the confidence to keep writing. I also blatantly stole one of my favorite lines from her, "It is disrespectful to the people who treat you well, to go after the people who don't't"

Rafael Vega criticized basically every single sentence I wrote, which forced me to question every sentence and every decision I made. Which then forced me to write and rewrite until I couldn't stand reading the book anymore.

Megan Gersch, who is in both the dedication and acknowledgments. Her continued support and friendship have meant the world to me. Also her art rocks, and very likely is on the cover of the book you are reading!

Jerry Brandt, who along with Megan gets the double whammy. Again, a friend who helped push me while I questioned even finishing the book. I was stuck with 130 thousands words of notes, and didn't think I would ever be able to turn them into any type of real book.

Heather Rabun. I didn't know where to put her in this book; in the dedication or in the acknowledgments? The rule for the dedication page was that the book would not exist without that person. And this is not true for Heather. However, Heather, in a very unexpected way, became one of the most important people in my life. She taught me how to dance. Ever since I was a kid, I hated to dance; I hated the way I felt on the dance floor. So I randomly signed up for ballet. I went all in, wearing tights and a dancers belt. I did the most uncomfortable thing I could possibly do, and in doing so, I learned to love dancing.

The Mystical Misfits, my Burning Man Camp. You took this young virgin in and showed him the ropes. I really cannot imagine my Burn without you guys.

The Windmill Factory, the art team that made the Pixel Forest, which I found in the Deep Playa on my last night of the Burn. Leah Siegal and Jon Morris. As I said then, it was my first Burn and thank you for ending it in such a perfect way.